BOOSTING
PAYCHECKS

BOOSTING PAYCHECKS

The Politics of Supporting America's Working Poor

Daniel P. Gitterman

BROOKINGS INSTITUTION PRESS
Washington, D.C.

Copyright © 2010
THE BROOKINGS INSTITUTION
1775 Massachusetts Avenue, N.W., Washington, D.C. 20036
www.brookings.edu

Library of Congress Cataloging-in-Publication data
Gitterman, Daniel Paul.
   Boosting paychecks : the politics of supporting America's working poor /
Daniel P. Gitterman.
     p.   cm.
   Includes bibliographical references and index.
   ISBN 978-0-8157-0285-6 (hbk. : alk. paper)—
   ISBN 978-0-8157-0308-2 (pbk. : alk. paper)
   1. Working poor—Government policy—United States.   2. Working poor—
Taxation—United States.   3. Minimum wage—United States.   I. Title.
   HD8072.5.G56 2010
   331.5'40973—dc22   2009041330

9 8 7 6 5 4 3 2 1

Printed on acid-free paper

Typeset in Adobe Garamond

Composition by R. Lynn Rivenbark
Macon, Georgia

Printed by R. R. Donnelley
Harrisonburg, Virginia

For American families,
who work hard,
play by the rules,
and raise children,
but many of whom would benefit from
a boost in paychecks or spirits.

Contents

Preface

The study of the politics of social policy (known as the "welfare state" to academics) traditionally has focused on the tax and spending programs that intervene when individuals, because of age, sickness, disability, poverty, or unemployment, are unable to earn from or to participate in the labor market. However, by focusing only on the most visible New Deal and Great Society social insurance or assistance programs such as Social Security or Transitional Aid to Need Families (TANF), we miss the major indirect policy tools that support hard-working families—the federal minimum wage and income tax credits, such as the Earned Income Tax Credit and the Child Tax Credit. This book analyzes the origins and development of our earnings support regime for poor working families, which I refer to as the "politics of boosting paychecks." By focusing on the politics as well as the distributional effects of our policy choices, I hope my efforts bridge a gap between the perspectives of welfare state scholars and social policy analysts, especially across the disciplinary boundaries and venues where we conduct research, teach, and advocate for improved social policies in the United States.

American politics has not always produced the optimal approaches to achieving the best social safety net, because our policies have emerged out of imperfect compromises and bargains within the legislative process, typically with contradictory goals and purposes. However, the challenge remains: we must build renewed bipartisan political support for a coordinated set of federal and state policy measures to enhance the economic well-being of our hardworking families. It represents the key challenge to America's policymakers, both Democrats and Republicans, in the twenty-first century. Indeed, what's at stake is a viable middle class, something America has always prided itself on.

Through the hundreds and hundreds of University of North Carolina at Chapel Hill students I have taught in my class, American Public Policy, I have come to learn that all our families will face risk and—at some moment in our lives—might need to rely on a social safety net during difficult economic and emotional times. In building my policy-oriented academic career, I have come to rely on the mentorship, support, and advice of many colleagues. This is the time for a heartfelt thank you to my mentors, James Morone (Brown University) and Robert Blendon (Harvard), as well as to Thomas Sugrue, Marie Gottschalk (University of Pennsylvania), Richard Scheffler, David Vogel, Robert Kagan (UC Berkeley), Chris Howard (College of William and Mary), Michael Sparer (Columbia), and Ted Marmor (Yale). My special thanks to Michael Stegman, Michael Luger, and Richard Andrews for launching me at the University of North Carolina at Chapel Hill—a special place where I can pursue research, teaching, and public service.

While this project had its origins in my dissertation on the political development of the minimum wage, my thanks to Bruce Katz and Alan Berube at the Brookings Institution for supporting my efforts to focus on tax credits as the new social policy for poor working families. At Brookings Institution Press, I discovered the dream team: my special thanks to Robert Faherty and Mary Kwak for their interest in and unyielding commitment to this project. The rest of the Brookings Press team has been just as wonderful: thanks to Starr Belsky, Larry Converse, Christopher Kelaher, Janet Walker, and Susan Woollen (for the great cover art). Finally, my thanks to a great group of freelance copy editors, Juliana Gruenwald Henderson, Leslie Kriesel, Kathleen O'Connor, who kept me out of tons of trouble, and Caitlin Winwood, my former student, for her assistance with data and figures.

Before I selected a dissertation topic on the American welfare state at Brown, Jim Morone had warned: "Whatever you do, make sure it passes the grandma test." That is, "think big, tackle an important topic, and write simply enough for your grandma to understand your argument." This was clairvoyant advice because my grandmothers are central to my own family's narrative. During the decades in the early twentieth century where this book begins, my own family faced unimaginable challenge and uncertainty. My maternal grandfather, Leon Pines, had emigrated to the United States from Russia in 1903; my maternal grandmother, Ilse Pines, fled Nazi Germany for what was then Palestine in 1933 and came to the United States in 1935; and my paternal families, the Hirsches and Schluessels, faced the 1939 Nazi invasion of Poland. My father was born into an unthinkable world in 1938. By the time he was seven at the end of World War II, only he, my grandmother, Frania Gitterman, my great aunt, Maria Rosenbloom, and my cousin, Menek Goldstein, had survived the Holocaust. And as I came to learn about the dislocation and tragedy they faced, each taught me the enduring values of courage, loyalty to family, and hope for a better day. My parents, Alex and Naomi Gitterman, then showed me the power of leveraging deeply personal empathy with public compassion. They were my role models as I forged my own vision of a life of collective caring.

My wife, Amy, often reminds me that this "book in progress" is older than our marriage. During this time, our own effort to build and care for our family has faced significant risk, tragedy, and uncertainty. Again, I have relied on the safety net of my grandmothers, my great aunt, my parents, my sister, and my in-laws (the Kahn family)—for courage, loyalty to family, and hope for a better day. There is no man who loves and appreciates his family and children more than I do. To Amy and to my children, Max Asher, Claire Isabel, and in memory of Ben Isaac—you know how much I love you: I love you—with both arms way out—this much.

1 Boosting Paychecks in America

S elf-sufficiency and hard work are core American values. Normatively, Americans expect their fellow citizens to work to support their families. Empirically, full-time participation in the labor market remains central to family economic well-being. Yet most Americans realize that work alone is not enough to keep all workers and their families out of poverty. Many of the 20 million working-age individuals in poverty are working, but even full-time work at the federal minimum wage does not provide enough income for a family of three to escape poverty. Therefore, in addition to programs to help individuals join the workforce, the federal government has devised a range of policies to boost the paychecks of low-income earners and their families. In a major Brookings report and the book *Government's Greatest Achievements: From Civil Rights to Homeland Security*, Paul Light identifies this effort as one of the greatest accomplishments of the twentieth century.[1]

This book analyzes the political origins and development of two critical pillars of the policy regime that supports low-income earners and their families in the United States: federal taxes on individual income and the minimum wage. My purpose is twofold: to explore the partisan and coalition politics that yield these policies and to highlight their economic and

---

1. Light (2000).

distributive consequences for low-income earners and their families. Ultimately, I seek to explain how American politics has shaped these policy bargains and to what degree they have succeeded in lifting poor and near-poor workers with and without families up and out of poverty.

Although disparities in the distribution of after-tax income have widened over the past quarter century, this book does not address America's political success or failure in reducing income inequality, measured as the size of the gap between those with the highest and lowest incomes. Rather, my focus is on policies that improve the economic well-being of low-wage workers and their families. By illuminating the politics of this issue and the consequences of the resulting bargains, I hope to bridge the perspectives of political analysts, who often account only for politics, and policy analysts, who focus on the distributional effects of alternative social policy choices.

The story told in this book shows that partisan distributional goals have been central to the politics of boosting paychecks for low-income working families. Democrats and Republicans have selected different policy tools not solely for technical or ideological reasons, but also based on their distributive consequences for core constituents and key interest groups. In forging the political coalitions needed to enact policy changes, Democrats and Republicans have sought to distribute tax relief or minimum wage increases to the earners or families who are perceived as crucial to their party's electoral success. Moderates or centrists in both parties have played a pivotal role in brokering and shaping these final policy bargains.

The resulting policy regime to support low-income working families reflects a core American belief: all able-bodied workers must participate in the labor market full time, and, if they do so, they should earn enough to keep a one- or two-parent family out of poverty. However, this consensus excludes low-wage single earners and married couples without children. For those without children, there is no guarantee that full-time work will generate enough income to escape poverty. Thus, despite nearly a century of efforts to help those at the bottom of the income distribution, we continue to face the challenge of making work pay for every American.

Rethinking the American Welfare State

This book expands our understanding of social policy in the United States in two ways. First, it looks beyond traditional social insurance and assistance programs (such as welfare) that have been considered the main tools of antipoverty policy to explore the importance of alternative policy instruments. Second, it moves beyond income support to nonworkers (the elderly, the disabled, nonworking mothers with dependent children, and others) to focus on efforts to support individuals who are active in the labor market. In so doing, it contributes to a recent wave of scholarship that has reshaped thinking about the welfare state in the United States by introducing such concepts as the "hidden welfare state" (which highlights the role of tax expenditures in social policy) and the "shadow" or "divided" welfare state (which focuses on the role of regulatory and tax policies in shaping employer-provided health and pension benefits).[2]

Scholars of the politics of U.S. social policy traditionally have focused on the income transfer programs that intervene when individuals—because of age, disability, or a sluggish economy—are unable to work.[3] Such social insurance and assistance programs typically redistribute cash and in-kind benefits. These benefits often appear meager when compared to their analogues in other advanced industrialized countries. Accordingly, many historical studies of U.S. social policy emphasize the political coalitions that did not come together to support large-scale social policy reform.[4] Seen in this light, the development of the American welfare state is often characterized as a long series of missed opportunities. However, as Christopher Howard observes, American social policy is exceptional not so much for its small size—in terms of spending—as for its reliance on an unusually broad range of policy tools to achieve social welfare objectives.[5]

Social insurance and assistance programs remain critical elements of American social policy. However, by focusing on these programs, analysts tend to overlook the broader set of tools that policymakers have used to assist low-wage workers and their families. These alternative policy instruments have recently moved to the forefront, as bipartisan consensus has shifted away from cash assistance for individuals outside the labor market and toward work-related income support for workers who are active in the labor market. Since 1980 federal income tax credits, such as the Earned Income Tax Credit (EITC), the Child Tax Credit, and, most recently, the Making Work Pay tax credit, have emerged as central elements of an ongoing political strategy to boost the paychecks of low-income working families

---

2. Howard (1997); Gottschalk (2000); Hacker (2002); Klein (2003).
3. Skocpol (1995); Amenta (1998); Marmor and others (1990); Graetz and Mashaw (1999).
4. Weir, Orloff, and Skocpol (1988); Katznelson (1989); Pierson (1995).
5. Howard (2007).

as well as moderate- and middle-income families.[6] However, their effectiveness in raising the incomes of the working poor can depend in part on regular increases in the federal minimum wage. Hence, the dual focus of this book.

Boosting Paychecks explores the political origins and development of taxes on individual income and the minimum wage as forms of earnings subsidies. Political conflict over these issues has largely mirrored major ideological and distributional divisions within American politics over the past century. Debates over the overall progressivity of the federal income tax code—tax rates, brackets, exemptions, and deductions—have been partisan and divisive. Tax credits for low- to middle-income earners with children have been a partial exception to this rule, drawing support across traditional partisan, ideological, and economic lines. Nonetheless, partisan conflict has recently emerged over the refundability of some tax credits, the budget costs of which have grown substantially over the past several decades. Similarly, there has been significant partisan conflict over increases in the minimum wage, driven by the trade-off between potential increases in workers' income and in labor costs for small business.

These policies are not the only ways in which the federal government can help low-wage workers and their families. The single factor that most benefits such workers and their families, experts agree, is a healthy macroeconomy with strong job growth.[7] In addition, government can invest in human capital through education and training programs that help workers prepare for higher-wage jobs. A range of "in-kind" supports also helps lower-income families with basic living expenses such as health care, food, and child care.[8] However, these means-tested benefit policies have been widely studied. In contrast, the politics of supplementing earnings through the income tax and the minimum wage remains largely unexplored.

The Nuts and Bolts of Supporting Low-Income Working Families

The federal government does not have official definitions of such terms as "low income," "moderate income," or "middle class," but it provides data that can help delineate these categories. According to the U.S. Department

6. Gitterman and Howard (2003); Steuerle (1990); Sammartino, Toder, and Maag (2002); Sawhill and Thomas (2001). See also William G. Gale, "Tax Credits: Social Policy in Bad Disguise," *Christian Science Monitor*, February 16, 1999.

7. Blank, Danziger, and Schoeni (2005); Blank (2000); Haveman and Schwabish (2000); Blank (2007).

8. Wilson and Stoker (2006).

of Commerce, real median income for all households in the United States was $50,303 in 2008.[9] Median income is the amount that divides the income distribution into two equal groups, half having incomes above the median, half having incomes below the median. Starting from this baseline, many analysts define *low income* as below 50 percent of the median income (roughly $25,000) and moderate income as 50 percent to 80 percent of the same figure ($25,000 to $40,000). Another approach starts with the federal poverty threshold, which was $21,834 for a two-parent family of four and $17,346 for a one-parent family of three in 2008, and defines *low income* as earnings at or below this level.[10] Moderate income can then be defined as earnings between 100 percent and 200 percent of the federal poverty threshold, or $43,688 for a family of four in 2008. Obviously, any such definitions are arbitrary, but they provide a sense of the economic challenges facing low- and moderate-income families.

The need for earnings supplements arises in large part from the nature of the jobs held by less-skilled, low-income workers. Such jobs are likely to be compensated on an hourly basis, as opposed to a salaried basis, and are less likely to be based on a full-time work schedule. Moreover, the wages that these jobs pay have declined significantly in relative terms. Over the past several decades, the real hourly wage rate in the United States grew substantially faster at the top of the wage distribution than at the middle, and grew faster at the middle than at the bottom.[11] This trend provides an important backdrop to efforts to use the tax system and federal minimum wage to help low-income earners and their families.

Role of the Federal Individual Income Tax

The tax system's effectiveness at supporting low-income earners and families depends largely on its progressivity. In a progressive tax system, the

9. U.S. Department of Commerce, "Income, Poverty and Health Insurance Coverage in the United States: 2008," press release, September 10, 2009 (www.census.gov/Press-Release/www/releases/archives/income_wealth/014227.html). The U.S. Census Bureau reported that real median household income in the United States fell 3.6 percent between 2007 and 2008, from $52,163 to $50,303. This broke a string of three years of annual income increases and coincides with the recession that started in December 2007.

10. For a single earner under sixty-five or a married couple under sixty-five with no children, the 2008 federal poverty thresholds were $11,201 and $14,417, respectively. U.S. Census Bureau, "Poverty Thresholds for 2008 by Size of Family and Number of Related Children under 18 Years" (www.census.gov/hhes/www/poverty/threshld/thresh08.html).

11. Congressional Budget Office, "Historical Effective Tax Rates: 1979 to 2004," Table 1C, December, 2006 (www.cbo.gov/ftpdocs/77xx/doc7718/EffectiveTaxRates.pdf).

share of earned income paid in tax rises with income, and after-tax income is more equally distributed than before-tax income. Over the course of the twentieth century, the federal individual income tax emerged as a relatively progressive tax that essentially exempts the poor, exempts some income from taxation at all income levels, taxes higher incomes at higher rates, and has no upper limit. Many provisions of the tax code have contributed to this outcome, including the tax rate structure and the definition of the tax base (defined as the portion of personal income subject to federal income tax at a positive rate).

INCOME TAX RATES AND BRACKETS.   Tax rates are applied by brackets. For example, imagine there are three tax brackets: 10 percent (for earned income under $10,000), 20 percent (for earned income between $10,000 and $19,999), and 30 percent (for income $20,000 and above). Under this system, a worker with $15,000 in taxable income would pay 10 percent on the first $9,999 and 20 percent on the rest, for a total of $2,000 and an average tax rate of 13.3 percent. In sum, a taxpayer's bracket defines her marginal rate—the rate paid on the "last dollar" earned—but, as a percentage of income, her tax liability is generally less than the marginal rate. The percentage of income that a household pays in income taxes is referred to as its average tax rate or tax burden.

The distribution of the overall tax burden can be reshaped dramatically by changing tax rates, the number and boundaries of tax brackets, or both. Broadly speaking, tax reforms that have reduced income tax rates by equal percentages have tended to redistribute income toward higher-income earners. To illustrate this effect, consider the situation of two families, one earning $15,000 and the other earning $50,000. Under the rate structure presented above, the low-income family would owe $2,000 in tax, and the middle-income family would owe $12,000 (an average tax rate of 24 percent). Now suppose that rates in all three brackets are cut in half to 5 percent, 10 percent, and 15 percent. The low-income family would then owe $1,000 (an average rate of 6.7 percent), and the middle-income family would owe $6,000 (an average rate of 12 percent). While both families have seen their tax liability cut in half, the low-income family's after-tax income has increased by only $1,000, or 7.7 percent, while the middle-income family's after-tax income has grown by $6,000, or 15.8 percent.

TAXABLE INCOME, EXEMPTIONS, DEDUCTIONS, AND CREDITS.   Tax rates are not the only determinant of a household's tax burden; an equally important factor is the way in which the household's taxable income is defined. For most low-income families, their taxable income is equal to their adjusted gross income less personal and dependent exemptions and a standard deduction. Since 1985 the U.S. Department of the Treasury has annually adjusted the personal exemption, standard deduction, and income tax tables to account for the prior year's change in the consumer price index.

The personal and dependent exemptions reduce the amount of earned income subject to federal income tax to account for differences in ability to pay based on family size. The tax benefits resulting from these exemptions depend on a family's marginal tax rate. As a result, an exemption is more valuable for high-income families than for low-income families.[12]

The standard deduction reduces taxable income for most workers by a fixed dollar amount that depends on their marital status, filing status, and age.[13] Many middle- and upper-income taxpayers choose to itemize deductions instead of taking a standard deduction. Itemized deductions, including for pension contributions and earnings, employer-paid health insurance premiums, mortgage interest on owner-occupied homes, and state and local income taxes, account for the majority of federal income tax relief.[14] However, most low- to moderate-wage workers and their families claim a standard deduction. The actual tax relief of a standard deduction equals the amount by which it exceeds deductions that would be itemized multiplied by the average tax rate on such deductions.

During the 1970s the standard deduction—known as the "zero bracket amount" from 1977 to 1986—became the preferred policy tool of federal policymakers who hoped to lessen the tax burden on low-income workers and their families. More recently, tax credits have taken over this role. While exemptions and deductions reduce taxable income, tax credits reduce income tax liability dollar for dollar. There are two types of credits: nonrefundable and refundable. Nonrefundable tax credits can reduce tax owed to zero but do not give rise to a refund. A refundable credit can reduce taxes below zero and generate a cash refund. Income tax credits can be structured in a number of ways, each with different distributional implications. They can be set at a fixed amount that does not vary by income; they can be structured to be more generous for some income groups than

12. Sammartino, Toder, and Maag (2002).
13. Blind taxpayers and taxpayers with blind spouses also qualify for a slightly higher standard deduction.
14. Sammartino, Toder, and Maag (2002).

for others; or like the EITC, which is designed primarily to help low-income and moderate-income working families, they can exclude some income groups altogether.

MARRIAGE PENALTIES AND BONUSES. Many of the factors just described—tax brackets and marginal rates, standard deductions, and the structure of tax credits, notably the EITC—interact to impose a marriage penalty on two-earner families. Under the current system, single individuals, heads of households, and married couples are subject to different standard deductions and tax rate schedules. Therefore, changes of marital and filing status can have important tax consequences. A married couple is generally required to file a joint tax return based on the combined income of husband and wife. When workers with similar earnings marry, their combined income often pushes them into a higher tax bracket than they would face as singles because most brackets for married couples are less than twice as wide as those for single filers. In contrast, when earners with dissimilar incomes marry, the individual with a higher income moves into a lower marginal tax bracket as a result of the change in marital and tax filing status, reducing the household's combined tax burden and increasing its after-tax income.[15]

In 2001 Congress alleviated the marriage penalty for lower-income families by redefining the two bottom brackets so that they would be twice as wide for married couples as for single filers. At the same time, it eliminated a second aspect of the marriage penalty by making the standard deduction for married couples twice the amount for single filers. (Like many provisions of the 2001 tax law, these measures were scheduled to sunset in 2010.) However, the marriage penalty remains a significant problem for low-income families who qualify for income-related tax credits such as the EITC. If a single working parent qualifies for the full EITC, marriage to another worker will usually result in a reduction in her credit or even its elimination because of the increase in her household income.[16] As this example suggests, low-income earners face some of the highest marginal tax rates because additional earned income not only increases the percentage paid on each dollar but also can cause them to forfeit tax credits.[17] On the other hand, the EITC offers a marriage bonus for couples consisting of a nonworking mother and a working man without children. In this case, her

15. Alm and Whittington (1999).
16. Ellwood and Sawhill (2000). See also McIntyre and McIntyre (1999).
17. Sammartino (2001).

children and his earnings allow them to receive the EITC when neither would qualify otherwise.

Compared to their lower- and higher-earning counterparts, moderate- to middle-income parents face what has been called a "middle-class parent penalty." Low-income workers with children receive tax benefits from the EITC, while higher-income earners with children benefit more from dependent exemptions. Parents in the middle receive substantially smaller child-related tax benefits. Middle-income families are increasingly likely to face marginal tax rates that are often as high as or higher than those that more affluent families face, due in large part to payroll taxes to finance Social Security and Medicare, as well as to marriage penalties.[18]

Role of the Federal Payroll Tax

Payroll taxes are mandated by the Federal Insurance Contributions Act, which finances Social Security and Medicare. Social Security provides benefits under the Old-Age, Survivors, and Disability Insurance trust fund. Medicare provides benefits under the Hospital Insurance trust fund. In contrast to the individual income tax, payroll taxes are levied on gross wages without exemptions or deductions. They are imposed on earnings, not investment income, and they apply at a single marginal tax rate. In the case of the Social Security tax, it also only applies up to an earned income ceiling ($106,800 in 2009). Thus payroll taxes have many regressive characteristics. However, the Social Security system as a whole is progressive. Social Security benefits are paid according to a formula that gives low-income earners a better rate of return on their contributions than high-income earners. It thus redistributes income from middle- and high-income earners to low-income households.

Role of the Federal Minimum Wage

While income and payroll taxes affect earners' after-tax income, the federal minimum wage is intended to boost the pretax earnings of workers in the lower tiers of the wage distribution.[19] It affects the earnings of all low-wage workers by establishing a floor for hourly wage compensation in covered sectors. It has taken on greater significance as the proportion of the U.S. workforce that has its wages set by collective bargaining has declined.

18. Ellwood and Leibman (2000); Davig and Garner (2006). See also U.S. Department of Commerce (2007).
19. Freeman (1994, 1996).

In 1983, 20.1 percent of U.S. workers were unionized. By 2008 the number had fallen to 12.4 percent.[20]

Proponents of the minimum wage view it as an important antipoverty tool. Opponents see it as a burden on employers and as unwarranted interference with the labor market. In particular, the employment effects of the minimum wage have generated considerable controversy. As early as 1941, economist George Stigler argued that "economists should be outspoken and singularly agreed" that the minimum wage does not reduce poverty.[21] Opponents continue to claim that the weight of the evidence over the past twenty-five years supports the traditional view that higher minimum wages reduce employment by forcing marginal businesses to lay off workers. However, research suggests that the most recent minimum wage increases have had little or no adverse effect.[22] Moreover, some economists believe that the minimum wage offers substantial benefits. They cite higher productivity, decreased turnover, lower recruiting and training costs, decreased absenteeism, and increased worker morale as gains that might offset some of the costs employers experience from a wage increase.[23]

Centrists in both parties have tried to minimize the negative economic (and political) consequences of the minimum wage by exempting various types of employers. The original 1938 minimum wage extended only to "businesses that were actually engaged in and substantially and materially affecting interstate commerce." Although the primary goal of this clause was to ensure the constitutionality of the legislation, it also made it politically more appealing by limiting its cost. Even after the Supreme Court upheld the federal minimum wage in 1941, agricultural and domestic service workers were exempt until 1966. These occupations—together with employees in the retail trade, who were similarly excluded until the 1960s—made up a large proportion of low-wage workers in the 1960s. By 2008, the highest proportion of workers earning at or below the federal minimum wage was in service occupations, about 9 percent. About 7 in 10 workers earning the minimum wage or less in 2008 were employed in service occupations, mostly in food preparation and serving related jobs.[24]

20. U.S. Department of Labor, Bureau of Labor Statistics, "Union Members in 2008," Economic News Release, January 28, 2009 (www.bls.gov/news.release/union2.nr0.htm).

21. Stigler (1946).

22. Card and Krueger (1995); Freeman (1996).

23. Fox (2006).

24. U.S. Department of Labor (2009); U.S. Department of Labor, Bureau of Labor Statistics, "B-2. Average Hours and Earnings of Production and Nonsupervisory Workers (1) On Private Nonfarm Pay-

More recently policymakers have sought to cushion the effects of the minimum wage on employers by packaging increases with small business tax relief. The Targeted Jobs Tax Credit (TJTC) that was enacted in 1978 provided employer tax credits to firms that hired workers in a number of categories, including low-income youth, low-income Vietnam veterans, low-income ex-convicts, and welfare recipients. In 1996 the Small Business Job Protection Act authorized the Work Opportunity Tax Credit (WOTC) to replace the TJTC. In 2007 Congress extended the WOTC until 2011 by passing the Small Business and Work Opportunity Tax Act. Currently, the WOTC provides a tax credit of up to 40 percent of the first $6,000 in wages paid during the first twelve months for each new qualified hire.[25] However, participation rates in WOTC are low, and its impact on employment is questionable.

Some recent research concludes that the EITC is more effective than the minimum wage in providing support for low-wage workers. Minimum wage critics argue, for example, that the EITC is better targeted than the minimum wage because many of the beneficiaries of minimum wage increases are not members of low-income families.[26] However, others conclude that the effectiveness of the EITC in raising the incomes of working poor families above the federal poverty threshold depends, in part, on regular increases in the minimum wage. Richard Freeman concludes that an appropriately set minimum wage can be a modestly effective redistributive tool—a risky but potentially profitable investment—particularly if it is linked with other social policies that support low-income earners and their families.[27]

Measuring the Distributional Impact

To understand how these policies affect the economic well-being of low-income earners and families, we must identify some appropriate metrics. In this book, I will focus primarily on how the federal income tax code and the

---

rolls by Major Industry Sector, 1964 to Date," 2009 (ftp://ftp.bls.gov/pub/suppl/empsit.ceseeb2.txt); U.S. Department of Labor, Bureau of Labor Statistics, "Characteristics of Minimum Wage Workers," table 4 (Employed Wage and Salary Workers Paid Hourly Rates . . .), 2008 (www.bls.gov/cps/min wage2008.htm).

25. Hamersma (2005).
26. Hotz and Scholz (2000, pp. 25–42).
27. Freeman (1996).

minimum wage affect a family's economic status relative to the federal poverty threshold. The federal poverty threshold represents "the minimum dollar amount needed for individuals, couples, or families to purchase food and meet other basic needs."[28] It increases with family size and is updated for inflation annually, using the consumer price index.[29] If total family income is less than the threshold appropriate for that family, the family is in poverty. Although the thresholds in some sense reflect families' needs, they are intended for use as a statistical yardstick, not as a complete description of what people and families need to live.

A useful way to think about the impact of the federal income tax on low-income working families is to compare the income tax entry threshold and the poverty threshold. The tax entry threshold is the maximum income a family can earn before owing federal income tax. If the income tax entry threshold for, say, a family of four, falls at or below the federal poverty threshold, tax liabilities will push such families below the poverty level. In recent decades policymakers have sought to avoid this outcome.

Another way to evaluate the impact of federal taxes is to examine the burden of the income and payroll tax.[30] The combination of income and payroll taxes can result in much higher effective tax rates and a higher total tax burden for lower-income households. (The effective tax rate measures the average rate at which an individual is taxed on his or her earned income.) It also shows that a higher portion of the total tax burden is being borne by labor income (as opposed to capital income, which is concentrated in higher-income households).

Like the tax system, the minimum wage can be evaluated relative to federal poverty thresholds. A key measure of the minimum wage's effectiveness is the annual income that a full-time, full-year worker who earns the minimum wage would earn relative to the poverty threshold for a family of three or four people. The ratio of the minimum wage relative to the average wage (which reflects the earnings of both skilled and unskilled workers) is another important metric, as is the real value of the minimum wage. In addition, many analysts focus on the number and percentage of workers who would be affected by a minimum wage increase.

---

28. U.S. Department of Labor (2005).
29. Maag (2004).
30. Center on Budget and Policy Priorities (1997).

A Brief History of the Federal Income Tax, Payroll Taxes, and the Minimum Wage

Federal income tax rates have varied widely since 1913, when the Sixteenth Amendment authorized Congress to levy an income tax, and now range from 10 to 35 percent of taxable income. (See figure 1-1.) From 1913 until World War II, high-income earners were the only group with any federal tax liability. This situation began to change in the early 1940s, when federal policymakers for the first time had to persuade low- and moderate-income earners to accept an individual income tax to help finance the nation's defense. With the emergence of inflation after World War II, these low- and moderate-income earners saw their tax rates increase through a phenomenon known as bracket creep: growth in their nominal incomes pushed them into higher tax brackets even when their real incomes remained the same or fell. High inflation rates played havoc on the after-tax income of low- to moderate-income earners because tax rate brackets, fixed exemptions, deductions, and credits were not indexed for inflation.

Because the personal exemption and the minimum standard deduction remained constant in nominal terms between 1948 and 1963, while the federal poverty threshold rose with inflation, the level at which low-income families started paying income taxes fell below the poverty line during this period. In 1964 Congress began to adjust tax entry thresholds—the amount a family could earn before having to pay federal income taxes—back up toward the federal poverty thresholds. But tax entry thresholds again fell below federal poverty lines during the late 1970s, and ad hoc increases were adopted in 1970, 1972, and 1979 to address the problem.[31]

The 1980s brought relief for low-income families in two forms. First, legislation passed in 1981 indexed the personal exemption, standard deduction, and tax brackets to inflation beginning in 1985. Second, the 1986 tax reform expanded the EITC, which had been introduced in more modest form in 1975, and indexed it to inflation as well. These changes, followed by further increases in the EITC in the 1990s under the Clinton administration, significantly reduced the tax burden faced by low-income earners with children. Since the 1990s the tax entry threshold for a family of four has exceeded the federal poverty threshold, due largely to the EITC and more recently to the Child Tax Credit.[32]

31. Bakija and Steuerle (1991).
32. U.S. House of Representatives (2000); Maag (2004).

Figure 1-1. *U.S. Individual Income Tax Rates, 1913–2009*

Tax rate (percent)

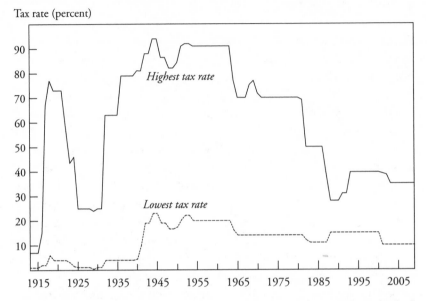

Source: Tax Policy Center, Tax Facts Online. Adapted from Tax Policy Center, "Historical Individual Income Tax Parameters," November 6, 2008 (www.taxpolicycenter.org/taxfacts/displayafact.cfm? Docid=543).

Payroll Taxes

When the federal payroll tax was first collected in 1937, it was only 2 percent of wages and salaries, evenly divided between employer and employee. (See figure 1-2.) By 1960 the rate had tripled to 6 percent, which approached the upper range of what President Franklin D. Roosevelt's Treasury Department had anticipated that low-income workers could bear without needing income tax relief. In 2009 the federal payroll tax rate was 15.3 percent of earnings (12.4 percent for Social Security and 2.9 percent for Medicare).[33]

Historically, the parties have disagreed over how to finance expansion of the Social Security program. Liberal legislators typically preferred to increase the income ceiling on the payroll tax base, which would increase the tax burden on higher-income workers, while their more conservative colleagues favored increasing the payroll tax rate, which would increase the tax burden on lower-income earners.[34] However, by the mid-1970s, both

33. Burman and Leiserson (2007).
34. Reese (1980, pp. 140, 169).

Figure 1-2. *Historical Payroll Tax Rates (OASDI and HI), 1937–2009*[a]

Percent

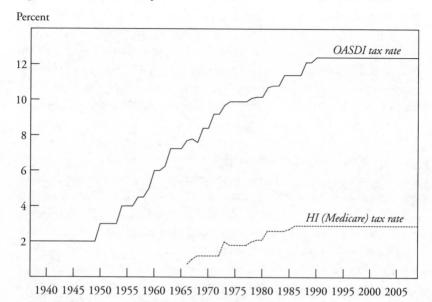

OASDI tax rate

HI (Medicare) tax rate

1940 1945 1950 1955 1960 1965 1970 1975 1980 1985 1990 1995 2000 2005

Sources: Social Security Administration, "Contribution and Benefit Base," January 15, 2009 (www.ssa.gov/OACT/COLA/cbb.html), and "Social Security and Medicare Tax Rates" (www.ssa.gov/OACT/ProgData/taxRates.html [January 8, 2009]).

a. OASDI, Old-Age, Survivors, and Disability Insurance trust fund; HI, Hospital Insurance trust fund. Amounts for 1937–74 and for 1979–81 were set by statute; all other amounts were determined under automatic adjustment provisions of the Social Security Act. Before 1989 the tax rate on self-employed persons was less than the combined tax rate on employers and employees. For 1991, 1992, and 1993, the upper limits on earnings subject to HI taxes were $125,000, $130,200, and $135,000 respectively. The upper limit was repealed by the Omnibus Budget Reconciliation Act of 1993.

Democrats and Republicans expressed growing concern about the regressive effects of the federal payroll tax, which when combined with the individual income tax, imposed a much higher effective tax rate on low-income earners than high-income earners. In fact, many low-income taxpayers owed more in payroll taxes than in federal income taxes. To help such families, in 1975 Congress adopted the Earned Income Credit—later known as the EITC—which significantly reduced their tax liability. Because of such programs, most low-wage workers now have net negative tax liabilities throughout their lifetimes.[35]

35. U.S. Congress (1997).

The Minimum Wage

Congress initially set the federal minimum wage at twenty-five cents per hour as part of the 1938 Fair Labor Standards Act.[36] At the time, most low-wage workers worked in sawmills and the apparel industry in the South. Today the impact of the minimum wage is not concentrated in one region. It largely affects teenagers and young adults; however, as the earnings distribution has widened in recent decades, an increasing number of adults have become its potential beneficiaries.[37]

Beyond its initial three-step increase to 40 cents per hour in 1945, Congress has increased the minimum wage numerous times over the past seven decades. (See figure 1-3.) Nonetheless, because the minimum wage has not been indexed to increase with the cost of living, it has not kept pace with inflation, and its real value has declined. The inflation-adjusted value of the minimum wage was 19 percent lower in 2008 than it was in 1979.[38]

The minimum wage was most effective as an antipoverty tool in 1968, when it allowed a full-time, full-year worker to earn an income equivalent to 118.7 percent of the poverty threshold for a three-person family. Since 1980 it has been below the poverty level for a full-time, full-year worker in a three-person family.[39] Today a worker who is employed full-time at the minimum wage of $7.25 per hour earns about $15,000 a year—more than $2,000 below the federal poverty threshold for a family of three and more than $6,000 below the poverty threshold for a family of four.

Similarly, the proportion of hourly workers earning the federal minimum wage or less has trended downward since 1979, when the government began to collect data on a regular basis.[40] In 1981, 15.1 percent of hourly paid workers were making less than the new minimum wage; in 2007, 2.3 percent of hourly paid workers were making less than the new minimum wage. Among those workers paid by the hour in 2007, 267,000 were reported as earning exactly the prevailing federal minimum wage.

36. Grossman (1978). For more historical background, see Storrs (2000); Hart (1994); Mettler (1998); Steinberg (1982); O'Brien (1998); Robertson (2000).

37. Freeman (1996).

38. Economic Policy Institute, "EPI Issue Guide: Minimum Wage," August 2008, p. 1 (www.epi.org/issueguides/minwage/epi_minimum_wage_issue_guide.pdf).

39. Tom Gabe, "Historical Relationship between the Minimum Wage and Poverty, 1959 to 2005," Congressional Research Service memorandum, July 5, 2005 (www.chn.org/pdf/crsminimumwage.pdf).

40. U.S. Department of Labor (2005).

Figure 1-3. *Nominal and Real Value of the Minimum Wage, 1947–2009*[a]

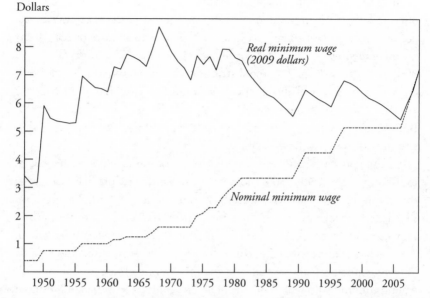

Dollars

Source: Economic Policy Institute analysis of Department of Labor and Bureau of Labor Statistics data (www.epi.org/publications/entry/tables_figures_data).

a. In May 2009 dollars, based on the Consumer Price Index Research Series Using Current Methods (CPI-U-RS).

Nearly 1.5 million were reported as earning wages below the minimum wage. Together, these 1.7 million workers with wages at or below the minimum made up 2.3 percent of all hourly workers.[41]

Boosting Paychecks: The Role of Partisan Preferences and Coalition Politics

In analyzing these policy approaches, I highlight the importance of partisan political control of the White House and Congress on the one hand and coalition politics within Congress on the other. Partisan control of the White House has already been shown to have a significant effect on the distribution of income nationwide. For example, as Larry Bartels concludes, "The striking differences in the economic fortunes of rich and poor under Democratic and Republican administrations evident in the historical record

41. Ibid., table 10.

do not seem to be an artifact of the different conditions under which Democrats and Republicans have happened to hold the reins of government, but a reflection of the fundamental significance of partisan politics in the political economy of the post-war U.S."[42] The average rates of real, after-tax income growth since 1980 for households at the 20th, 40th, 60th, and 80th percentiles of the income distribution scale show that households at every income level did about equally well under Democrats Jimmy Carter and Bill Clinton, while Republicans Ronald Reagan and George H. W. Bush produced weaker income growth at the top of the income distribution and little or none at the bottom.

Partisan political control is also important for understanding the federal minimum wage. Keith Poole and Howard Rosenthal report that changes to the nominal value of the minimum wage since World War II have depended largely on which party controls Congress and the White House.[43] The federal minimum wage increased at an average annual rate of 7.1 percent when Democrats controlled both the House and the Senate. When Democrats had political control of the White House as well, the federal minimum wage grew 9.3 percent a year. Under a Republican president and a Democratic Congress, its annual growth rate was only 4.6 percent.

The differences between the parties over key issues have increased in recent decades as partisan polarization has soared. According to Nolan McCarty, by almost all measures, the divide between Democratic and Republican members of Congress has widened over the past twenty-five years, reaching levels of partisan conflict not witnessed since the 1920s.[44] Polarization contributes to gridlock and stalemate, making it more difficult for Congress to respond to economic shocks and to pass contested measures such as increases in the minimum wage.

Nonetheless, bipartisan coalitions have continued to form around important policy issues. In the case of the income tax, centrists in both parties have embraced the goal of progressivity and worked together through the House Ways and Means and Senate Finance Committees to incorporate such policies as the EITC and other tax credits into omnibus budget packages. Moderates have also joined coalitions in support of minimum wage increases by crafting agreements that allowed them to secure the elec-

---

42. Bartels (2004, p. 13).
43. Poole and Rosenthal (1991).
44. McCarty (2007).

toral benefits of a modest minimum wage increase without imposing industry-, group-, or geography-specific costs.[45]

In examining each of these bargains, the major analytical challenge is to identify the coalition that made the political agreement possible. Thus, rather than examine only the preferences of the ardent supporters and opponents of each policy approach, I attempt to identify the centrist members of the enacting coalition whose preferences had to be taken into account in order to reach a bargain.[46]

Plan of the Book

In the chapters that follow, I offer an analytically grounded narrative that abstracts from the historical details and identifies broad partisan and coalitional patterns in the politics of supporting low-income earners and their families since the early twentieth century. Chapters 2 and 3 explain the political development of the federal income and payroll tax and the minimum wage, with a particular focus on the period between the New Deal and 1980. Chapters 4–6 focus on the political evolution of the federal income and payroll tax and the minimum wage (and their potential interactions or lack thereof) from 1981 to the 2008 election. Chapter 7 focuses on initial efforts by Obama and Democrats in Congress to extend additional income tax relief to working families. Chapter 8 assesses the distributive implications of the federal government's policy regime to support low-income working families and concludes by moving from the retrospective to the prospective: the immediate political future of boosting the paychecks of low-wage workers and their families in America.

Why is boosting paychecks so important? It is simply because, for the foreseeable future, many less-skilled workers will continue to face low and even falling real wages. Declining demand has pulled down the wages of the less skilled, both men and women, so employment often does not lead to economic self-sufficiency. Consequently, the construction of a new policy regime that balances the flexibility of the labor market with economic security for low-wage workers and their families remains a key political challenge in the twenty-first century.

45. Arnold (1990).
46. McCubbins, Noll, and Weingast (1992, 1994).

2 | The Political Origins of Federal Taxes on Individual Income

The goal of this chapter is to explain the political development of the federal individual income and payroll taxes, as their basic parameters emerged in the four decades between the New Deal and the late 1970s, and to characterize their impact on low-income earners and their families. Throughout this period, partisan conflict over the federal income and payroll tax largely mirrored broader ideological and distributional divisions within American politics. By 1980 the result was a system that included a higher income tax rate on high-income earners, a lower or zero rate on low-income earners, and a moderate amount exempted from tax liability for middle-income earners. However, even families living below the federal poverty threshold who owed no individual income taxes still faced substantial payroll taxes.

Origins of the Federal Individual Income Tax

The federal government first imposed a personal income tax in 1861 to help finance the Civil War.[1] However, such levies faced constitutional challenges until 1913, when the ratification of the Sixteenth Amendment opened the way for the creation of the federal income tax. That same year, Congress adopted an income tax with rates ranging from 1 percent to 7 percent and

1. Baack and Ray (1985).

approved a personal exemption of $4,000 for a married person (worth roughly $87,000 in 2009) and $3,000 for a single taxpayer, thereby creating an initial tax bracket with no tax liability that encompassed more than 99 percent of the working-age population. The legislation also provided deductions for such expenses as state and local taxes but made no allowance for dependents.[2] In establishing this system, Democrats in Congress argued that no tax should be due on the minimum sum that a taxpayer required for his or his family's daily expenses. They believed that "$4,000 [was] a reasonable amount for an American family to live upon, with a proper standard of living, and that a sum below that ought not to be taxed."[3] However, over the next thirty-five years, federal policymakers changed the exemption level frequently, in both directions, to produce sizable increases or decreases in tax revenues.[4] (See figure 2-1 for the history of personal exemption.)

Following the country's entry into World War I, Congress raised the lowest tax rate to 2 percent and the highest tax rate, which applied to earners with incomes in excess of $1.5 million, to 15 percent. Further wartime increases brought the lowest rate to 6 percent and the top rate to 77 percent by 1918. Driven by wartime revenue needs, in 1917 Congress also reduced the exemptions of married taxpayers and heads of families by half to $2,000. (Single heads of families had been granted the same exemption as married filers in 1916.) The exemption for a single filer fell even more in percentage terms from $3,000 to $1,000. The impact of this sharp drop was somewhat softened by the introduction of a personal exemption allowance for dependents, then termed a credit, of $200 for each child or dependent relative living with the taxpayer.[5]

By 1921 both Democrats and Republicans believed that high wartime tax rates were not justified in times of peace and that tax avoidance had reduced the revenue collected from higher-income Americans, thus shifting the tax burden toward lower-income earners.[6] Although there was general agreement that income tax rates should be cut, there was major disagreement over how much progressivity should be written into a new tax rate schedule. The Republican majority favored substantial rate cuts and less progressivity while Democrats wanted larger tax rate reductions for the lowest-income earners

2. Blakey and Blakey (1940, p. 97).
3. Seltzer (1968, p. 38-57).
4. See Talley (2001).
5. Seltzer (1968, p. 40). See also "Defines Tax Exemptions," *New York Times,* February 10, 1918.
6. Smiley and Keehn (1995).

Figure 2-1. *History of the Personal Exemption, 1913–2009*

Amount (dollars)

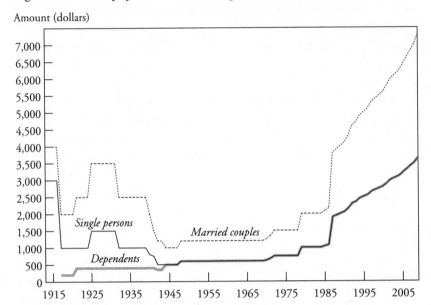

Source: Adapted from Tax Policy Center Online, "Tax Facts: Historical Individual Income Tax Parameters" (www.taxpolicycenter.org/TaxFacts/TFDB/TFTemplate.cfm?Docid=543 [July 2009]).

and smaller reductions for higher-income earners, and progressive Republicans pushed for an even steeper set of progressive tax rates.

The combination of a booming economy and Republican control of both Congress and the White House resulted in five income tax cuts over the 1920s, including both across-the-board rate reductions and an increase in personal exemptions for married taxpayers, single filers, and dependents. In 1921 Congress raised the exemptions for married filers and heads of families from $2,000 to $2,500 for those with net incomes of no more than $5,000 ($60,000 in 2009 dollars) and increased the credit for each dependent from $200 to $400. In 1926 personal exemptions rose again from $2,500 to $3,500 for married filers and heads of families and from $1,000 to $1,500 for single persons. These levels were retained until 1932.

The across-the-board income tax rate cuts shifted the federal income tax code in a less progressive direction.[7] By 1929 the marginal rate facing the highest earners had been reduced to 24 percent. Thus the Democrats

7. Ibid.

lost their battle to retain steep marginal rates on the nation's highest-income earners. However, by increasing personal exemptions, they did manage to target some relief at the lower end of the income distribution, removing many from the tax rolls entirely.[8]

Origins of the Payroll Tax

The Great Depression ended Republican tax reductions and led to significant changes in the federal income tax. The 1932 Revenue Act, enacted five months before Franklin Roosevelt won his first bid for the White House, established the enduring framework for 1930s federal income tax policy.[9] With bipartisan support, Democrats in control of Congress approved across-the-board increases in tax rates, cut personal exemptions (to $2,500 for married taxpayers and $1,000 for single filers), and imposed a federal sales tax on a limited number of items, including gasoline and electricity.[10] Three years later the Democratic majority in Congress again increased the rates on high-income earners.[11] By 1936 the lowest tax rate was 4 percent and the top tax rate was 79 percent.[12] However, only 2 million households—out of 32 million—had any federal tax liability—largely due to the personal exemption.[13]

President Franklin D. Roosevelt championed progressivity in the income tax code, arguing that "long ago the United States, through the Congress, accepted the principle that citizens should pay in accordance with their ability to pay, and that identical tax rates on the rich and on the poor actually worked an injustice to the poor."[14] However, by 1938 a coalition of conservative Democrats and Republicans began to block any additional New Deal tax reform.[15] FDR denounced these efforts as the "abandonment of an important principle of American taxation"—taxing according to ability to pay.[16]

---

8. Joseph J. Thorndike, "The Republican Roots of New Deal Tax Policy," *Tax Notes*, September 1, 2003.

9. Ibid.

10. The limitation of the sales tax represented a victory for Democratic House insurgents, led by a member of the House Ways and Means Committee, who had opposed their leaders' support for a general federal sales tax on the grounds that it would be highly regressive (Brownlee 1996, pp. 72–73).

11. Brownlee (1996, p. 83).

12. Ibid.

13. Brownlee (2004).

14. Franklin D. Roosevelt, "Message to Congress on Terminating Tax Exemptions, April 25, 1938," *American Presidency Project* (www.presidency.ucsb.edu/ws/?pid=15633).

15. Leff (1984).

16. Ibid., p. 99.

Nevertheless, the president was also responsible for a significant increase in the regressivity of the federal tax system because of his decision to champion the payroll tax, which was introduced in 1935 to fund the Social Security program. FDR opted not to finance Social Security through an increase in income taxes, fearing congressional opposition.[17] At the time— and for decades to come—tax legislation was tightly controlled by the Ways and Means Committee in the House and the Finance Committee in the Senate. Ways and Means, in particular, had developed a high degree of autonomy from—and even significant power over—the House majority.[18] In addition, the seniority system that guided committee assignments gave control of the committee to conservative Democrats from the one-party South. Rather than confront the conservative wing of his party head-on, Roosevelt proposed that his new program rely on earmarked federal payroll taxes. This approach also allowed him to insist that Social Security was not an income transfer program but a form of insurance, with workers paying premiums (through the payroll tax) in return for future benefits.[19] Therefore, FDR claimed, a "future president and Congress could not repeal the entitlement character of the program."

The 1935 Social Security Act created a federal old-age insurance program financed by a federal payroll tax of 2 percent, to be shared between the employer and employee, on a covered worker's first $3,000 in wages.[20] At the time, only 3 percent of covered workers earned more than $3,000 annually.[21] The payroll tax was scheduled to increase in steps to 6 percent by 1949, despite a warning from the president's Committee on Economic Security that a payroll tax higher than 5 percent "might impair the living standards of workers and that the employer's 2.5 percent rate might actually fall on workers."[22]

Democratic backers of Social Security recognized that the federal payroll tax was regressive. However, they believed that this approach to funding would make the system more politically palatable. As Edward Berkowitz observes, the original proponents of Social Security "managed to sustain

17. Steinmo (1996, p. 99).
18. Zelizer (1998).
19. Ibid., p. 232.
20. Derthick (1979, pp. 229, 429).
21. Derthick (1979, p. 229).
22. Ibid. The Committee on Economic Security had proposed that the combined payroll tax should reach a maximum of 5 percent by 1965, after which general revenue funds would support future financing of Social Security.

what was probably the closest thing to a popular tax in American political history by emphasizing the close connection between payments and benefits."[23] Democrats also believed that the payroll tax represented a form of forced savings that would fund employees' retirement and facilitate the transition from a "living wage" during their active employment years to an "adequate minimum income" during their retirement.[24] Moreover, the formula by which benefits were allocated was designed to deliver a higher return to lower-income workers. For FDR and New Deal Democrats, the overall progressivity of the Social Security benefit formula outweighed the short-term economic burden that the payroll tax might impose on lower-income earners and their families.

Income Taxes for Everyone: The Impact of World War II

The approach of World War II led Democrats in Congress to increase income tax rates again in 1940. Of greater importance, it broadened the income tax base by reducing the personal exemption for a married taxpayer by 20 percent to $2,000. (The exemption for single filers fell to $800, but the exemption for dependents remained at $400.)[25] This move extended federal tax liability to an additional 2.19 million low- to moderate-income earners and families.[26] Further rate increases and cuts in the personal exemption followed, as Congress and the president struggled to finance a massive two-front war.

As a result of such steps, the individual income tax, which had applied to only a small percentage of the population until the early 1940s, had been extended to most earners in the labor market by the middle of the decade. As FDR's Treasury Secretary Henry Morgenthau Jr. remarked, "For the first time in our history, the income tax is becoming a people's tax."[27] The significant change of an income tax into a "people's tax" was a major political development in shaping later efforts to provide income tax relief. The number of individual taxable returns grew from 3.9 million in 1939 to more than 40 million in 1943, giving rise to the introduction of the modern withholding system.[28] To help new low- and moderate-income taxpayers, Congress

23. Berkowitz (1996, p. 153).
24. Ibid., p. 153.
25. Tempalski (2006, p. 9).
26. Kent (1941, p. 163).
27. U.S. Senate (1942, p. 3).
28. Witte (1985, p. 113).

created a standard deduction, as an alternative to itemized deductions, in 1944. Individuals were granted the option of taking a standard deduction amounting to 10 percent of adjusted gross income or $1,000, whichever was less, in lieu of itemizing personal deductions.[29] This innovation was an immediate success. More than 82 percent of earners selected the standard deduction over itemized deductions in 1944.[30] In addition, the 1944 tax legislation created a uniform personal exemption of $500 per person, replacing the previous system of different amounts for single filers, married taxpayers, and dependents.[31] This measure was intended to facilitate the construction of simple tax tables for the use of taxpayers with incomes under $5,000. From 1944 to 1969, the standard deduction was equal to 10 percent of adjusted gross income, up to a maximum of $1,000. Figure 2-2 shows the evolution of the standard deduction from 1970 to 2009.

Until World War II, the personal exemption functioned primarily to limit the number of workers with federal tax liability. Thereafter, although the precise purpose of the personal exemption was never explicitly stated by Congress, it served multiple purposes. First, it excluded from income tax altogether individuals and families with the smallest incomes. Second, it provided a deduction from otherwise taxable income for the essential living expenses of all earners. Third, it provided significant additional allowances for earners with dependents. And finally, when combined with a low first bracket tax rate, it created a "progression of effective tax rates in the lower part of the income scale."[32]

Although income tax rates increased sharply in wartime, with the top tax rate reaching 94 percent in 1944, the federal payroll tax followed a different trajectory. Under the original Social Security Act, the payroll tax was scheduled to begin increasing in 1940, ultimately reaching a combined employer–employee rate of 6 percent in 1949. However, since Social Security was not scheduled to begin paying benefits until 1942, it quickly built up a sizable reserve. Responding in part to pressure from business groups, Congress agreed to freeze the federal payroll tax rate until 1942. FDR supported the initial freeze of the scheduled payroll tax increases but opposed future deferrals.[33] In 1943 he vetoed a freeze of a scheduled payroll tax increase, but

29. Woodworth (1969, p. 713).
30. Ibid., pp. 711–25.
31. Tempalski (2006, p. 10).
32. Strayer (1955, p. 339).
33. Schieber and Shoven (1999).

Figure 2-2. *Historical Standard Deduction Amounts, 1970–2009*[a]

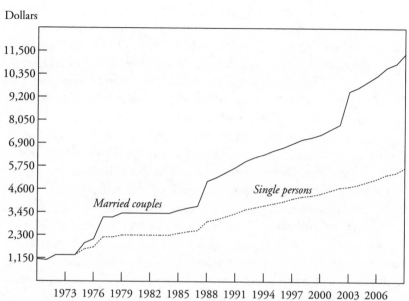

Dollars

Sources: Bakija and Steuerle (1991); Pechman (1987, appendix A.1); U.S. Census Bureau, "Historical Statistics of the United States, Colonial Period–1970 (www.census.gov/prod/www/ abs/statab.html); IRS Form 1040 instructions, various years; James Young, "Inflation Adjustments Affecting Individual Taxpayers in 2007," *Tax Notes*, October 9, 2006; Internal Revenue Service, "Revenue Procedure 2007-66" (www.irs.gov/pub/irs-drop/rp-07-66.pdf [November 1, 2007]); and Tax Policy Center, "Personal Exemption and Standard Deduction 2001–2009" (www.taxpolicycenter.org/taxfacts/displayafact.cfm?Docid=389).

a. Note: the standard deduction was first adopted in 1944. From 1944 to 1969, it was equal to 10 percent of adjusted gross income up to a maximum of $1,000.

Congress overrode the veto. A bipartisan coalition, consisting of Democrats who did not want to impose an additional burden on low-wage earners and Republicans who opposed a large Social Security trust fund reserve, rejected all subsequent payroll tax increases throughout the decade.[34]

Truman, a Republican Congress, and Across-the-Board Tax Relief

Partisan battles over federal income tax rates, which had been muted in wartime, reemerged after 1945. Broadly speaking, Democrats increasingly saw a progressive income tax code as an important mechanism for financing

34. Leff (1984, pp. 282–83).

domestic discretionary spending, while Republicans opposed larger government and higher taxes.[35] To bridge this divide, changes to the tax code had to deliver benefits to constituents of both parties and satisfy the powerful conservative coalition of Republicans and southern Democrats.[36] Each new proposal required the construction of an enacting coalition through logrolling and a broad distribution of income tax relief.[37] This maneuvering continued "to the point where no one was satisfied but few could afford to see the package defeated," as John Witte has observed.[38]

The first steps in postwar tax reform focused on rolling back the tax rate increases that had been adopted during World War II. In 1945 a Democratic Congress adopted income tax reductions that dropped the top rate from 94 percent to 86.5 percent and the bottom rate from 23 percent to 19 percent. Despite these rate cuts, the eightieth Congress—the first under Republican control since 1930—proposed across-the-board income tax relief in 1947. These proposals were opposed by President Harry S. Truman, who concluded that "in the present economic situation, it is clear that it would be unsound fiscal policy to [further] reduce individual income taxes," and by House minority Democrats, who argued that the reductions gave insufficient relief to low-income earners.[39] Confident of victory, House Republicans rejected Democratic efforts to aid low-income earners by increasing the personal exemption. However, in an effort to build a veto-proof majority, Senate Republicans included some tax relief for lower-wage earners as part of their package, introducing an entry-level 15 percent tax bracket.[40]

The Republican strategy succeeded. Truman vetoed three income tax relief packages in 1947 and 1948, arguing in one case that "the tax [cut] is inequitable as well as untimely. Nearly 40 percent of the reduction would go to individuals with net incomes in excess of $5,000, who constitute less than 5 percent of all taxpayers."[41] However, the Republican Congress overrode all three vetoes. Truman tried to counter the Republicans by propos-

35. Pollack (1996).

36. Steinmo (1996, p. 137).

37. Ibid.

38. Witte (1985).

39. Harry S. Truman, "Special Message: The President's First Economic Report to the Congress, January 8, 1947," *American Presidency Project* (www.presidency.ucsb.edu/ws/?pid=12828).

40. "Taxes and Economic Policy," *CQ Almanac*, 1948, pp. 336–37.

41. Harry S. Truman, "Veto of the Income Tax Reduction Bill, April 1, 1948," *American Presidency Project* (www.presidency.ucsb.edu/ws/?pid=13142).

ing a $40 "cost-of-living" tax credit for each worker and an additional $40 credit for each dependent in 1948. Although the credits would be extended to all earners, Truman believed they would be particularly helpful to those in the low-income group.[42] However, this effort failed.

The Republican Congress did provide some relief to low-income earners by increasing the personal exemption from $500 to $600 in 1948.[43] Republicans also provided relief to married couples by allowing them to file jointly and to compute their tax liability as though their combined incomes were divided equally between the spouses. Income splitting essentially doubled the width of tax brackets for married couples, thereby creating a "marriage bonus." However, Democrats claimed that this plan "would provide much more tax relief to the middle and upper brackets than to the lower."[44] The great majority of low-income married couples did not benefit at all or benefited little from joint filing because under both single and joint filing, their incomes fell within the first tax bracket.

With the outbreak of the Korean War, the national focus shifted from income tax relief to the renewed need to finance defense programs. In his 1951 Special Message to the Congress, Truman proposed an increase within each tax bracket while opposing any decrease in the personal exemption, which would adversely affect low- and moderate-income workers and their families. This time he found a more receptive audience in Congress, which had been retaken by Democrats in 1948. The Democratic Congress temporarily increased tax rates (through 1953) and approved an additional exemption for dependents age nineteen or older who were not students and who had no more than in $600 in earnings.

Congress also addressed a new problem created by the 1948 decision to allow income splitting for married couples. This provision created a substantial penalty for single persons with dependents, who found themselves placed in higher tax brackets than married couples with the same income. In 1951 Congress created a new filing category by allowing unmarried individuals with dependents to file as "head of household" and to claim a larger standard deduction.[45] The legislation created a separate rate schedule for heads of household that incorporated approximately half the benefits of income splitting. In 1954 the head of household category was expanded to

42. Ibid.
43. Seltzer (1968).
44. "Taxes and Economic Policy," *CQ Almanac*, 1948, p. 346.
45. Webster (1951).

include single persons who supported one or more parents in a separate home. In later decades, it became a mechanism for boosting the after-tax income of single-earner parents.

Eisenhower, Congress, and Reducing the Income Tax Burden

With the return to a peacetime economy, federal income tax politics took on a familiar pattern. Democrats continued to champion progressivity and to support increases in the personal exemption and a minimum standard deduction to "remove as many lower-wage workers as possible from federal income tax liability."[46] Republicans favored lower taxes on dividends in order to stimulate investment. However, Republicans within Congress were not united on taxes. Fiscal conservatives supported only limited tax cuts while other Republicans preferred major across-the-board income tax rate reductions, arguing that they would promote investment and productivity.

President Dwight D. Eisenhower, who took office in 1952 together with a newly Republican Congress, was a moderate Republican and a fiscal conservative. He opposed the Democrats' proposals to offer each earner a new income tax credit and to increase the personal exemption to $1,000, arguing that the latter measure "would excuse one taxpayer in every three from all federal income taxes." "The share of that one-third," he continued, "would have to be paid by the other two-thirds. I think this is wrong. I am for everybody paying his fair share."[47] But Eisenhower's tax reform plan did not include the more far-reaching tax reductions favored by congressional Republicans.[48] In addition, he offered some tax relief to low- and moderate-income working families by proposing a broader definition of the dependent exemption (to include unrelated but financially dependent individuals and children over nineteen who were full-time students) and a maximum deduction of $600 for child care expenses incurred by "gainfully employed women, widowers, and legally separated or divorced men."[49]

Most of Eisenhower's proposals were adopted with little partisan disagreement as the 1954 Internal Revenue Code (IRC). Over the next decade, there were no significant changes in the federal tax system. After Democrats

46. Reese (1980, p. 182).

47. Dwight D. Eisenhower, "Radio and Television Address to the American People on the Tax Program, March 15, 1954," *American Presidency Project* (www.presidency.ucsb.edu/ws/?pid=10181).

48. Pollack (1996).

49. Buehler (1998, p. 209); "Revision of Internal Revenue Laws," *CQ Almanac,* 1954, p. 476.

regained control of Congress in 1955, they proposed a $20 tax credit for every earner and dependent. However, Eisenhower opposed the measure on the grounds of cost.[50] Eisenhower was backed by Republicans and southern Democrats, who blocked the plan within the Senate Finance Committee.[51]

Because of the lack of federal government action, tax burdens climbed as inflation increased. As wages and salaries rose in nominal terms, they became more highly taxed, even though in real terms their value had not increased. In short, income taxes rose because the tax rates were not adjusted to compensate for inflation. Such "bracket creep" emerged as a political instrument for Democrats and Republicans alike because it allowed federal income taxes and revenues to increase without Congressional action. These inflation-driven increases in revenues enabled Congress to appease specific constituencies by offering targeted income tax relief through exclusions, deductions, and credits, such as tax-favored treatment for medical expenses, employer contributions to health plans, retirement income, and scholarship income. Many of these measures principally benefited middle- and higher-income families.[52]

End of a Political Freeze on the "Regressive" Federal Payroll Tax

In contrast to the back-and-forth over income tax rates, the federal payroll tax initially generated little partisan dissension. Throughout the 1940s, as Martha Derthick observed, "without regard to party or ideology, elected representatives of the people were not willing to argue for increases in an earmarked [payroll] tax if a current need for them could not be demonstrated."[53] Congress repeatedly postponed a federal payroll tax increase between 1942 and 1947, concluding that revenues were adequate to cover benefit payments.[54]

By 1950 Republicans and Democrats agreed on the desirability of expanding Social Security benefits and eligibility but held divergent preferences on how to finance this expansion. Democrats generally preferred to

---

50. Dwight D. Eisenhower, "The President's News Conference, February 23, 1955," *American Presidency Project* (www.presidency.ucsb.edu/ws/?pid=10418).

51. "Tax Policy, 1954" (*Congressional Quarterly*, 1965, pp. 416–18).

52. Witte (1985, p. 147).

53. Derthick (1979, p. 237).

54. The 1942 Revenue Act, a joint resolution regarding the 1943 Tariff Act, the 1943 Revenue Act, the 1945 Federal Insurance Contributions Act, the 1946 Social Security Amendments, and the 1947 Social Security Amendments all temporarily froze the combined rate at 2 percent. The 1947 act called for it to rise to 3 percent in 1950 and to 4 percent in 1952. See Derthick (1979, pp. 429–30); Solomon (1986).

raise the wage ceiling (the level of wages subject to the tax), which would increase the burden on higher-wage workers. Republicans generally favored an increase in the payroll tax, which would increase the burden on lower-income earners, both directly (through a decrease in take-home pay) and indirectly (through lower wages, as employers passed on their share of the tax).[55] Support among more conservative Democrats helped the Republican viewed prevail, and Congress increased the federal payroll tax four times during the 1950s. Lawmakers also adopted changes to Social Security in 1950, 1952, and 1954 that doubled monthly benefits for current and future recipients and added millions of new beneficiaries.[56] By 1960 the Federal Insurance Contributions Act (known as FICA) tax rate had reached 6 percent, split between employer and employee.

Kennedy, Johnson, and the Great Society

By the early 1960s, there was new movement to cut income tax rates, this time on the Democratic side. President John F. Kennedy and the Democratic majority in Congress supported tax reductions to stimulate the economy, which had begun to slow down.[57] In 1963 Kennedy proposed rate cuts that would reduce the top rate from 91 percent to 65 percent and lower the bottom rate from 20 percent to 14 percent. These cuts, he argued, would be reflected "immediately in lower withholding deductions and higher take-home pay for millions of Americans."[58]

Kennedy's plan included a number of proposals targeting earners at the bottom of the economic ladder.[59] In addition to cutting rates in the lower brackets, Kennedy urged that the first bracket be split into two groups so that married couples with adjusted gross incomes of $2,000 or less would receive a 30 percent reduction in their tax rate. He also recommended the adoption of a minimum standard deduction of $300 plus $100 per dependent up to the existing maximum of $1,000 (roughly $7,000 in 2009 dollars). At the time, the standard deduction could not exceed 10 percent of a person's income. The establishment of a minimum standard deduction would provide about $220 million of tax relief, primarily to those with

55. Reese (1980, p. 140).

56. Derthick (1979, p. 431). See also Kollmann (2000).

57. Reese (1980, p. 138).

58. John F. Kennedy, "Annual Message to the Congress on the State of the Union, January 14, 1963," *American Presidency Project* (www.presidency.ucsb.edu/ws/?pid=9138).

59. Ibid.

incomes below $5,000.[60] Kennedy believed these reforms were preferable to increasing the personal exemption because they focused relief "more directly on those who needed it most."[61] Kennedy also recommended an increase in the maximum allowable deduction for child care expenses, the amount of income that families with two working parents could earn and remain eligible for the child care deduction, and the age limit on qualifying children.[62]

President Lyndon B. Johnson, who pushed the tax package through after Kennedy's assassination, summed up its implications for a low-income family of four at the signing ceremony for the Revenue Act of 1964: "If you earn less than $3,000 a year, you will no longer pay federal income taxes. If you receive wages of $5,200 a year, your taxes will be reduced by $135 a year, nearly one-third of what you are now paying. Your take-home pay will go up around $10 a month."[63] In addition, for the first time, the new legislation set the federal income tax entry threshold to correspond to the official federal poverty threshold, by adjusting the personal exemption and standard deduction.[64] The introduction of the minimum standard deduction in 1964 enabled earners to shield from tax an additional $200 plus $100 for each personal exemption (up to a maximum of $1,000), thus increasing tax-free income to $900 for a single person, $1,600 for a married couple, and $3,000 for a married couple with two children.

Thus the individual income tax came to be seen as an antipoverty tool to move working poor families above the federal poverty threshold.

Combating poverty was one of President Johnson major goals. Although most attention focused on his proposals for ambitious new Great Society spending programs, tax policy was also part of his antipoverty agenda. In the mid-1960s, the White House charged several antipoverty task forces with investigating the impact of nonindexation of the personal exemption and standard deduction, as well as the effects of the federal payroll tax, which rose to 6.25 percent in 1962 and 7.25 percent in 1963.[65] The 1964 Presidential Task Force on Sustaining Prosperity reported that an individual income tax with fixed exemptions became "more burdensome for average and below-average income recipients" as the average level of income grew

60. Ibid.

61. Kennedy, "Annual Message to the Congress."

62. Witte (1985, p. 165).

63. Lyndon B. Johnson, "Radio and Television Remarks upon Signing the Tax Bill, February 26, 1964," *American Presidency Project* (www.presidency.ucsb.edu/ws/index.php?pid=26084).

64. Atrostic and Nunns (1990, p. 352).

65. Ventry (2000, p. 986).

over time. The task force also warned that a steady increase in the payroll tax would reduce the progressivity of the overall federal tax system. "Further cuts in tax rates and increases in payroll taxes would force an increasingly large share of the total federal income tax burden to fall on lower-income families," the task force concluded. "This cannot be justified simply by reference to the contributory aspect of the Social Security program."[66]

One year after the task force reported, payroll taxes were scheduled to increase yet again as a result of the creation of Medicare, a hospital and supplementary medical insurance program for seniors.[67] The Medicare payroll tax was set at 0.7 percent for 1966, and the Social Security tax was increased to 7.7 percent, for a combined rate of 8.4 percent. By 1969 the Medicare tax had risen to 1.2 percent and the rate for Social Security had reached 8.4 percent, for a total of 9.6 percent. Initially, the Medicare tax applied to the same wage base as the Social Security tax, but since 1994 it has been imposed on all wages and self-employment earnings.

The rising payroll tax burden helped fuel interest among some Democrats in a proposal known as the negative income tax (NIT). The NIT would be a mirror image of the regular income tax. Instead of tax liabilities varying positively with income according to an income tax rate schedule, benefits would vary inversely with income according to a negative tax rate (or benefit reduction) schedule. Unlike the traditional tools of tax relief, such as rate cuts or increases in the personal exemption, this approach would allow policymakers to increase the after-tax income of low-wage earners whose federal income tax liability was already zero but who faced increasingly burdensome payroll taxes. More broadly, it would provide an additional policy tool for pushing low-income working families above the federal poverty threshold and keeping them from turning to welfare or other cash assistance programs. However, President Johnson did not endorse the NIT.[68]

Nixon, a Democratic Congress, and Bipartisan Income Tax Relief

His successor, Richard Nixon, promised like Eisenhower that he would "bring equity to the federal tax system." His goal was to "lighten the burden on those who pay too much, and increase the taxes of those who pay

66. Samuelson (1964, p. 11).
67. Kollmann (2000).
68. Ventry (2000, p. 987).

too little."[69] In 1969 Nixon proposed targeted tax relief for lower-income earners. Notably, a new low-income allowance would remove more than 2 million low-income families from the federal tax rolls and "ensure that persons or families below the federal poverty threshold had no federal income tax liability."[70] Under the plan, a family of four would begin paying taxes only at the $3,500-a-year income level instead of at $3,000 under the existing law; even then such a family would not pay the full tax rate until its income reached $4,500 a year (about $26,500 in 2009 dollars).[71] Thus workers just above the federal poverty threshold would pay individual income taxes at reduced rates.[72]

The Democratic majority in Congress joined forces with the Republican president to adopt the low-income allowance. The low-income allowance was a two-part tax deduction consisting of a "basic allowance" and an "additional allowance." The basic allowance was the old minimum standard deduction: $200 plus $100 for each personal or dependent exemption up to a maximum of $1,000. The additional allowance was computed by subtracting the basic allowance from a base figure set at $1,100 in 1970, $1,050 in 1971, and $1,000 in 1972.

This reduction of the base figure was offset by planned increases in personal exemption levels from $650 in 1971 to $700 in 1972 and $750 in 1973. The net effect of the low-income allowance was to increase the amount of an earner's income shielded from tax to the amount of exemptions plus $1,100.[73] These changes were expected to give about 43 million earners some boost in after-tax income and remove more than 9 million low-income individuals from the tax rolls.[74] In addition, Congress and the president approved an inflation adjustment, which instituted scheduled increases in the amount of the personal exemption and standard deduction.

As part of the 1969 legislation, Nixon and Democrats in Congress also addressed the disparity between single and married persons, which had been introduced by income splitting, by creating a new tax schedule for single taxpayers under which the difference between the tax liability of a single person and that of a married couple with the same income could not

69. Richard Nixon, "Special Message to the Congress on Reform of the Federal Tax System, April 21, 1969," *American Presidency Project* (www.presidency.ucsb.edu/ws/?pid=2010).
70. Ibid.
71. "Nixon's Tax Package: A Modest Start on Reform," *Time*, May 2, 1969.
72. Nixon, "Special Message."
73. Dodyk (1971).
74. Nixon, "Special Message."

exceed 20 percent. Although there was no actual change in the tax burden imposed on married couples, the introduction of the new single schedule caused their relative position to worsen. This change transformed the "marriage bonus" into a "marriage penalty": in a reversal of the previous situation, the combined tax liability of two single people often increased with marriage. Since the reforms of 1969, numerous modifications to the income tax code have altered the magnitude of the marriage penalty.[75]

Two years later, the Nixon administration and Democratic Congress delivered further tax relief for low-income working families by again increasing the personal exemption, the standard deduction, and the minimum income at which earners must file tax returns. They also authorized greater income tax deductions for child care expenses.[76] Soon, however, attention began to shift from reducing tax liability to assisting low-income earners whose tax liability already was zero.

Although President Nixon had not mentioned the NIT in the 1968 election, he included it as part of his Family Assistance Plan in 1969. Under this proposal, a family of four with no income would receive $1,600 from the federal government—a guaranteed minimum income. However, the idea was blocked by conservative Democrats, who argued that it would undermine the incentive to work. As an alternative, Senate Finance Committee Chair Russell Long (D-La.) proposed a plan to distribute income tax relief only to those "willing to work." This proposal called for wage subsidies to low-income workers, known as a "work bonus," equal to 10 percent of the wages subject to payroll taxes. Long argued that his measure would offset federal payroll taxes, act as an earnings subsidy, and "prevent the taxing of people onto the welfare rolls."[77] One major attraction of the earnings subsidy, which eventually became known as the Earned Income Credit (EIC), was that its benefits rose positively with earnings up to a phase-out point, increasing incentives for very low income earners to work. However, liberal Democrats in the House rejected the proposal three years in a row in the hope of passing a negative income tax instead.

In its place, a group of Democratic liberals, led by Representative Martha Griffiths (D-Mich.), endorsed a proposal that replaced cash assistance programs ("welfare") with a federal system of income tax credits and allowances. Introduced as the Tax Credit and Allowances Act, the plan

75. Alm and Whittington (1996).
76. "Nixon Tax Plan Enacted after Major Partisan Clash," *CQ Almanac,* 1971, pp. 430–58.
77. Ventry (2000, p. 986).

proposed to replace personal exemptions and deductions for low-income families with refundable income tax credits. A bipartisan coalition, made up largely of conservative members, rejected this proposal because it did not fit an emerging political consensus that was pro-work, pro-growth, and low-cost.[78] A variety of other plans to help low-income earners—through increases in the personal exemption, refundable tax credits, tax deductions for Social Security taxes, reductions in payroll taxes, and even the abolition of payroll taxes altogether—similarly failed.[79]

Ford and the Origins of the Earned Income Credit

This was the backdrop against which President Gerald Ford took office in 1974. With the national economy heading toward recession, Ford proposed a one-year tax reduction, including an increase in the minimum standard deduction and cuts in tax rates.[80] He also proposed an $80 tax rebate for the country's poorest taxpayers.[81] Al Ullman (D-Ore.), the Democratic chairman of the House Ways and Means Committee, went further by proposing a refundable income tax credit, worth 5 percent of earned income, up to a maximum of $200 (worth roughly $800 in 2009), for lower-income earners with little or no tax liability.[82] This EIC, which closely matched the payroll tax on the first $4,000 of earned income, was expected to stimulate the economy because low-wage earners generally spent much of their increases in after-tax income.[83]

House Democrats viewed a one-time EIC as a way of offsetting the regressivity of the federal payroll tax, a subject of growing concern within both parties.[84] The House Ways and Means Committee report accompanying the legislation creating the EIC concluded: "If the problems of low-wage workers are the regressive effects of payroll taxes then the credit should be available to all low-income individuals, regardless of marital status or children."[85] Senate Democrats, in contrast, portrayed the EIC as

---

78. Ibid.
79. Ibid.
80. Gerald R. Ford, "Address before a Joint Session of the Congress Reporting on the State of the Union, January 15, 1975," *American Presidency Project* (www.presidency.ucsb.edu/ws/?pid=4938).
81. Gerald R. Ford, "Address before a Joint Session of the Congress Reporting on the State of the Union, January 19, 1976," *American Presidency Project* (www.presidency.ucsb.edu/ws/?pid=5677).
82. U.S. House of Representatives (1975).
83. Ibid.
84. U.S. House of Representatives (1975, p. 10).
85. Ibid.

work-to-welfare reform and sought to restrict the credit to low-income married couples with children. Many low-wage workers were from non-poor families; therefore, a Senate report argued, extending earning subsidies to all workers would be expensive and inefficient in reaching the poor.[86] By limiting eligibility for the EIC, the Senate plan reduced the number of earners who would see a boost in their paychecks from 28 million to 6.4 million.

Ultimately, the measure that was adopted in 1975 created only a one-year refundable income tax credit of up to $400 for earners with dependents and incomes below $8,000 (roughly $32,000 in 2009 dollars).[87] Nonetheless, the EIC emerged as a new policy tool to boost the paychecks of lower-income working families.[88] Over the next ten years, it would be made permanent and take on an increasingly central role in government efforts to support such families.

Carter and the Growing Payroll Tax Burden

President Jimmy Carter, who regained control of the White House for Democrats in 1976, promised to make the federal income tax more progressive, to broaden its base, and to "avoid a piecemeal approach to change."[89] He proposed a one-year, $50 nonrefundable rebate for all earners and dependents up to the limit of their tax liability. For families eligible for the EIC, this could increase their EIC payment by up to $50 per person, making it a benefit of particular value to working poor families.[90] He also brought new attention to the "marriage penalty" for low-income parents by proposing a tax credit for the lesser-earning spouse.[91] This proposal was intended not only to boost the after-tax income of low-income families with two working parents but also to encourage labor force participation among lower-earning spouses in two-earner families. While neither of these measures was adopted, Carter and Democrats in Congress

86. U.S. Senate (1975).

87. Marguerite Casey Foundation, "The Earned Income Tax Credit: Analysis and Proposals for Reform" (www.caseygrants.org/documents/reports/MCF_EITC_Paper.pdf).

88. The EIC might also have had significant appeal to business groups seeking to reduce demands for a minimum wage increase, but there was little evidence that either labor or business groups lobbied for this proposal. See Howard (1994).

89. Brownlee (1996, p. 112).

90. Jimmy Carter, "Economic Recovery Program: Message to the Congress, January 31, 1977," *American Presidency Project* (www.presidency.ucsb.edu/ws/?pid=7344).

91. Ibid.

simplified and increased the standard deduction as part of the 1977 Tax Reduction and Simplification Act. In place of the previous two-track system, which included a minimum standard deduction that had grown to $2,100 and a regular standard deduction of 16 percent of income up to $2,800 for joint filers, the 1977 act created a single standard deduction—renamed the "zero bracket amount"—of $3,200 for married couples and $2,200 for unmarried filers. In presenting his original version of this plan, Carter argued that it would allow an additional 4 million earners to claim the standard deduction, rather than itemize deductions each year, and excuse 3.7 million low-income earners from federal income tax liability.[92]

The following year, in an effort to battle economic stagflation, Carter proposed substantial tax relief for virtually all Americans, principally through a simple, across-the-board reduction in personal tax rates. Carter also recommended a $240 income tax credit, which would exempt millions of earners at or below the federal poverty threshold from tax liability. For earners in the lower tax brackets, this would yield a large net reduction in their combined income and payroll taxes even after scheduled payroll tax increases were taken into account. Without a reduction in income taxes, according to Carter, the payroll tax increases would cause a reduction in the after-tax income of American workers.[93]

Although the Democrats controlled Congress, all of Carter's proposals were rejected. Even among Democrats, there was little support for Carter's broader reforms. However, Democrats in Congress did reduce income taxes in the 1978 Revenue Act by widening tax brackets, reducing the number of rates, and increasing the amount of the personal exemption (from $750 to $1,000) and the standard deduction (from $3,200 to $3,400 for married couples).[94] Congress also made the EIC, which was renamed the Earned Income Tax Credit (EITC), a permanent part of the income tax, increasing the maximum credit to $500 and allowing EITC payments in advance of annual tax filing.[95] These increases nearly restored the credit's original value, which had eroded due to inflation since 1975.[96]

However, these immediate gains were countered by the growing burden of federal payroll taxes, which reached a combined rate of 11.7 percent on

92. Ibid.

93. Jimmy Carter, "Tax Reduction and Reform Message to the Congress, January 20, 1978," *American Presidency Project* (www.presidency.ucsb.edu/ws/?pid=31055).

94. Anderson (2007).

95. Nellen (2001).

96. Campbell and Peirce (1980, p. 6).

the first $16,500 in earned income in 1977. Although Carter pledged that year not to increase the federal payroll tax and recommended unsuccessfully that employers be allowed to take an income tax credit equal to 4 percent of their share of payroll taxes to help them cope with this burden, he eventually agreed with the Democratic Congress to accelerate previously scheduled increases, approving small increases in the payroll tax rate in 1979 and 1980, and more significant scheduled increases in 1981 and later. Under the 1977 agreement, the federal payroll tax was scheduled to reach a combined employer-employee contribution of 15.3 percent by 1990.

Three Decades of Individual Income Tax Policy

Between World War II and the mid-1970s, the individual income tax remained essentially progressive. However, this progressivity was constantly threatened by inflation, which first peaked in the late 1940s, increased during the late 1960s, and continued throughout the 1970s, reaching 13.3 percent by 1979. In the absence of congressional action, rising price levels shifted more and more low- and moderate-income earners into higher income tax brackets and reduced the value of both the personal exemption and standard deduction, which like tax brackets were not indexed for inflation. The largest percentage increases in taxes were faced by low-income earners, who moved from paying little or no tax to a more significant income tax liability.[97]

Between 1948 and 1969, the personal exemption stagnated at $600, losing much of its value to inflation.[98] The exemption was not restored to its initial nominal level of $1,000 until 1979 (where it remained until 1984).[99] Similarly, the standard deduction remained at the lesser of 10 percent of adjusted gross income or $1,000 until the passage of the Revenue Act of 1964. As a result, the tax entry threshold for families fell as a percentage of the federal poverty threshold between 1948 and 1963, forcing some low-income working families to pay federal income tax. In 1964, when the White House began publishing statistics on the number of people living in poverty, the Democratic majority in Congress began to adjust tax entry levels back up toward the federal poverty level, at least for taxpayers filing joint returns with zero to two dependents. By the 1970s, the

97. Steuerle (1995).
98. Steuerle and Hartzmark (1981).
99. Bakija and Steuerle (1991, p. 460).

tax entry threshold had emerged as a primary focus for policymakers seeking to support low-income families.[100] Ad hoc legislative increases were adopted in 1970, 1972, and 1979 to realign falling tax entry thresholds with the federal poverty line.[101]

In contrast to income tax rates, which have moved up and down, the federal payroll tax has risen steadily throughout its existence. Between the 1950s and the early 1970s, Democrats sought repeatedly to expand Social Security. The success of their efforts yielded a 3 percentage point increase in the payroll tax each decade.[102] In 1950 the combined payroll tax was 3 percent, in 1960 it was 6 percent, and by 1970 it was 9.6 percent. The combination of the federal income and payroll taxes yielded much higher effective tax rates for lower-income earners than for higher-income earners. By 1974 the average effective tax rate on low-income working families exceeded 13 percent.[103] In 1975 policymakers responded to their plight by adopting the EIC, which directly offset federal tax liability for the lowest-income workers with children. In addition, political debate over the future of Social Security in the mid-1970s focused new attention on the payroll tax and proposals to exempt low-income earners from future payroll refinancing.

Thus, by the late 1970s, the major pillars of post–New Deal federal tax policy—the individual income and payroll tax—had become inextricably linked within the political debate. By 1979 payroll taxes exceeded individual income taxes for 44 percent of families.[104] The tax burden facing such families became a central focus in American politics in the 1980s.

100. Bakija and Steuerle (1991, p. 462).
101. Ruggles (1990).
102. Steuerle (1996, p. 420).
103. Scholtz (2007).
104. Mitrusi and Poterba (2000).

3 | The Political Origins of the Federal Minimum Wage

The federal minimum wage emerged from the later New Deal as a mechanism to boost the pretax earnings of low-wage workers, regardless of their family size. It is based on a simple principle, as put forth by Franklin Delano Roosevelt: all able-bodied American workers should receive a "fair day's pay for a fair day's work."[1] Nonetheless, from its inception, it has been one of the most contested issues in U.S. public policy. This chapter traces the debate around the minimum wage from its origins in the late 1930s until the late 1970s and highlights the degree to which it has been shaped by partisan competition, intraparty maneuvering, and cross-party coalitions.

The federal minimum wage was created through the 1938 Fair Labor Standards Act in an effort to support workers who were not organized for collective bargaining. In crafting this mandate on employers, a conservative coalition of southern Democrats and Republicans in Congress chose to retain direct legislative control over the minimum wage rather than delegate wage-setting authority to an independent body, as FDR's White House proposed. This decision ensured that a new enacting coalition had to be built each time policymakers sought to increase the minimum wage

1. Franklin D. Roosevelt, "Message to Congress on Establishing Minimum Wages and Maximum Hours, May 24, 1937," *American Presidency Project* (www.presidency.ucsb.edu/ws/?pid=15405). See also Grossman (1978).

or expand its coverage. This coalition had to include key members of the House and Senate Labor committees, the House Rules Committee, the leadership of the majority party in each chamber, and the president.

Initially, southern Democrats played a key role in securing many of the bargains that took shape around the minimum wage. In the early 1930s, they generally favored an assertive role for the federal government in economic affairs and supported many of President Roosevelt's labor-related initiatives, albeit with reservations and only after securing protection for their regional interests. During these years, the House Rules Committee, which decided which legislation would be sent to the House floor and under what rules, always sent the president's proposals to the full House under "closed" rules that prevented any additional amendments.

However, by the second half of the decade, many southern Democrats were increasingly concerned about efforts to foster national labor union organization and to nationalize labor markets.[2] Southern rural, conservative Democrats, who held the balance of power in Congress, began to form coalitions with midwestern Republicans to block unwanted policy changes and to resist the expansion of national regulatory authority.[3] Between 1936 and 1940, the Rules Committee ceased to be an unquestioned ally of the House Democratic majority leadership. Together southern Democrats and Republicans formed a 9-5 majority on the committee. They exploited this position to block minimum wage increases from being reported to the House floor or to extract concessions, such as different wage rates for different regions or exemptions for particular industries.

Rather than work for outright political repeal of the minimum wage, which was not in its members' electoral self-interest, this conservative coalition opposed any expansion of coverage from 1938 until 1961, as well as efforts to index the minimum wage to inflation. However, they did agree to modest and periodic increases in the minimum wage. Throughout this period, liberal Democrats and their labor group allies were forced repeatedly to scale back their ambitions in order to win any support for wage increases from conservative legislators and the agricultural and small business groups to which they were linked. In the 1960s, however, moderates began to replace conservatives among southern Democrats within Congress, leading in 1961 and 1966 to the first major expansions of minimum wage coverage since the New Deal.

2. Farhang and Katznelson (2005).
3. Katznelson, Geiger, and Kryder (1993).

Origins of the Federal Minimum Wage

The Great Depression had reached unprecedented depths by 1932–33, with more than half of all Americans living below a minimum subsistence level. The central challenge was to lift wages and prices at the same time. FDR's initial political response was the 1933 National Industrial Recovery Act (NIRA), through which Democrats in Congress empowered the president to set minimum prices, wages, and competitive conditions in all industries. The minimum wage (and maximum hour) requirements were intended to increase workers' purchasing power and to spread the available hours of work among more employees. However, there was widespread evasion of these labor codes, and, in 1934 the Supreme Court declared the recovery program an unconstitutional delegation of legislative power to the president.[4]

Led by President Roosevelt, Democrats in Congress responded by adopting the 1935 National Labor Relations Act (NLRA), which authorized most private-sector employees to join unions, to bargain collectively with their employers, and to strike. Congress established an independent federal agency, the National Labor Relations Board, with the power to investigate and decide allegations of unfair labor practices and to conduct elections in which workers were given the opportunity to choose whether to be represented by a union. Senator Robert Wagner (D-N.Y.), a prime sponsor of the NLRA (also known as the Wagner Act), declared that the "rise of business activity . . . collapsed in short order because no adequate purchasing power had been built up to sustain it. The key to national prosperity, then, was to strengthen labor's ability to take home more pay."[5] Under the patronage of the NLRA, unionization rates doubled to more than one in four workers by 1940.[6]

However, collective bargaining was not a realistic option for many of the lowest-wage workers. To help these unorganized workers, FDR proposed a federal minimum wage. Under his plan, Congress would delegate authority to a Fair Labor Standards Board, analogous to the National Labor Relations Board, which would determine "industries, establishments, occupa-

---

4. Finegold and Skocpol (1995); Bernstein (1987); Himmelberg (1976); Weinstein (1980); Skocpol, Finegold, and Goldfield (1990).

5. Robert F. Wagner, "Under a New Law He Expects Labor to Hold Its Gains and Peace in Industry to Be Advanced," *New York Times*, May 26, 1935, p. E10.

6. VanGiezen and Schwenk (2001).

tions, and employments within the scope of interstate commerce" (that is, determine who would receive protection as "covered employees") and set a minimum wage on an industry-by-industry basis. This board would also be empowered to adjust the minimum wage to keep pace with inflation.[7] If Congress retained direct political control over minimum wage increases, FDR warned, policymakers "would face intense political pressure as groups would request the minimum wage be raised or lowered based on economic self-interest rather than on the basis of sound investigation of changes in economic conditions."[8]

To win passage of this proposal, Roosevelt had to secure the support of rural conservative southerners, who dominated the Democratic Party. Between 1933 and 1952, southerners never constituted less than 40 percent of the Democrats in Congress. Equally important, due to the seniority system and the southern phenomenon of one-party rule, they chaired about half of the committees. There were never fewer than 115 southern Democrats in the House, and even at the height of the New Deal, southerners were required as coalition partners to approve any New Deal policy. To ensure that their voices would be heard, southern Democrats had two powerful weapons: the threat of a filibuster in the Senate, where they made up 30 percent of the body, and the very real possibility that the House Rules Committee would prevent a bill proposed by the president from being considered by the full House.

Despite the heterogeneity of the Democrats' electoral base, the Democratic House majority leadership in the early stages of the New Deal was able to forge an enacting coalition by logrolling legislation around the issue of trying to alleviate the Depression. Rural southern Democrats supported the NIRA in exchange for industrial northern Democrats' support for the 1933 Agricultural Adjustment Act and Rural Electrification Act. During the early phase of the New Deal, they did not appear to regard as a threat the employment regime that was emerging because of the NIRA and NLRA. However, by 1937–38, when the minimum wage came before Congress, southern Democrats were beginning to join Republicans on a range of issues to form a conservative coalition.[9] In particular, concern

---

7. Board members would be appointed by the president, without Senate confirmation, and serve staggered five-year terms. Congress would set only a minimum wage to be used as a guide by the wage-setting board (see U.S. Congress 1937).

8. Ibid.

9. Fleck (2002); Sinclair (1978).

about New Deal labor policies was increasingly dividing southern Democrats from their urban northern brethren.

Labor issues were central to the voting identity of southern Democrats. As historian Gavin Wright has observed, "All the distinguishing differences between the South and the rest of the U.S. had their roots in the separateness of the southern labor market."[10] Given the importance of this divide, FDR's proposed minimum wage–setting board was bound to provoke opposition among southern Democrats. As one policymaker who represented low-wage southern industries, such as lumber, tobacco, and textiles, claimed, "What southern industry is mortally afraid of is the domination of U.S. industry by an independent labor board . . . with the power of life and death over practically every industry in America."[11] Southern Democrats strongly preferred to keep political control of a minimum wage in congressional hands rather than delegate authority to a board appointed by the president.[12] At the same time, they had to weigh the threat to the integrity of the South's insular regional labor market against their interest in the success of the party as a whole.[13]

Faced with the specter of open rebellion within his party, FDR limited the proposed federal minimum wage to "businesses that were actually engaged in and substantially and materially affecting interstate commerce."[14] In addition, the president offered an exemption for agricultural and domestic service workers, occupations that were dominated by African Americans and women—two groups that were politically weak.[15] (These exemptions also applied to the 1935 Social Security Act and the NLRA.) Finally, an agreement on regional minimum wage differences and the exemption of business of a "purely local nature" pacified most of the measure's remaining Democratic opponents.[16] In the House, a majority of southern Democrats and a minority of Republicans voted for a minimum wage set at 25 cents an hour.[17]

10. Wright (1986, p. 8).

11. U.S. Congress (1937, p. 762).

12. Patterson (1967); Brady and Bullock (1980); Shelley (1983); Brady (1988, p. 29).

13. See Schulman (1991); Wright (1986); Nordlund (1988); Paulsen (1996); Douglas and Hackman (1938).

14. U.S. Congress (1937).

15. See Linder (1987, p. 1336). For a similar criticism of the Fair Labor Standards Act for leaving many women workers without protection, see Mettler (1998, p. 635).

16. Patterson (1967).

17. Ibid.

President Roosevelt embraced this political agreement, declaring, "Except perhaps for the Social Security Act, it is the most far-reaching, far-sighted program for the benefit of workers ever adopted here or in any other country."[18] However, as the price of victory, Roosevelt had to surrender political control over the minimum wage to Congress. Moreover, at 25 cents an hour, the initial minimum wage was far below the original 80 cents an hour proposed by FDR. Under the final provisions of the Fair Labor Standards Act, Congress did agree that the minimum wage could increase to no less than 30 cents (by 1944) and then to 40 cents (by 1945) "without substantially curtailing employment or earning power."[19] However, by the time the increase was fully phased in, seven years later, inflation had largely erased its value.

Altogether, at its inception, the minimum wage covered about 11 million of the country's 33 million nonsupervisory wage and salary workers.[20] To form an enacting coalition, Congress limited coverage to low-wage workers in a subset of interstate industries (manufacturing, mining, quarrying, and forestry) and approved a range of exemptions for employees in executive, administrative, and professional positions; for retail businesses and service businesses doing less than 50 percent of their business in interstate commerce; and for farm workers.[21] Consequently, a large number of the lowest-paid workers did not receive minimum wage protection.

Notably the federal minimum wage had little impact on workers in the industries and occupations with the largest number of less-skilled workers in the South. Even within large "covered" industries, such as lumber, the majority of employers avoided paying the federal minimum wage either by withdrawing from interstate commerce or by paying less than the minimum wage in violation of federal labor standards.[22] Only 300,000 southern workers were affected by the minimum wage in 1938. This number rose with the nominal value of the minimum wage, reaching 1.4 million workers in 1945.[23]

By retaining political control over the minimum wage, Congress could claim credit for an increase, which had strong public support across all

18. Franklin D. Roosevelt, "Fireside Chat, June 24, 1938," *American Presidency Project* (www.presidency.ucsb.edu/ws/?pid=15662).

19. U.S. House of Representatives (1938, p. 1).

20. Daugherty (1939).

21. U.S. House of Representatives (1949).

22. See Selzter (1997).

23. Ibid.

regions, as well as minimize anger among groups who feared its impact on labor costs by limiting coverage and the amount of the increase. Over the following decades, it made the most of this ability by fine-tuning minimum wage increases in response to the dictates of electoral politics. Congress adopted minimum wage increases in a series of incremental annual steps rather than one large increase, often directly before an election. For example, the original minimum wage took effect on October 24, 1938—eight days before the midterm election. Similar examples of election-related timing can be found throughout the history of the minimum wage.[24]

Truman and the Birth of an Enduring Bargain

Between 1938 and the end of the 1970s, Congress agreed to six statutory phased-in increases in the minimum wage—in 1949, 1955, 1961, 1966, 1974, and 1977. (See table 3-1 for a history of minimum wage increases between 1938 and 1981.) Each of these increases was made possible by intraparty bargaining between conservative southern and liberal northern Democrats. The pattern was set in the mid-1940s, when Democratic leaders sought to increase the minimum wage to 60 cents or even 75 cents an hour. Although Democrats had only a small majority in the Seventy-Ninth Congress (1945–46) and were the minority party in the Eightieth Congress, President Harry S. Truman proposed annually that Congress increase the minimum wage in three annual steps. In a 1945 message, Truman concluded, "The goal of a 40-cent-per-hour minimum wage was inadequate when established. It has now become obsolete."[25] Indeed, every year that Congress did not act, inflation eroded the buying power of the minimum wage.

Truman and Democratic congressional leaders faced a predictable battle. The conservative coalition, which had mobilized against the New Deal, opposed any expansion of the minimum wage to workers in the agricultural industry, as it might throw farm prices and labor costs out of balance.[26] More broadly, Republicans were intent on overhauling New Deal labor relations policies, especially after winning political control of Congress in 1946

24. Sobel (1999).
25. Harry S. Truman, "Special Message to the Congress Presenting a 21-Point Program for the Reconversion Period, September 6, 1945," *American Presidency Project* (www.presidency.ucsb.edu/ws/?pid=12359).
26. Campbell (1962).

Table 3-1. *History of Federal Minimum Wage under the Fair Labor Standards Act, 1938–81*

			1966 and subsequent amendments[c]	
			Minimum hourly wage of workers in jobs first covered by	
Effective date	*1938 Act*[a]	*1961 amendments*[b]	*Nonfarm*	*Farm*
Oct. 24, 1938	0.25			
Oct. 24, 1939	0.30			
Oct. 24, 1945	0.40			
Jan. 25, 1950	0.75			
Mar. 1, 1956	1.00			
Sept. 3, 1961	1.15	1.00		
Sept. 3, 1963	1.25			
Sept. 3, 1964		1.15		
Sept. 3, 1965		1.25		
Feb. 1, 1967	1.40	1.40	1.00	1.00
Feb. 1, 1968	1.60	1.60	1.15	1.15
Feb. 1, 1969			1.30	1.30
Feb. 1, 1970			1.45	
Feb. 1, 1971			1.60	
May 1, 1974	2.00	2.00	1.90	1.60
Jan. 1, 1975	2.10	2.10	2.00	1.80
Jan. 1, 1976	2.30	2.30	2.20	2.00
Jan. 1, 1977			2.30	2.20
Jan. 1, 1978	2.65 for all covered, nonexempt workers			
Jan. 1, 1979	2.90 for all covered, nonexempt workers			
Jan. 1, 1980	3.10 for all covered, nonexempt workers			
Jan. 1, 1981	3.35 for all covered, nonexempt workers			

Source: U.S. Department of Labor, Employment Standards Administration (www.dol.gov/esa/min wage/chart.htm).

a. The original 1938 Fair Labor Standards Act (minimum wage) covered employees engaged in interstate commerce or in the production of goods for interstate commerce.

b. The 1961 minimum wage amendments extended coverage primarily to employees in large retail and service enterprises as well as to local transit, construction, and gasoline service station employees.

c. The 1966 minimum wage amendments extended coverage to state and local government employees of hospitals, nursing homes, and schools, and to laundries, drycleaners, and large hotels, motels, restaurants, and farms. The 1974 minimum wage amendments extended overage to the remaining federal, state, and local government employees who were not protected in 1966; to certain workers in retail and service trades previously exempted; and to certain domestic workers in private household employment.

for the first time since 1931. In 1947, for example, Congress adopted the Taft–Hartley Act, which significantly restricted the activities and power of labor unions, despite Truman's veto of what he called a "slave-labor bill."[27] However, the public sided with the president on the minimum wage, with more than two-thirds of those polled in May 1947 supporting his request for an increase to 65 cents an hour.[28]

In 1948 Truman made the Republicans' refusal to raise the minimum wage an important campaign issue.[29] This strategy helped keep Truman in the White House and restore control of Congress to the Democrats. The following year, the minimum wage emerged front and center in Truman's economic recovery program, with the White House arguing that it was important "to maintaining adequate consumer purchasing power among America's lowest-wage workers."[30]

Truman and Democratic leaders proposed an increase in the minimum wage to 75 cents an hour and an expansion of coverage to all activities "affecting" interstate commerce.[31] House Democratic leaders maintained that "a 75-cent federal minimum wage takes into account, and gives desperately needed help to workers in the lowest-paid occupations and industries; it prevents disastrous wage cutting, and bolsters purchasing power against any future economic recessions."[32] However, the conservative coalition on the House Rules Committee blocked the administration's original proposal from consideration by the full House and ultimately exacted a high price for its acquiescence in a minimum wage increase.[33] Rather than reduce the number of exemptions, the final agreement exempted an additional 500,000 retail and service workers from minimum wage protection, including those employed in the laundry, cleaning, and clothing repair service industries, while raising the minimum wage to 75 cents an hour.

---

27. Tomlins (1985).
28. Gallup (1996).
29. Harry S. Truman, "Address in Wilkes-Barre, Pennsylvania, October 23, 1948," *American Presidency Project* (www.presidency.ucsb.edu/ws/?pid=13060).
30. Harry S. Truman, "Special Message to the Congress: The President's Midyear Economic Report, July 11, 1949," *American Presidency Project* (www.presidency.ucsb.edu/ws/?pid=13240).
31. U.S. Senate (1949).
32. U.S. House of Representatives (1949, p. 6).
33. "House Rules Change," *CQ Almanac*, 1949, pp. 577–78; Herzberg (1986).

Eisenhower and the Politics of the Minimum Wage

A similar bargain was reached in the 1950s during the administration of Dwight D. Eisenhower, a moderate Republican who preached a doctrine of "dynamic conservatism" throughout his presidency. This approach helped him secure many political victories in Congress, even though Democrats were in the majority for six of the eight years he was in the White House.[34]

As the first Republican president to confront the minimum wage, Eisenhower supported a modest increase. He believed that a minimum wage would not protect or benefit low-wage workers if it were set so high as to push up the "whole scaffolding of wages and costs of doing business," leading either to inflation or to the elimination of less efficient employers and workers. Cautiously, therefore, he concluded that the exact "nature and timing" of an increase should depend on economic growth and that Congress should "increase the minimum wage only when national economic growth could support it, thus minimizing the risk of unemployment for the workers the minimum wage attempted to help."[35]

In addition, Eisenhower supported expanding coverage to workers in "multistate enterprises that were not local or intrastate in terms of ownership, control, financing, or management."[36] Under this proposal, workers in retail and service industries that were primarily "local" in character would still be exempted from the minimum wage while low-wage workers in interstate department stores, variety stores, and grocery chains, national motion picture theater chains, interstate hotel chains, and loan companies would be covered.[37] Even though these multistate chains were just more than 2 percent of all retail business, they employed 34 percent of private industry workers.[38] However, Eisenhower was unable to persuade Congress to follow his lead. A large bipartisan majority agreed to increase the minimum wage to $1 an hour in 1955, but the conservative coalition succeeded

34. O'Neill (1995).

35. Dwight D. Eisenhower, "Radio and Television Address to the American People on the Tax Program, March 15, 1954," *American Presidency Project* [(www.presidency.ucsb.edu/ws/?pid=10181).

36. Dwight D. Eisenhower, "Annual Message Presenting the Economic Report to the Congress, January 20, 1955," *American Presidency Project* (www.presidency.ucsb.edu/ws/?pid=10332).

37. "Wage and Hour Legislation after World War II," *Congress and the Nation* I (1945–64), pp. 633–51.

38. Ibid.

in blocking efforts to expand coverage to new groups of workers or consider any form of indexation to account for changes in the cost of living.

After picking up additional congressional seats in the 1958 midterm election, Senate Democrats, led by John F. Kennedy of Massachusetts, tried again to expand coverage and to increase the minimum wage to $1.25 an hour. Kennedy proposed to extend the minimum wage to cover "employees of large enterprises engaged in retail trade or services and other industries engaged in activities affecting interstate commerce." This would include low-wage workers in large retail and service businesses; laundry, cleaning, and related businesses; firms operating street, suburban, or interurban transit systems; taxi companies; building and construction firms; and other enterprises with one or more employees engaged in commerce or in the production of goods for commerce.[39] Kennedy's proposal would extend the benefits of minimum wage protection to an additional 4.3 million low-wage workers. Of the approximately 45 million wage and salary workers in the United States, only about 24 million were protected at that time under the federal minimum wage.

Eisenhower initially supported a modest expansion of coverage and no wage increase, but public opinion swayed him in favor of an increase to $1.10 or $1.15 by 1960. Nonetheless, a special session of Congress held in 1960 failed to produce agreement. In conference, the Senate agreed to accept the House's proposal to limit the increase to $1.15 an hour. However, Senator Kennedy, by then the Democrats' presidential nominee, refused to compromise with the House on the Senate's intention to expand coverage to 4 million low-wage workers (as opposed to the 700,000 new workers who would be covered by the House), and went on to make the minimum wage a central issue in the 1960 election.[40]

The New Frontier and the Federal Minimum Wage

With Kennedy's election to the White House in 1960, Democratic leaders sought fundamental changes to the rules of the game when it came to the minimum wage and other major policies. Liberal Democrats in the Eighty-Seventh Congress—organized internally as the 100-member Democratic Study Group—pushed to change the structure of the House Rules Com-

---

39. See U.S. Senate (1959).
40. "Minimum Wage," *CQ Weekly*, August 26, 1960, pp. 1481–75.

mittee, acting on its "firm conviction of the absolute necessity of corrective action which will insure House consideration of legislation reported by committees and in accord with the House leadership's legislative program."[41] Democratic leaders attempted to enlarge the committee, which they hoped would break the conservative coalition's political control. President Kennedy took no formal position on the proposal, but as an "interested citizen," he said he hoped that a "small group of men would not have the power to keep important legislation from the floor."[42] Although a majority of southern Democrats voted against the rules change, House Speaker Sam Rayburn (D-Tex.) had enough support from both Democrats and moderate Republicans to win passage of the reform.[43] Thus Democratic House leaders were empowered to assert new political influence over a broad range of issues.

Kennedy, who had helped Democrats secure large majorities in both chambers, urged Congress "to raise the minimum wage . . . to improve the incomes, level of living, morale, and efficiency of many of our lowest-paid workers, and provide incentives for their more productive utilization."[44] Of the approximately 45 million full-time wage and salary workers, only about 24 million were covered under the federal minimum wage. Kennedy proposed to expand coverage to 4.3 million additional workers in retail trade and services by stipulating that all low-wage employees of businesses of a certain size would receive minimum wage protection even if they were not individually involved in interstate commerce or in producing goods for commerce.[45] However, Kennedy agreed to continue to exempt low-wage workers in service industries such as hotels, motels, and restaurants, who depended on tips for a significant part of their earned income.

Following Kennedy's lead, Democrats in Congress approved a two-step increase to $1.25 by 1963 for workers already covered, while newly covered low-wage workers would receive a three-step increase to $1.25 by 1966.[46] The conservative coalition had defeated similar provisions in 1960. Nevertheless, with the replacement of some conservative southern Democrats

41. "House Committees: Rules," *CQ Almanac* XVI, 1960, p. 58.

42. "House: Democratic Caucus," *CQ Weekly*, January 6, 1961, p. 4; "Floor Action: House Votes to Expand Rules Committee," *CQ Weekly*, February 3, 1961, pp. 170–75.

43. "House Committees: Rules," *CQ Almanac* XVI, 1960, p. 58.

44. John F. Kennedy, "Special Message to the Congress: Program for Economic Recovery and Growth February 2, 1961" (www.presidency.ucsb.edu/ws/?pid=8111).

45. U.S. Senate (1961, p. 41).

46. See U.S. House of Representatives (1961a, p. 13).

with moderates following the 1960 election and a change in the chair-manship of the key House Education and Labor Committee, the House succeeded in adopting this agreement in 1961.[47] Upon the bill's passage, Kennedy proclaimed, "This advance in one of our great pieces of social legislation is one of the most important domestic accomplishments so far of this administration . . . This is the first time since the act came into existence under the administration of President Roosevelt in 1938 that we have been able to expand coverage."[48]

The final parameters of the 1961 agreement maintained the president's basic preferences but reduced the increase in coverage from 4.3 million to 3.62 million by excluding laundries and dry cleaning establishments (140,000 workers), urban and interurban transit systems with annual revenues under $1 million (17,000 employees), and auto and farm equipment dealers (305,000 workers). The expansion included all low-wage workers in retail trade businesses with sales exceeding $1 million annually as long as two or more employees did work that was closely connected to instate commerce, although individual establishments within those covered enterprises were exempt if their annual sales fell below $250,000.

But small retail and service firms and "mom-and-pop" businesses employing only family members remained exempt from the minimum wage. In addition, the bill created a subminimum wage for full-time students in jobs normally held by full-time employees.[49] This bargain extended coverage from 250,000 workers to 2.2 million in the retail trade industry.

Johnson's Great Society, the Federal Minimum Wage, and Antipoverty Policy

President Lyndon B. Johnson sought to build on these gains as part of his Great Society campaign. In 1964 he proposed to expand protection to 735,000 low-wage workers in the hotel, motel, restaurant, laundry, dry cleaning, agricultural, processing, and logging industries.[50] Johnson con-

47. "Kennedy Wins Minimum Wage Victory," *CQ Almanac* XVII, 1961, pp. 471–82.
48. John F. Kennedy, "Statement by the President on the Increase in the Minimum Wage," September 3, 1961 (www.presidency.ucsb.edu/ws/?pid=8305), p. 587.
49. U.S. House of Representatives (1961b).
50. Lyndon B. Johnson, "Annual Message to the Congress: The Manpower Report of the President, March 9, 1964," *American Presidency Project* (www.presidency.ucsb.edu/ws/?pid=26103).

cluded, "Certain groups in the nation have not shared fully in the benefits of our unprecedented economic expansion. We must provide all possible assistance to those who seek work and decent living conditions for those who do work."[51] In 1966 the Democratic majority in Congress responded by extending minimum wage protection to workers on farms and in public schools, nursing homes, laundries, and the construction industry, as well as federal employees and those employed on federal contracts.[52] This move extended protection to agricultural workers for the first time since the New Deal, over the opposition of the farm lobby, bringing the total number of low-wage workers covered to 41.4 million.[53] At the same time, Congress lowered the sales threshold at which businesses became covered by the minimum wage to $500,000, with a further reduction to $250,000 in 1969. Congress also established a "tip credit" that allowed employers to count tips as up to 50 percent of the compensation they were required to provide under the minimum wage. (A tipped employee was defined as a worker who received more than $20 a month in tips.)

For already covered employees, Democrats increased the minimum wage from $1.25 to $1.40 in 1967 and then to $1.60 in 1968. Newly covered workers received a minimum wage of $1 in 1967, with annual 15-cent increases to $1.60 by 1971.[54]

Moderate southern Democrats were pivotal in securing this new bargain on the federal minimum wage, which encompassed both a significant increase in the wage and an important expansion of coverage.[55] On the campaign trail in 1968, Johnson cited these reforms as a key Democratic achievement:

> We raised the minimum wage, the wages that poor people earn at the bottom of the ladder, we raised it to bring a decent income to every workingman . . . and Republicans, more than two out of every three, voted to recommit that bill . . . then after they couldn't stick a dagger in its heart because there were too many Democrats for them to succeed,

51. Lyndon B. Johnson, "Annual Message to the Congress: The Manpower Report of the President, March 8, 1966," *American Presidency Project* (www.presidency.ucsb.edu/ws/?pid=27473).

52. See U.S. House of Representatives (1966).

53. "Expansion of Minimum Wage Law Approved," *CQ Almanac* XXII, 1966, pp. 821–30.

54. Ibid.

55. "Kennedy Wins Minimum Wage Victory," *CQ Almanac* XVII, 1961; "Wage and Hour Legislation after World War II," *Congressional Quarterly* (1965), pp. 633–51.

they did a flip-flop . . . they voted for final passage so they could come home and say look what I did for minimum wages.[56]

Nixon's New Federalism and the Minimum Wage

Despite Johnson's campaign trail rhetoric, not all Republicans opposed increasing the minimum wage. President Richard Nixon, who won control of the White House in 1968, believed that "both fairness and decency require that we raise the minimum wage. We cannot allow millions of America's low-income families to become the prime casualties of inflation."[57] Like Eisenhower, Nixon expressed "support for the basic purpose to increase the minimum wage" but harbored "reservations regarding the size and timing of an increase."[58] Nixon also opposed expanding protection to state and local government workers as "an unwarranted interference with state prerogatives" and a mandate that would run counter to the principles of his New Federalism. In addition, he distinguished between adult and teenage workers, who had the highest jobless rate of any group—more than four times the unemployment rate for adult workers in 1971.[59] To help teen workers, Nixon proposed a youth subminimum wage that would apply to workers under eighteen, all eighteen- and nineteen-year-olds during their first six months on the job, and full-time students under twenty.

Nixon typically pursued a "floating" coalition strategy with Congress, trying to solidify political support for policies, then reaching out to either northern or southern Democrats depending on his particular political goals.[60] But in the face of stark divisions within Congress, he was unable to assemble an enacting coalition around his proposals for the minimum wage.

House Republicans charged that an increase in the minimum wage would "only stoke the flames of inflation, while doing little or nothing to help reduce unemployment among those of our people who are, propor-

56. Lyndon B. Johnson, "Remarks at a Democratic Party Rally in Newark, October 7, 1966," *American Presidency Project* (www.presidency.ucsb.edu/ws/?pid=27909).

57. Richard Nixon, "Veto of the Minimum Wage Bill," September 6, 1973 (www.presidency.ucsb.edu/ws/?pid=3950).

58. U.S. House of Representatives (1971a, p. 547).

59. Richard Nixon, "Message to the Congress Transmitting Annual Manpower Report of the President," March 15, 1972 (www.presidency.ucsb.edu/ws/?pid=3771).

60. Reichley (1981).

tionately, its most numerous victims."[61] House Democrats argued, "Belated and gradual increases, approximately equivalent to productivity and cost-of-living increases in recent years, could be absorbed by the national economy as easily as all previous increases."[62] Despite this stand-off, both the House and Senate passed bills increasing the minimum wage in 1972. However, the proposal died when conservative Democrats joined House Republicans in refusing to send it to a conference committee, arguing that Democratic conferees would likely ignore the House's provisions in favor of those adopted by the more liberal Senate.[63] As in 1960, squabbling within the Democratic Party doomed the effort to increase the minimum wage.

Yet the following year, House Democrats rallied around a proposal to expand the minimum wage to federal, state, and local government workers as well as domestic service workers, and to phase in coverage to workers in progressively smaller retail and service chain stores.[64] At the same time, Democrats in Congress rejected Nixon's youth subminimum wage. This time a larger bargain held the key to party unity: southern Democrats traded support for a minimum wage increase in return for urban northern Democrats' backing of an omnibus farm package.[65]

Nixon vetoed the measure in 1974, becoming the first president to veto a minimum wage increase, and House Democrats failed to produce the two-thirds majority needed to override the veto. Nixon then asked Congress to adopt a "responsible" minimum wage increase, with a youth subminimum wage. Despite the threat of another veto, the Democratic majority in Congress approved essentially the same package for a second time.[66] Due to increases in the cost of living, the likelihood that House Democrats had the votes to override a veto, and House Republicans' electoral vulnerability in the wake of the Watergate scandal, Nixon accepted the expansion and increase just one year after he had vetoed a nearly identical proposal.[67]

61. U.S. House of Representatives (1971b, p. 2).
62. Ibid., p. 105.
63. "House Vote Kills Legislation Raising the Minimum Wage," *CQ Almanac* XXVIII, 1972, pp. 361–71.
64. The sales threshold at which a business became covered would remain at $250,000 for one year, fall to $225,000 in 1974, fall to $200,000 in 1975, and then be repealed in 1976. U.S. House of Representatives (1973, p. 23).
65. "Urban-Rural Coalition Emerges on Minimum Wage," *CQ Weekly*, June 16, 1973, p. 1560.
66. U.S. House of Representatives (1975).
67. Reichley (1981).

More than 6.6 million low-wage workers would receive minimum wage protection for the first time, including workers for local and state governments as well as those working on federal contracts.

By then doubts were gathering about the effectiveness of the minimum wage. In the early 1970s, the congressional Joint Economic Committee's Subcommittee on Fiscal Policy considered the overall effectiveness of the minimum wage as part of a broad three-year, nineteen-volume study of the U.S. income tax and transfer system. The panel affirmed a growing consensus that many of the covered workers whose wages were lowest were not in poor families and that minimum wage increases might make matters worse for large numbers of both needy and non-needy low-wage workers by increasing unemployment.[68] Therefore, instead of adjusting the minimum wage, the Joint Economic Committee recommended addressing the problem in ways that "attempt to retain the allocative efficiency of the market."[69]

Nonetheless, Democratic support for the minimum wage remained strong as the party's electoral strength increased. In the 1974 midterm elections, the Democrats secured their largest House majority since the Seventy-Fifth Congress, which had approved the original minimum wage. On paper they had one more vote than the two-thirds majority needed to override a presidential veto. In addition, the conservative coalition had dropped in number from 176 to 163 in the House.[70] Buoyed by these gains, House Democratic leaders renewed their efforts to index the minimum wage to inflation. Linking the minimum wage to the consumer price index, they maintained, was the "only way for Congress to commit to a minimum wage that kept pace with increases in the cost of living, to maintain the purchasing power of the minimum wage in the future, and to ensure that workers would share in the benefits of increased productivity."[71] In the absence of indexation, House Democrats argued, "even though Congress has attempted to set the rate close to half the prevailing average hourly earnings, the gap between it and average wages has widened dramatically by the time Congress has gotten around to taking another look."[72]

---

68. U.S. Congress (1974).

69. Ibid., p. 142.

70. Reichley (1981, p. 317).

71. U.S. House of Representatives (1975, p. 8).

72. Martha V. Gottron, "House Hearings: Minimum Wage Increase," *CQ Weekly*, November 1, 1975, pp. 2305–06.

Post-Watergate Democrats, Carter, and the Minimum Wage

With the election of Jimmy Carter as president in 1976, congressional Democrats saw a new opportunity to index the minimum wage to annual changes in the cost of living. They backed Carter's proposal to increase the minimum wage to $2.85, with future automatic increases to keep it at 60 percent of the average manufacturing wage.[73] In addition, House Democrats proposed the repeal of the "tip credit" over a four-year period. Rejecting claims that repeal of the tip credit would be inflationary or result in job losses in restaurants, hotels, and motels, Democrats argued that low-wage workers who depended on the spending of discretionary income "feel the impact of economic downturns more immediately and drastically than all others."[74]

However, a House majority defeated indexation and replaced it with a three-step plan to increase the minimum wage to $3.05 by 1980. Despite efforts by majority leader Jim Wright (D-Tex.) to reject the phase-in, ninety-seven northern and southern Democrats joined Republicans to defeat automatic indexation. The conservative coalition also voted to expand the exemption for small businesses (by raising the threshold at which they became covered from $250,000 to $500,000 in annual sales), removing 3.8 million workers from minimum wage coverage, and to retain the 50 percent tip credit. For their part, liberal Democrats defeated a subminimum wage by one vote, with House Speaker Tip O'Neill breaking a tie.[75] Ultimately, the two chambers reached a compromise that increased the minimum wage in four steps to $3.35 by 1981, and for the first time since the New Deal, extended the same minimum wage to all eligible workers regardless of when they had become eligible for protection.[76] Congress also retained the tip credit at 50 percent until 1978, but agreed to decrease it by 5 percentage points annually over the next several years.[77] Finally, Congress agreed to increase the annual sales threshold at which businesses became covered by minimum wage legislation to $362,500 by 1981. This measure would increase the number of exempted low-wage workers by 800,000, in contrast to the 3.8 million workers who would have been affected by the conservative coalition's proposal to increase the sales threshold to $500,000.[78]

73. Dark (1994, p. 778).
74. U.S. House of Representatives (1977a).
75. "Four-Step Minimum Wage Increase Approved," *CQ Almanac* XXXIII, 1977, pp. 138–44.
76. U.S. House of Representatives (1977b).
77. Ibid.
78. Ibid.

Figure 3-1. *U.S. House Political Control by Party, 1937–2011*[a]

Number of representatives

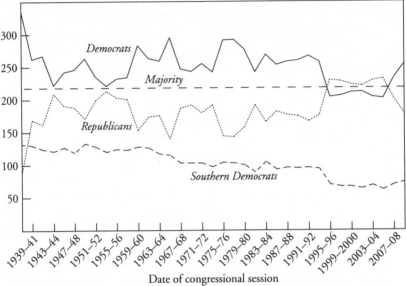

Date of congressional session

Sources: voteview.com; www.senate.gov.

a. Southern Democrats are from the following states: Maryland, Virginia, North Carolina, South Carolina, Georgia, Tennessee, Kentucky, Alabama, Mississippi, Louisiana, Arkansas, Missouri, West Virginia, and Texas.

Four Decades of the Minimum Wage

Between 1938 and 1978, every Democratic and every Republican president—FDR, Harry S. Truman, Dwight D. Eisenhower, John F. Kennedy, Lyndon B. Johnson, Richard M. Nixon, and Jimmy Carter—all approved minimum wage increases throughout the period. In sum, the original 1938 bargain was revisited and revised in 1949, 1955, 1961, 1966, 1974, and 1977. Minimum wage supporters—generally liberal Democrats—repeatedly advocated an expansion of coverage as well as a significant increase in the minimum wage rate; opponents—generally Republicans—preferred to let inaction and inflation reduce the value of the minimum wage. The outcome of this tug-of-war was determined by centrist southern Democrats (see figures 3-1 and 3-2 on southern Democrats in the House and Senate). This group succeeded repeatedly in restricting coverage and minimizing

Figure 3-2. *U.S. Senate, Political Control by Party, 1937–2011*[a]

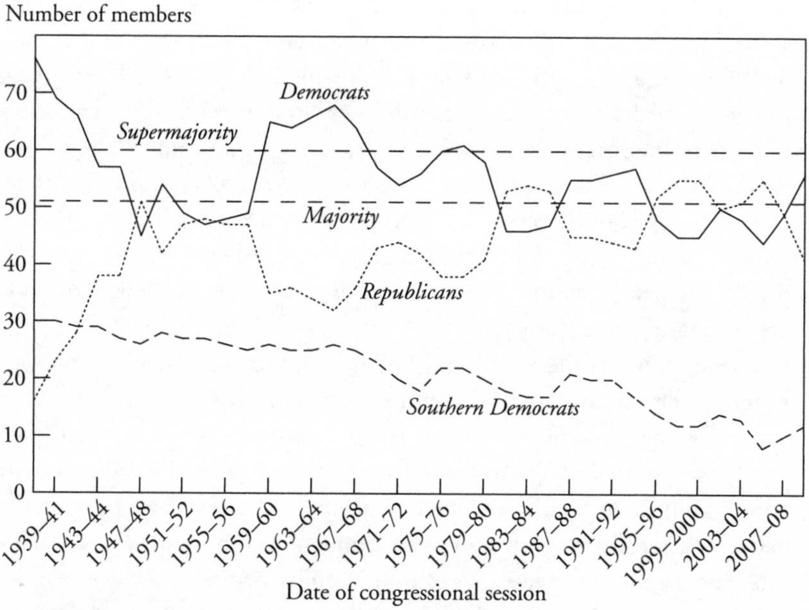

Number of members

Date of congressional session

Sources: voteview.com; www.senate.gov.

a. Southern Democrats are from the following states: Maryland, Virginia, North Carolina, South Carolina, Georgia, Tennessee, Kentucky, Alabama, Mississippi, Louisiana, Arkansas, Missouri, West Virginia, and Texas.

the magnitude of an increase by amending the bills introduced by their more liberal colleagues. Time and again, liberal Democrats were forced to join forces with the conservatives on final minimum wage votes, after their proposals had been defeated and substitutes had been adopted on the floor of each chamber.

Given these constraints, how effective was the minimum wage in providing support to low-income earners and their families? If the focus is growth in the number of affected workers, the results were considerable, despite periodic efforts to roll back coverage. The federal minimum wage originally applied only to workers directly engaged in interstate commerce or in the production of goods for interstate commerce—roughly 11 million workers. By 1985 about 73 million nonsupervisory workers—almost 90 percent of that part of the workforce—were subject to the minimum wage, although the fraction of covered workers varied considerably among industries. However, the value of the minimum wage did not fare as well over time. In nominal terms, the minimum wage, which was originally set at $0.25 an hour in 1938, rose to $1.00 an hour in 1956, $2.00 an hour in 1974, and $3.35 by 1981 (where it remained until 1990). The purchasing power of the minimum wage was lower in the early 1980s than at any time since the mid-1950s. Similarly, the federal minimum wage fell as a share of average wages over the same period. After reaching around 50 percent of average hourly earnings in private nonagricultural industries during the 1950s and 1960s, the minimum wage averaged just over 45 percent in the 1970s. By the mid-1980s, the minimum wage had fallen to about 36 percent of average wages.[79]

During most of the 1960s and 1970s, a person working full time year-round at the minimum wage would have earned an income roughly equal to the poverty threshold for a three-person family. By 1985 a similarly situated worker earned less than the federal poverty threshold for a two-person family. And many minimum wage workers fared even worse because they had less than full-time, full-year work. Some minimum wage workers, however, had access to the earnings of other family members—which could be significant—complicating efforts to establish the effectiveness of the minimum wage at lifting individuals and families out of poverty.

Frustrated by such complications, by the 1980s a number of lawmakers were seeking to replace the federal minimum wage with alternative policy tools, such as an earned income credit, for helping poor working families. The alternative approach gained an official endorsement with the 1980 election of Ronald Reagan, who proclaimed, "The minimum wage has caused more misery and unemployment than anything since the Great Depression." With the support of Senate Republicans, who secured a majority in 1980, Reagan rejected any efforts to increase the federal minimum wage, which fell to 33 percent of the average hourly wage by 1989. Faced with this political roadblock, some centrist Democrats joined centrist Republicans in a search for other mechanisms to boost the paychecks of low-income earners and their families. These efforts and the debates they inspired are the focus of the following chapters.

79. Kai Filion, "EPI's Minimum Wage Issue Guide," updated July 21, 2009 (www.epi.org/publications/entry/issue_guide_on_minimum_wage).

4 | Reagan, Bush, and a New Era in the Politics of Boosting Paychecks

Following the election of Ronald Reagan in 1980, major differences emerged between Democrats and Republicans over the appropriate distribution of federal income and payroll tax burdens and the antipoverty effectiveness of the federal minimum wage. Nonetheless, President Reagan forged a coalition with conservative House Democrats (then known as Boll Weevils) and Senate Republicans to adopt some of the most significant changes to the federal income tax since World War II. The across-the-board income tax reductions that lay at the heart of the Reagan reforms primarily benefited higher-income taxpayers. However, they were accompanied by important changes to the Earned Income Tax Credit (EITC) that significantly reduced effective tax rates for low-income workers with families.

At election time, both Democrats and Republicans claimed credit for increasing the after-tax income of "average working Americans" and for freeing poor and near-poor working families from federal tax liability. However, these gains were offset in part by a decline in the real value of the federal minimum wage throughout the 1980s. In 1989 President George H.W. Bush accepted a two-step minimum wage increase from $3.35 to $4.25 an hour as part of an agreement that included an expansion of the small employer exemption as well as a new, entry-level, youth subminimum wage. But the two-step increase did not compensate for the drop in the minimum wage's real value over the preceding decade.

For most of the 1980s, debate focused on the impact of tax reforms on those at the top and the bottom of the income scale. However, toward the end of the decade, attention began to shift to the plight of moderate- and middle-income taxpayers and their families. The Reagan reforms offered relatively little targeted relief to this group, while the burden of payroll taxes continued to rise.

End of the New Deal Regime

President Reagan came into office determined to cut taxes, reduce government spending, and shrink the role that the federal government played in Americans' lives. This agenda amounted to a wholesale rejection of the broad principles that had shaped policy over the previous forty to fifty years. As one political historian summed it up: "When Ronald Reagan assumed office in January of 1981, an epoch in the nation's political history came to an end. The New Deal, as a dominant order of ideas, policies, and political alliances, died."[1] Reagan's landslide victory helped him argue that he had a mandate for sweeping change. Buoyed by anger over mismanagement of the economy as well as foreign crises, notably the takeover of the U.S. Embassy in Iran, the Reagan-Bush ticket beat the Carter-Mondale team by almost 10 percentage points in the popular vote and captured forty-four states, leaving the incumbent with only six states plus the District of Columbia.

Equally important, Reagan's popularity fueled a Republican electoral resurgence across the South and restored control of the Senate to the Republicans for the first time in more than twenty-four years. Of the twelve Senate seats that switched to the Republican side, four were in the South, as were nine of the thirty-three House seats. Many Democrats feared that they had no better than a 50-50 chance of maintaining their majority in the House in the midterm elections unless they won back conservative southern voters. Representative Beryl Anthony (D-Ark.) spoke for many when he warned, "Republicans have us on the run in the South, and we Democrats must concentrate on a southern strategy or else we could lose the whole region."[2] These concerns greatly enhanced the influence of conservative House Democrats, who held the balance of power

1. Fraser and Gerstle (1989).
2. Richard E. Cohen, "They're Still a Majority in the House, but Are Democrats Really in Control?" *National Journal*, January 31, 1981, pp. 189–91; Cohen, "In the Conservative Politics of the '80's: The South Is Rising Once Again," *National Journal*, February 28, 1981, pp. 350–54.

between the Republican Senate and the Democratic House. Soon after the election, this group (composed largely but not exclusively of southerners) formed the forty-seven-member Conservative Democratic Forum (CDF).[3] The CDF forged an alliance with the White House to enact tax cuts, roll back economic regulation, and strengthen the military. Some members of the CDF eventually defected to the Republican Party; the remainder reorganized as the "Blue Dogs" by the end of the decade.[4]

The Economic Recovery Tax Act of 1981

Addressing his first joint session of Congress in February 1981, President Reagan put forward a program based on the premise "that the percentage of people's earnings taken by the federal government in taxes should be reduced."[5] To bolster his case, he dwelt on the situation of the average taxpayer: "Not only have hourly earnings of the American worker, after adjusting for inflation, declined 5 percent over the past five years, but in these five years, Federal income taxes for the average family have increased 67 percent."[6] The average taxpayer, he argued, would benefit from his plan just as much as the rich and the poor: "This is not merely a shift of wealth between different sets of taxpayers. This proposal for an *equal* reduction in everyone's tax rates will expand our national prosperity, enlarge national incomes, and increase opportunities for all Americans."[7]

Reagan's proposal called for tax rates in all brackets to fall by 10 percent each year for three years.[8] Since the 10 percent reductions would apply to a smaller base in each successive year, the cumulative reduction in each tax rate over three years would be roughly 27 percent. Due to inflation, this proposal offered more relief to high-income earners than low-income earners. For low-income earners, some of the benefits of rate cuts would be offset as inflation pushed them into higher tax brackets. In contrast, earners in the top tax bracket would have little exposure to bracket creep and get the full benefit of the 27 percent rate cut.[9]

3. "The South Rises Again in Congress," *Time,* May 18, 1981.

4. Lisa Leiter, "The Blue Dogs Have Their Day: Conservative Democratic Legislators," *Insight on the News,* June 5, 1995, pp. 6–8.

5. Ronald Reagan, "Address before a Joint Session of the Congress on the Program for Economic Recovery, February 18, 1981," *American Presidency Project* (www.presidency.ucsb.edu/ws/?pid=43425).

6. Ibid.

7. Ibid.

8. Gravelle (2001).

9. Brownlee (2004, p. 141).

To address this issue and protect the full value of his proposed tax relief, Reagan proposed that tax brackets be indexed to inflation. As he explained in a July 1981 address, "As it is now, if you get a cost-of-living [wage] raise that's intended to keep you even with inflation, you find that the increase in the number of dollars you get may very likely move you into a higher tax bracket, and you wind up poorer than you would [have been]. This is called bracket creep."[10] To send home his point, Reagan offered a hypothetical example:

> If you earned $10,000 a year in 1972, by 1980 you had to earn $19,700 just to stay even with inflation. But that's before taxes. Come April 15th, you'll find your tax rates have increased 30 percent. Now, if you've been wondering why you don't seem as well-off as you were a few years back, it's because government makes a profit on inflation. It gets an automatic tax increase without having to vote on it.[11]

Bracket creep was a relatively invisible, politically low-cost means of increasing tax revenues. However, once the issue had been forced into the open, eliminating bracket creep became a popular cause.

House Democratic leaders made a token effort to withstand the Reagan bandwagon. In place of his three-year plan, they proposed a single-year tax reduction targeted at earners with moderate to middle incomes ($20,000 to $50,000) combined with an increase in the standard deduction. However, conservative House Democrats joined forces with Republicans to support the president's package, leaving their own party leaders with little role to play.[12]

Ultimately, the Economic Recovery Tax Act of 1981 enacted a 23 percent cut in tax rates for all earners over three years. Congress scaled back the president's 10-10-10 formula for rate cuts to a 5-10-10 schedule. Measured in percentage points, the rate reductions were larger as workers moved up the income distribution. The top rate was scheduled to fall from 70 percent to 50 percent, while the bottom rate would fall from 14 percent to 11 percent. As a result, the lowest-income earners received the smallest percentage increase in their after-tax income.

10. Ronald Reagan, "Address to the Nation on Federal Tax Reduction Legislation, July 27, 1981," *American Presidency Project* (www.presidency.ucsb.edu/ws/?pid=44120).

11. Ibid.

12. Brownlee (2004).

As Reagan had proposed, the tax package protected earners against bracket creep by indexing the brackets to inflation. In addition, Democrats secured some additional tax relief for low- and moderate-income working families by increasing and indexing the personal exemption and the zero bracket amount, as the standard deduction had been renamed. However, in all three cases, indexing did not take effect until 1985.[13] Thus inflation continued to have a significant impact on the take-home income of low-income earners in the early 1980s. During this time, a worker whose income increased at the rate of inflation could move from paying no income tax to paying $200 simply because the personal exemption and the standard deduction remained fixed.

Democrats also pushed successfully for an increase in the Child and Dependent Care Tax Credit to offset child care expenses and to make up for the effect of inflation on child care costs since 1976.[14] Between 1976 and 1981, earners could claim a credit of 20 percent of qualified child care expenses, with a maximum credit of $400 for each of the first two dependents. The 20 percent credit was the same for taxpayers at all income levels. The new 1981 provisions raised the ceiling on expenses to account for inflation over the past five years. Congress and Reagan also broadened eligibility requirements, eliminated family income limits, and awarded the credit on a sliding scale based on income. Thus families with lower incomes could claim a larger credit than families with higher incomes.[15] The applicable percentage is inversely correlated to the adjusted gross income of the earner—the higher the adjusted gross income, the lower the percentage. These efforts delivered some support to low- and moderate-income working families. However, since the credit remained nonrefundable, it did little to help very low wage parents with little or no federal income tax liability. For two decades thereafter, Congress failed to adjust the value of the credit for inflation, though it came close on several occasions. (See figure 4-1 for average child and dependent care credit amounts.)

President Reagan's aversion to higher taxes also extended to the federal payroll taxes that funded Social Security and Medicare. Although Social Security faced an acute funding crisis in the early 1980s, he opposed efforts to raise the federal payroll tax, arguing that it was already too high. By the beginning of the decade, federal payroll taxes exceeded individual income

13. Steuerle (2008, p. 86).
14. Dunbar and Nordhauser (1991); Zeitlin and Campbell (1982).
15. Zeitlin and Campbell (1982).

Figure 4-1. *Historical Child and Dependent Care Credits, 1976–2007*

Average credit (dollars)

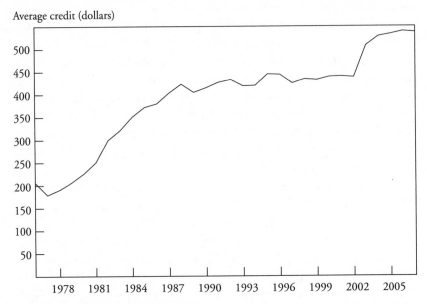

Source: Tax Policy Center, "Historical Dependent Care Credits," August 10, 2009 (www.taxpolicy center.org/taxfacts/displayafact.cfm?Docid=180).

taxes for 44 percent of families.[16] "For the nation's work force, the Social Security tax is already the biggest tax they pay," the president declared in September 1981. "In 1935, we were told the tax would never be greater than 2 percent of the first $3,000 of earnings. It is presently 13.3 percent of the first $29,700, and the scheduled increases will take it to 15.3 percent of the first $60,600."[17]

Nonetheless, in 1983 the bipartisan National Commission on Social Security Reform (also known as the Greenspan Commission) recommended an acceleration of the scheduled increases in the payroll tax to address projected revenue shortfalls in Social Security. The commission

16. Mitrusi and Poterba (2000). Due to differences in the composition of family income (including earnings, transfer income, property income, and income from other sources) across income levels, federal payroll taxes rose as a proportion of income from the low to middle ranges of family income, remained at a roughly constant proportion through the middle range, and declined at the top. The ceiling on income subject to the federal payroll tax also contributed to this trend.

17. Reagan, "Address to the Nation on Federal Tax Reduction."

recommended that the 1985 payroll tax rate increase be moved to 1984 and that part of the 1990 rate increase be moved to 1988; the rate for 1990 and after would not be changed. (This solution was supported largely by commissioners appointed by Democratic leaders in Congress; the Republican-appointed commissioners favored cuts in reductions.) To offset these increases, the commission explored a variety of options, such as making part of the payroll tax deductible. Eventually it recommended a one-time, refundable tax credit in an amount equaling the increase in the worker's payroll tax. This credit would be applied against his or her tax liability in 1984.[18]

In the 1983 amendments to Social Security, Congress and the president adopted the commission's proposal to accelerate previously scheduled increases in the payroll tax but not the plan for a one-time refundable tax credit.[19] Between 1980 and 1990, the federal payroll tax increased from 12.26 percent to 15.3 percent of wages, and the maximum payroll tax burden more than doubled to $7,849.[20] Many low-income earners came to owe more in payroll tax than in federal income tax.

The regressivity of the payroll tax became an increasingly visible issue as payroll taxes grew both in absolute terms and as a proportion of federal taxes.[21] Democratic leaders, seeking a balance between the solvency of Social Security and the desire to reduce the burden of payroll taxes, began to explore policy options that would leave the payroll tax untouched while targeting relief to low- and moderate-income workers and their families. In 1984, for example, House Democrats accepted a Senate Republican provision improving the tax treatment of capital gains in exchange for agreement to increase the maximum EITC available to working poor families from $500 to $550. The measures also raised the income level at which the credit would be completely phased out from $10,000 to $11,000 a year.[22]

18. See SocialSecurityOnline, "Dissenting Views of Congressman Bill Archer to the Report of the National Commission on Social Security Reform," *Appendix C of the 1983 Greenspan Commission on Social Security Reform* (www.socialsecurity.gov/history/reports/gspan7.html).

19. Ibid.

20. "Summary of Major 1983 Congressional Action: Labor/Social Security," *CQ Weekly*, November 26, 1983, p. 2480.

21. Ronald D. Elving, "Social Security Tax Offset?" *CQ Weekly*, February 24, 1990, p. 572.

22. Pamela Fessler, "$63 Billion in Cuts, Taxes: First Installment of 'Down Payment' Clears," *CQ Weekly*, June 30, 1984, pp. 1539–44.

Toward Bipartisanship and the 1986 Tax Reform Act

More broadly, despite supporting much of the president's 1981 plan for tax reform, between 1982 and 1986, Democrats increasingly challenged the fairness of Reagan's federal tax and budgetary policies. As part of this effort, House Democrats directed the General Accounting Office (now the Government Accountability Office) and the Congressional Budget Office to study the distributional effects of Reagan's tax and budget reductions. The Congressional Budget Office reports concluded that the gains from federal tax reductions rose substantially with household income and the reductions in federal benefit payments for individuals were greatest for households with incomes below $10,000.[23] Armed with this information, Democrats reached out to antipoverty groups, which had been focused on protecting traditional cash assistance programs from federal budget reductions, to highlight the growing importance of the federal individual income tax code as a way to support low-income workers and families.[24]

However, Democrats did not seek to overturn all of the 1981 reforms. Like Reagan, Representative Dan Rostenkowski (D-Ill.), who chaired Ways and Means, believed that the federal individual income tax must be revised to allow working Americans to "keep more of their salaries." Democratic House leaders supported Rostenkowski's effort to prevent Reagan from running off with "their" issue—tax fairness.[25] For his part, in February 1984, President Reagan asked the Treasury Department to "develop a plan of action with specific recommendations to make our tax system fairer, simpler, and less of a burden on our nation's economy."[26] Nine months later, Treasury Secretary Donald Regan submitted his department's report on *Tax Reform for Fairness, Simplicity, and Economic Growth*.[27]

Known as Treasury I, the plan provided for three tax brackets—15 percent, 25 percent, and 35 percent—which would be indexed to keep pace with inflation. It also proposed increases in the personal exemption (to $2,000) and zero bracket amount (to $3,800 for a married couple and $2,800 for a single filer), which would remain indexed in order to "virtu-

23. Congressional Budget Office (1982).

24. Howard (1997, p. 147).

25. Elizabeth Wehr, "Veteran Dealer: Rostenkowski: A Firm Grip on Ways and Means," *CQ Weekly*, July 6, 1985, pp. 1316–19.

26. Ronald Reagan, "Message to the Congress Transmitting the Annual Economic Report of the President, February 2, 1984," *American Presidency Project* (www.presidency.ucsb.edu/ws/?pid=39222).

27. U.S. Department of the Treasury (1984).

ally eliminate from taxation families with incomes below the poverty level," and the indexation of the EITC.[28] However, low-income families were likely to be hurt by the proposal to replace the existing credit for children and dependents with a deduction, which would be capped at $2,400 for one child and $4,800 for two or more children.

Treasury I was designed to be both revenue neutral and "distribution-ally" neutral. In other words, based on Treasury calculations, the plan altered neither the total tax revenue collected by the federal government nor the existing distribution of tax payments across income classes. Treasury officials calculated that the share of total income taxes paid by taxpayers with annual incomes between zero and $10,000, then 0.5 percent, would remain essentially the same under its plan, at 0.3 percent.[29] However, as analysts later pointed out, the Treasury's definition of distributional neutrality—"as equal percentage reductions in tax liabilities at all income levels"—was not the only one available.[30] According to two economists involved in the preparation of Treasury I, "A reasonable alternative was an equal percentage increase in after-tax incomes at all income levels. . . . The implications of these two definitions differ substantially, as the definition of distributional neutrality chosen by the Treasury Department results in far greater tax reductions for high-income taxpayers than does adoption of the second alternative."[31]

Although these authors believed the Treasury definition was chosen "without full appreciation of the political importance of that decision," many Democrats in Congress believed the definition was selected with a specific partisan distributional goal in mind.

Greatly watered down, Treasury I provided the basis for the Tax Reform Act of 1986, widely regarded as the most significant set of changes to the federal tax system since the 1940s. The president set the stage for the debate that led up to this landmark legislation in his February 1985 State of the Union address. Although calling for "an historic reform of tax simplification for fairness and growth," he acknowledged the "steep tax barriers that make hard lives even harder" for low-income families. To "encourage opportunity and jobs rather than dependency and welfare," he said,

28. Pamela Fessler, "More Concern for Deficit Reduction on Hill: Treasury Tax Overhaul Excites Little Interest," *CQ Weekly*, December 1, 1984, pp. 3016–19.

29. U.S. Department of the Treasury (1984).

30. McLure and Zodrow (1987, p. 44).

31. Ibid.

"we will propose that individuals living at or near the poverty line be totally exempt from Federal income tax."[32] As the White House later explained, under the president's plan, "by taking the basic deductions, the average family earning up to $12,000 . . . would be dropped completely from the tax rolls—not one penny of tax to pay."[33] Under existing law, four-person families became liable for income tax once their household income reached roughly $9,500.

Reagan's proposal to provide tax relief for low-income working families was embraced by Republicans and Democrats alike. Senator Max Baucus of Montana, a moderately conservative Democrat and member of the Finance Committee, claimed, "I think we're all going in this direction."[34] Democrats and Republicans also agreed, as the White House had demanded, that any tax package would be distributionally neutral.[35] This meant that anyone in Congress who proposed additional tax relief for higher-wage earners had to add an equal tax reduction for lower-income earners (and vice versa).[36] Nonetheless, the initial plans approved by the House and Senate were quite far apart.

In the House, the Democratic majority approved a measure to replace the existing fourteen individual tax rates ranging from 11 percent to 50 percent with four rates—15 percent, 25 percent, 35 percent, and 38 percent. Democrats also increased the standard deduction and the EITC.[37] In the Senate, a bipartisan coalition approved a plan with two brackets, 15 and 27 percent. The 15 percent bracket would include 80 percent of all taxpayers. In addition, more than 6 million workers with incomes at or slightly above the officially defined poverty level would be removed from the tax rolls.[38]

Ultimately, the 1986 Tax Reform Act provided for another across-the-board reduction in tax rates, this time lowering the top rate from 50 per-

32. Ronald Reagan, "Address before a Joint Session of the Congress on the State of the Union, February 6, 1985," *American Presidency Project* (www.presidency.ucsb.edu/ws/?pid=38069).

33. Robert Rothman, "Bipartisan Support on Hill: Reagan Critics Praise Tax Cuts for the Poor," *CQ Weekly*, July 6, 1985, pp. 1323–24.

34. Eileen Shanahan, "Tax Reform Warm-up: Harmony on Some Points," *CQ Weekly*, July 1986, pp. 1566–68.

35. Ibid.

36. Ibid.

37. Pamela Fessler, "House Reverses Self, Passes Major Tax Overhaul," *CQ Weekly*, December 21, 1985, pp. 2705–11.

38. Eileen Shanahan, "Finance Panel OKs Radical Tax Overhaul Bill," *CQ Weekly*, May 10, 1986, pp. 1007–13.

Figure 4-2. *Historical EITC Parameters, 1975–2009*

Maximum credit (dollars)

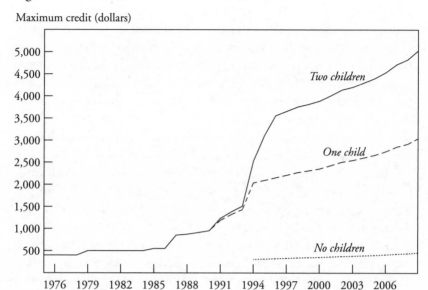

Sources: For 1975–2003: U.S. House of Representatives (2004). For 2004–2007: Internal Revenue Service, Form 1040 Instructions. For 2008: Internal Revenue Service, "Revenue Procedure 2007-66 (www.irs.gov/pub/irs-drop/rp-07-66.pdf [November 1, 2007]). For 2009: Internal Revenue Service, "Revenue Procedure 2008-66" (www.irs.gov/pub/irs-drop/rp-08-66.pdf [November 3, 2008]), and Internal Revenue Service, "ARRA and the Earned Income Tax Credit" (www.irs.gov/newsroom/article/0,,id=205666,00.html [August 2009]).

cent to 28 percent.[39] The legislation replaced the existing fourteen tax brackets (fifteen for single taxpayers) with a temporary five-bracket system for 1987 only, and a two-bracket system, with rates of 15 percent and 28 percent, thereafter. With bipartisan support, the new law reduced federal tax liability on low-income workers and families by increasing the personal exemption, increasing the standard deduction, expanding the EITC, and indexing the EITC for inflation.[40] The maximum credit for a family with one or more children rose from $550 in 1986 to $874 in 1988. (See figure 4-2 for history of maximum EITC amount.)

The 1986 Tax Reform Act overcame previous partisan divides by combining tax loophole–closing reforms long sought by liberal Democrats with

39. Brownlee (2004, p. 174); "Major Provisions of Tax Bill Conference Agreement," *CQ Weekly*, August 23, 1986, p. 1952. For a fuller discussion of all the provisions, see "Major Provisions of the Tax Reform Act of 1986," *CQ Weekly*, October 4, 1986, pp. 2350–58.

40. Steuerle (2008, p. 130).

income tax rate reductions favored by conservative Republicans. Due to its complexity, many of the policymakers who helped negotiate the 1986 package were uncertain about its final distributional consequences. One of the major goals of the Tax Reform Act was an increase in the equity of the tax system, but equity was and is a concept that is difficult to evaluate. According to some, "[the 1986 tax reform] was so progressive that it essentially offset the regressive effects of the 1981 across-the-board tax reductions and the post-1983 increase in the schedule of the federal payroll tax."[41] However, others concluded that the changes left the progressivity of the federal income tax code unchanged.[42]

The official documentation of the Tax Reform Act, contained in the Joint Tax Committee's General Explanation of the 1986 Tax Reform Act, reported data estimating the tax reductions by income levels. These data showed that tax liabilities were cut by 65 percent and 22 percent, respectively, in the two lowest brackets; by 8–10 percent in the next three brackets; and by 1–2 percent at the higher-income levels. However, the proportional change in tax liability was not the most meaningful measure of the effect of the tax on progressivity. If tax liabilities were extremely small at lower-income levels, even a large percentage change could mean very little in terms of increased income. A better measure of the distributional effects was the percentage change in after-tax income. Based on the official data, this measure suggested that lower-income earners received larger percentage increases in after-tax incomes than higher-income earners, but the differences did not appear nearly as dramatic.[43]

The Bipartisan 1990 Omnibus Budget Act and Low-Income Working Parents

Efforts to aid low-income families with at least one working parent continued under Reagan's successor, George H.W. Bush. In his first State of the Union address, President Bush emphasized the importance of helping low-income families pay for child care, declaring: "Our help should be aimed at those who need it most—low-income families with young children. I support a new child care tax credit that will aim our efforts at ex-

41. Brownlee (2004, p. 176).
42. Ibid., p. 176.
43. Gravelle (1992, pp. 27–44).

actly those families, without discriminating against mothers who choose to stay at home."[44] In place of the existing $720 nonrefundable credit, he proposed a refundable credit of up to $1,000 per child. The new child care tax credit would be offered in addition to the EITC and would be available in advance as a payment in parents' monthly paychecks. In addition, he proposed to increase the standard deduction for families with children under age one—a provision that became known as the "wee tot allowance."

The goal of helping working families pay for child care had bipartisan political support, but Congress had difficulty agreeing on a specific proposal. Although Republicans supported the president's plan, liberal Democrats viewed the proposed tax credits as inadequate and favored a plan to use federal funds to help states subsidize child care centers serving families with low to moderate incomes. Centrist Democrats supported a hybrid of both approaches. Eventually House Democrats reached agreement on a plan to support poor working families by expanding the EITC instead of creating a refundable child care tax credit. As approved by the Ways and Means Committee, the plan would increase the EITC for families with one child and would adjust it for family size, providing larger credits for families with two children and those with three or more children.[45] The House leadership packaged this proposal with plans to increase funding for the Social Services Block Grant (Title XX of the Social Security Act) that provides funding to the states for day care, counseling, and other social services; to expand Head Start, the federal school readiness program; and to create a school-based program for before-school and after-school care.

In contrast to their colleagues in the House, Democrats in the Senate, who had retaken control of the chamber in 1986, agreed both to a refundable child care tax credit, as the president had requested, and to direct grants to the states for subsidies to child care providers and cash payments to parents. In addition, at the initiative of Finance Committee Chair Lloyd Bentsen (D-Tex.), the Senate approved an additional tax credit to offset the premiums that low-wage parents paid for health insurance. To promote agreement with the House, Senate Democrats made the Child and Dependent Care Tax Credit only 90 percent refundable, which meant that

44. George H. W. Bush, "Address on Administration Goals before a Joint Session of Congress, February 9, 1989," *American Presidency Project* (www.presidency.ucsb.edu/ws/?pid=16660).

45. Julie Rovner, "Ways and Means Approves Major EITC Expansion," *CQ Weekly,* July 22, 1989, pp. 1862–63.

working parents who did not earn enough to owe federal income taxes would nonetheless get 90 percent of the benefit.[46]

The final agreement approved by Congress, as part of the 1990 Omnibus Budget Reconciliation Act, incorporated elements of both plans. It provided for an increase in the EITC, to be phased in over three years. Under previous legislation, the maximum credit was projected to be $995 in 1991. The new measure increased it to a maximum of $1,186 for parents with one child and $1,228 for those with two or more—giving families with more than one child a larger credit for the first time. Acknowledging the EITC's interaction with other means-tested programs (food stamps, Medicaid, and Aid to Families with Dependent Children), Democrats demanded that the credit not be considered as earned income in determining eligibility for other federal social safety net programs.[47]

Contrary to the wishes of the Bush White House, the package did not create a refundable child care tax credit, but it included a refundable tax credit for low-wage parents who purchased health insurance for their children, as the Senate had proposed. (The maximum credit for 1991 was expected to be $426.)[48] In addition, it provided an additional tax credit for each child less than one year old. This measure replaced the president's proposal to increase the standard deduction for families with infants. Although the wee tot allowance had been a key White House demand, Democrats argued that it would not help families with little or no tax liability and would not serve the intended goal of encouraging mothers to stay at home.[49]

Democrats portrayed the final 1990 agreement as an important step toward restoring "fairness" to the federal income tax after a decade of policy changes that had hurt low-income working families.[50] Together with the 1986 Tax Reform Act, the 1990 Omnibus Budget Reconciliation Act was also an important step forward for the EITC, which was emerging as a favored way to alter the distributional characteristics of various deficit

46. Julie Rovner, "Senate's Child-Care Measure Would Broaden U.S. Role," *CQ Weekly,* June 24, 1989, pp. 1543–46.

47. "Provisions: Budget-Reconciliation Bill," *CQ Weekly,* December 1, 1990, pp. 4012–36.

48. Pamela Fessler, "Taxes: This Year's Battle May Be Over, But the War Has Just Begun," *CQ Weekly,* November 3, 1990, pp. 3714–17.

49. Julie Rovner, "Families Gain Help from Hill on Child Care, Medicaid." *CQ Weekly,* November 3, 1990, pp. 3721–22.

50. Pamela Fessler, "Search for a Tax Compromise Ends with a New Layer of Complications," *CQ Weekly,* October 27, 1990, pp. 3576–77.

reduction packages. EITC expansions in both 1986 and 1990 helped low-income working families by increasing their tax entry threshold—the income below which no federal income tax was owed. During this period, the EITC continued to be supported by both Democrats and Republicans who favored reducing the income tax burden on low-income working families and rewarding work. However, as the budgetary cost of the EITC rose in succeeding years, this bipartisan political support would erode.

Decline of the Federal Minimum Wage

Throughout the 1980s, there was bipartisan support for efforts to use the tax code, especially the EITC, to boost the paychecks of low-income working families. However, this consensus did not include the minimum wage. The federal minimum wage had reached its highest value relative to the federal poverty threshold in 1968, when it amounted to 118.7 percent of the poverty level for a full-time, full-year worker supporting three dependents. Throughout the 1970s, a full-year, full-time, minimum wage job had kept a single worker with two children above the federal poverty threshold. By 1980 this was no longer true.[51]

Nonetheless, in the early 1980s, the minimum wage was "political enemy number one" for Reagan and the Republicans. By the time Ronald Reagan took office, he was calling it an injustice, the cause, in his opinion, of "more misery and unemployment than anything since the Great Depression."[52] In 1983 Reagan proposed a youth opportunity wage of $2.50—or 25 percent below the federal minimum wage of $3.35.[53] To address Democrats' fears that adult workers would be displaced by younger entry-level workers, Reagan suggested that the subminimum wage be effective only during the summer and that employers be prohibited from using it to

---

51. Tom Gabe, "Historical Relationship between the Minimum Wage and Poverty, 1959 to 2005," Congressional Research Service memorandum, July 5, 2005 (www.chn.org/pdf/crsminimum wage.pdf).

52. As quoted in Jimmy Carter, "Wyoming, Michigan Remarks and a Question-and-Answer Session with High School Students, October 24, 1980," *American Presidency Project* (www.presidency.ucsb.edu/ws/?pid=45369).

53. Singer (1981, p. 146); "Message on Structural Unemployment," *CQ Almanac*, 1983, p. 18E; Janet Hook, "Labor Opposition Remains Strong: White House Resurrects Youth Summer Wage," *CQ Weekly*, May 19, 1984, p. 1177. See also Ronald Reagan, "Message to the Congress Transmitting Proposed Employment Legislation, March 11, 1983," *American Presidency Project* (www.presidency.ucsb.edu/ws/index.php?pid=41038).

displace adult workers.[54] Senate Republicans supported the proposal, calling it a "non-bureaucratic and cost-effective proposal" to address youth unemployment.[55] However, a majority of House Democrats refused to act on the president's plan, arguing that its main impact would be to create a windfall profit for McDonald's and other fast-food chains.[56]

Meanwhile, inflation continued to erode the purchasing power of the minimum wage. Between January 1981 and January 1986, average prices increased by about 26 percent. Over the same period, the minimum wage remained $3.35. In order to maintain its purchasing power, it would have had to rise above $4.00 an hour. In 1981 the income of a full-time, full-year worker earning the minimum wage fell just below the poverty threshold for a family of three; by 1986 the gap had grown to 20 percent.[57]

After regaining control of the Senate in 1986, Democrats in Congress aimed to increase the minimum wage to "roughly half of the average wage."[58] To preserve the future value of the federal minimum wage, House Democratic leaders also proposed indexing it to remain at 50 percent of the average private, nonsupervisory, nonagricultural hourly wage.[59] The president responded by threatening to veto any minimum wage increase. Reagan argued in 1987, "The last time I looked, we wanted the minimum (wage) lower, not higher. I don't think that's changed. And in the meantime, we've got what we asked for, because inflation has in fact cut the real value of the minimum wage."[60] He was joined in his opposition by moderate-to-conservative Democrats, who shared his belief that "a higher minimum wage would do more harm than good, creating unemployment and causing the collapse of companies already in financial distress."[61] Conservative Democrats also opposed indexation and supported an increase in small business exemption from the minimum wage.[62]

---

54. "Message on Structural Unemployment," *CQ Almanac*, 1983.

55. U.S. Senate (1984, pp. 9–10).

56. Ibid.; Bill Keller, "Fast-Food Industry Expands Its Lobby Franchise to Cover Jobs and Commodities Issues," *CQ Weekly Report*, June 1981, pp. 1095, 1097; James W. Singer, "A Subminimum Wage: Jobs for Youths or a Break for Their Employers," *National Journal*, January 24, 1981, p. 146.

57. Smith and Vavrichek (1986); Ellwood (1989, p. 110).

58. Nadine Cohodas, "Minimum Wage Getting Maximum Attention," *CQ Weekly*, March 7, 1987, pp. 403–07.

59. U.S. Department of Labor (2008).

60. Timothy Clark, "Raising the Floor," *National Journal*, March 21, 1987, pp. 702–05.

61. Ibid., p. 705.

62. Ibid.

Nevertheless, it was Senate Republicans who repeatedly blocked Democratic efforts to increase the minimum wage toward the end of President Reagan's second term. In 1988 the Senate agreed to a debate on a minimum wage increase only after Vice President Bush, as the GOP nominee, indicated that he would support a modest increase if it were coupled with a lower "training" wage for new entry-level workers.[63] After two attempts to end a Republican filibuster in the Senate, Democrats failed to secure the votes needed to move forward.[64]

Many opponents of a minimum wage increase saw expansion of the EITC as an alternative policy tool to support low-income earners and their families. Expanding the EITC, advocates pointed out, would target assistance to low-income working families, whereas increasing the minimum wage would benefit low-wage workers with or without children. This view was shared by moderate-to-conservative Democrats and by centrist Republicans, who wanted to avoid being forced to take a position on the minimum wage. As Representative Thomas E. Petri (R-Wis.) proclaimed, "We who are against the minimum wage are led into this valley and slaughtered. We'd like to begin shifting the debate."[65] Liberal Democrats supported the EITC but believed that the EITC and the minimum wage should reinforce each other. As one policymaker warned, "It's [the EITC] best seen as a complement to the minimum wage."[66]

By 1989 the ratio of the minimum wage to the average hourly wage for production, nonsupervisory workers had dropped to 33 percent. The new president, George H.W. Bush, supported a two-step increase in the minimum wage from $3.35 to $3.80 in 1990 and from $3.80 to $4.25 the following year. However, he supported it only as part of a package that included a six-month subminimum training wage of $3.35 an hour, an expansion of the tip credit from 40 percent to 50 percent, and an increase in the sales ceiling for exempted small businesses from $362,500 to

63. Macon Morehouse, "Senate Opens Debate on Minimum-Wage Hike," *CQ Weekly Report*, September 17, 1988, p. 2587; Morehouse, "GOP Seeks Action on Judgeships: Minimum-Wage Bill Snared in Partisan Power Struggle," *CQ Weekly*, September 24, 1988, p. 2641.

64. Macon Morehouse, "Election-Year Politicking: Senate Fills Its Spare Time Feuding over 'Family Issues,'" *CQ Weekly*, October 1, 1988, pp. 2708–09.

65. Patrick Knudsen, "Bill to Boost Minimum Wage Encounters Resistance, Delays," *CQ Weekly Report*, February 27, 1988, p. 506.

66. Macon Morehouse, "House GOP Adopts Old Democratic Plan: Tax Credit Pushed as Alternative to Wage Hike," *CQ Weekly*, July 30, 1988, pp. 2078–79.

$500,000 a year.[67] House Democratic leaders secured agreement with conservative Democrats and moderate Republicans on a plan providing for a large increase in the minimum wage to $4.55 an hour, a two-month training wage equal to 85 percent of the minimum wage, and an expansion of the small business exemption.[68] However, Bush vetoed the final package that emerged from the Senate-House conference, insisting that the minimum wage could not be raised above $4.25 an hour and that the training wage should be equal to 80 percent of the minimum wage and apply to a worker's first six months on the job.[69]

In explaining his veto, Bush highlighted his support for income tax credits for low-income families as a preferred alternative to increases in the minimum wage. Tax credits, he argued, "can be much more precisely targeted, to help only those who need the help, with none of the job-loss or inflationary effects of raising the minimum wage."[70] However, Congressional Democrats continued to press the minimum wage issue as a test of President Bush's pledge to promote a "kinder, gentler America." Senate Majority Leader George J. Mitchell (D-Maine) contrasted Mr. Bush's support for a reduction in the capital gains tax with his opposition to a larger increase in the minimum wage: "How can anyone justify wanting to give a $30,000-a-year tax cut to the richest Americans and at the same time opposing 30 cents an hour more for the poorest Americans?"[71]

Finally, in late 1989, the president and Democrats in Congress agreed to increase the minimum wage in two steps to $4.25 by 1991, to create a training wage for teenagers in their first three months of employment (a temporary provision to expire in 1993), and to increase the small business exemption as the White House had sought.[72] As part of the agreement, Democrats agreed to abandon their proposal for a minimum wage review board, which would recommend annual changes in the minimum wage— a plan that Republicans viewed as an attempt at "backdoor indexing." The final bipartisan bargain was the result of Bush's desire to avoid vetoing a

67. U.S. Senate (1989, p. 19).

68. Macon Morehouse, "House Defies Threatened Veto, Passes Minimum-Wage Bill." *CQ Weekly*, March 25, 1989, pp. 641–42.

69. "Bush Sends Congress Veto of Minimum-Wage Bill," *CQ Weekly*, June 17, 1989, pp. 1501–02.

70. Ibid.

71. Susan F. Rasky, "Senate, Rejecting Bush Program, Backs Minimum Wage of $4.55," *New York Times*, April 12, 1989.

72. Alyson Pytte, "Labor: Minimum-Wage Bill Cleared, Ending 10-Year Stalemate," *CQ Weekly*, November 11, 1989, p. 3053.

second Democratic minimum wage proposal and Democrats' reluctance to confront Bush for uncertain electoral advantage.[73]

For workers the gains were modest. The increase to $4.25 in 1991 did not make up for the drop in the real value of the minimum wage over the previous decade. Since 1980 the minimum wage has remained below the federal poverty line for a single, full-time, full-year worker supporting a family of three.

Helping More Middle-Income Working Families

By the early 1990s, the politics of boosting paychecks was shifting away from aiding working poor families toward a debate about delivering tax relief to the middle class. Over the course of the 1980s, low-income families benefited from two expansions of the EITC. However, middle-income families received little help in a decade when the maximum payroll tax burden more than doubled. Helping middle-income families cope with this problem emerged as a significant political challenge for both Democrats and Republicans. As a direct result, the 1990s became the first decade in more than half a century in which American politics did not yield an increase in the federal payroll tax.[74]

In the run-up to the 1992 election, Democrats began making the case for boosting the paychecks of families in the middle of the income distribution.[75] In February 1992, House Democrats put forward a tax plan that included a two-year income tax credit based on a worker's payroll tax contributions. Most workers would receive 20 percent of the amount they contributed through their share of the 15.3 percent payroll tax, up to a cap of $200 for individuals and $400 for couples. To win the support of liberal Democrats for more middle-class tax relief, Ways and Means Committee Chair Dan Rostenkowski (D-Ill.) agreed to make the temporary tax credit refundable, ensuring that earners too poor to owe federal income taxes would get some increase in their monthly paychecks.[76]

73. Ibid. See also "Legislative Summary: Labor," *CQ Weekly*, December 2, 1989, p. 3304.

74. Steuerle (1996, p. 436); Ronald D. Elving, "Moynihan Seeks to Roll Back Social Security Tax Rate," *CQ Weekly*, January 6, 1990, pp. 32–33; Elving, "Moynihan Tax Cut Proposal Draws Cheers, Barbs," *CQ Weekly*, January 20, 1990, p. 192; George Hager, "Senate OKs Fiscal Blueprint, Rejects Payroll Tax Cut," *CQ Weekly*, April 27, 1991, pp. 1040–43.

75. David S. Cloud, "The Cry for Middle-Class Cuts: Looking behind the Rhetoric," *CQ Weekly*, January 18, 1992, pp. 105–10.

76. David S. Cloud and John R. Cranford, "Democrats Hone Tax Plan as Challenge to Bush," *CQ Weekly*, February 15, 1992, pp. 347–52.

Senate Democrats rejected the House proposal in favor of a $300-per-child tax credit. The Senate's child tax credit would be permanent and non-refundable, while the House plan was for a temporary refundable credit. The Senate child tax credit would go to 20 million earners with children (out of 113 million earners), while the House's credit would go to 90 million earners.[77] Senate liberals, such as Bill Bradley (D-N.J.) and Jay Rockefeller (D-W.Va.), lobbied Finance Committee Chair Lloyd Bentsen (D-Tex.) for changes to the plan that would aid low-income working families. For example, Bradley proposed that the child tax credit be refundable. However, more conservative Senate Democrats argued that tax relief ought to be targeted to the middle class—not to the working poor, who had received a boost in their paychecks due to the last EITC expansion. As a compromise, Bentsen proposed to make the EITC easier to claim and to broaden its eligibility by repealing the credit targeted to children under age one year and committing the resulting revenue to the EITC.[78]

Ultimately, in 1992 Congress approved a package of middle-income tax relief that included a trimmed-down version of the two-year credit based on payroll taxes that originated in the House, as well as the Senate's permanent $300-per-child tax credit, which was made available to working parents with children under age sixteen. Both credits were offered only to families earning up to $70,000 and began to phase out at $50,000. To finance these tax cuts, the bill increased the rate in the top tax bracket to 36 percent and levied a 10 percent surcharge on income over $1 million.[79] Despite the growing signs of recession, Bush vetoed the Democrats' plan because it "would increase taxes on the wealthy to finance a $28 billion tax cut for the middle class." In announcing his veto, he claimed, "The Democrat package gives typical Americans only about 25 cents a day for two years. But it increases taxes permanently. I believe a Congress that has consistently shown it spends too much of hard-working Americans' tax dollars should not be allowed to tax and spend any more."[80]

The outcome was a stalemate between a Democratic Congress and a Republican White House over which workers and their families needed a

77. Ibid.

78. David S. Cloud, "Finance Committee Sends Doomed Bill to Senate," *CQ Weekly*, March 7, 1992, pp. 517–21.

79. Adam Clymer, "Tax Bill Is Passed by the Democrats and Bush Vetoes It," *New York Times*, March 21, 1992.

80. George H.W. Bush, "Statement on House of Representatives Action on Tax Legislation, February 27, 1992," *American Presidency Project* (www.presidency.ucsb.edu/ws/?pid=20662).

boost in their paychecks, and more important, who should finance it. Weighed down by concern about the economy, Bush lost his bid for reelection in 1992.

Conclusion: A New Bargain

The 1980s were marked by first a steady climb and then a sharp fall in the effective tax rates faced by low-income working families. A household's effective tax rate is the total taxes it pays measured as a percentage of its pretax income. Effective tax rates vary across types of households because of differences in sources and levels of income and in how the tax system treats earners in different situations.[81] The average effective tax rate for families with incomes at the federal poverty line fell sharply in 1975 with the creation of the EITC but then rose over the next ten years, reaching 15.3 percent in 1986 for a family with one working adult and two children—nearly the highest rate in forty-five years. The decision not to index tax brackets, exemptions, the standard deduction, and the EITC contributed largely to this distributive outcome.[82] Another important factor was the growth of the payroll tax, which rose from 7.25 percent in 1965 to 14.3 percent in 1986.

The Reagan tax reforms helped low-income earners in several ways. The Economic Recovery Tax Act of 1981 resulted in the indexation of tax brackets, personal exemptions, and the zero bracket amount (or standard deduction) beginning in 1985. The 1986 Tax Reform Act expanded and indexed the EITC. Both packages increased the personal exemption and standard deduction. Together these changes brought effective tax rates for working poor families back down to roughly their level in 1975.

The 1980s also saw the emergence of a bipartisan consensus in support of the EITC as a mechanism to boost the paychecks of low-income working families.[83] This development was particularly important in light of the stalemate around the minimum wage, which remained at the same level from 1981 to 1990. According to Eugene Steuerle, "Democrats found that they could achieve social policy goals using the tax code. In doing so, they were taking a page from the playbook of Republicans, who had long used

81. Roberton Williams, "Effective Tax Rates for Different Kinds of Households," *Tax Notes*, January 14, 2008, p. 327.
82. Scholtz (2007).
83. Toder (1998, p. 41). See also Steuerle (2008, p. 41).

the tax code to encourage business investment."[84] The EITC reduced or eliminated the federal income taxes paid by low-wage parents and operated as a wage subsidy for their employers. However, this boost in after-tax income only modestly offset the increases in payroll and other taxes being paid by moderate-income families. Based on evidence on the level and distribution of income and payroll tax burdens for U.S. families over the period, payroll taxes became an increasingly important component of the tax burden for many low- and middle-income families.[85]

By the 1992 election, political pressure was building for Democrats to challenge Republicans on the issue of "tax fairness" for moderate- and middle-income families. During the campaign, Democratic presidential nominee Bill Clinton launched a broad attack on the distributive consequences of the Reagan-Bush tax and budget policies, arguing, "For 12 years the Republicans in Washington have praised the virtues of hard work, but they have hurt hard-working Americans."[86] Clinton declared that he would both cut the deficit and provide income tax relief to the middle class, proposing a new income tax credit or deduction for families with taxable income up to $60,000.[87] He also pledged that full-time work at the federal minimum wage plus the EITC (and any food stamps for which a family was eligible) would be enough to raise a family's income, net of the payroll tax, above the federal poverty line. To achieve this distributional goal, the EITC would need to be increased, particularly for families with two or more children. Someone would have to pay for these proposals. Thus as a new Democratic administration took office, political attention focused on who would get a boost in their paychecks, how much of an increase would they get, and who would finance it.

84. See Daniel Altman, "A Tax Code Not Intended for Amateurs," *New York Times*, February 4, 2003, p. C1.

85. Mitrusi and Poterba (2000).

86. O'Connor (2002, pp. 396–411).

87. Chuck Alston, "Clinton's Program: The President's Position on Taxes: Reversal or 'Healthy Evolution'?" *CQ Weekly*, February 20, 1993, pp. 384–86; "Clinton's Promises," *CQ Weekly*, February 20, 1993, p. 385.

5 | Clinton and the Fight over Tax Relief for the Working Poor or the Middle Class

I n the 1990s, tax relief for more moderate- and middle-income earners emerged as a major partisan distributional goal for Democrats and Republicans alike. By then the combination of a refundable Earned Income Tax Credit (EITC), which aided the working poor, and a variety of nonrefundable credits and exemptions, which largely helped higher-income earners, had created a situation that had working families in the middle feeling left out. Middle-income families earned too much to qualify for the EITC and too little to gain much benefit from other tax provisions. In other words, they faced a "middle-class parent penalty" relative to their poorer and richer counterparts.[1]

Over the course of the decade, both Democrats and Republicans sought to cultivate partisan advantage through income tax proposals to help more middle-income families. These efforts often stalemated over such critical issues as how to define the middle class and who exactly deserved such help. Although there was bipartisan support for expanding the EITC in 1993 to offset the rising burden of the payroll tax, partisan strife emerged over the refundability of the EITC and the proposed refundability of a child tax credit. Once the Republicans took control of Congress in 1994, agreement between the White House and Congress on tax

---

1. Ellwood and Liebman (2000).

relief for working families was largely limited to the adoption of the non-refundable Child Tax Credit (CTC) in 1997. In addition, in 1996 both sides agreed to a package that coupled an increase in the minimum wage with small business tax relief.

Throughout this period, intraparty divisions were often as important as differences between the parties in shaping policy. In the House, moderate-to-conservative Democrats exercised significant influence over questions related to the income tax and the minimum wage by threatening to form blocking coalitions with like-minded Republicans. However, this minority began to cede its power as conservatives left the Democratic Party or were replaced by southern Republicans. After the 1994 midterm election, six of the most conservative Democrats switched parties.[2] However, a similar dynamic gained force on the other side of the aisle. As conservative Republican leaders sought to push forward with the radical program embodied in the Contract with America, they were held back by centrists within their own party, often from the Northeast. This group of moderate Republicans helped push policy back toward the center and played an essential role in forging coalitions to bring about changes in policy.

The Omnibus Budget Reconciliation Act: Expanding the EITC

At the start of his term, President Bill Clinton pledged that Democrats would "put government back on the side of the hard-working middle-class families of America who think most of the help goes to those at the top of the ladder, some goes to the bottom and no one speaks for them."[3] However, economic realities soon forced him to abandon the goal of middle-class income tax relief in favor of deficit reduction, on the one hand, and assistance for the working poor and very moderate income families, on the other.

Facing projections of a large budget deficit in early 1993, the Clinton White House proposed a broad-based energy tax that became known as the all fuels British thermal unit or BTU tax. The White House proposed to help offset the energy tax for low- to moderate-income families by expanding the EITC. Clinton also relied on in-kind benefits such as food

2. David Hosansky, "Special Report: Conservative Coalition: Southern Democrats Not Needed for Republicans to Win Votes," *CQ Weekly*, January 27, 1996, pp. 202–04.

3. Chuck Alston, "Clinton's Program: The President's Position on Taxes: Reversal or 'Healthy Evolution'?" *CQ Weekly*, February 20, 1993, pp. 384–86; see also "1992 Democratic Convention Supplement. The Platform: Party's Statement of Policies Mirrors Clinton's Goals," *CQ Weekly*, July 4, 1992, pp. 59–67.

Figure 5-1. *Historical Average Tax Credits (EITC and CTC) per Family,*
1975–2007

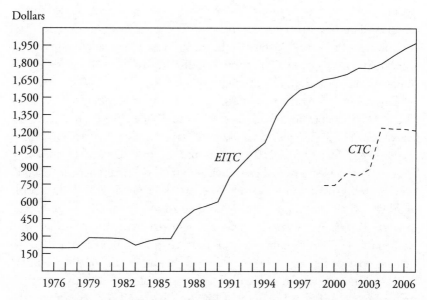

Dollars

Sources: Tax Policy Center, "Earned Income Tax Credit: Number of Recipients and Amount of Credit, 1975–2007," August 7, 2009 (www.taxpolicycenter.org/taxfacts/displayafact.cfm?Docid=370); "Credit Type and Amount by AGI 1999–2007," August 10, 2009 (www.taxpolicycenter.org/taxfacts/ displayafact.cfm?Docid=393).

stamps to shield low-income families from the burden of this tax increase. However, middle-income families were left on their own.

In 1993 an estimated 13.7 million families were due to receive the EITC, with an average boost to their annual paychecks of $872 each.[4] (See figure 5-1 for historical average EITC amounts. CTC average amounts are also listed, which begin in 1998). To qualify for the credit, families had to have incomes of less than $22,370. Under Clinton's plan, families with two children and earning up to $30,000 a year would qualify for the EITC, as would one-child families with income up to $28,500 and childless couples making up to $9,000.[5] The White House estimated that the net result would be no additional tax burden for the average family making $20,000

4. David S. Cloud, "Clinton Looking to Tax Credit to Rescue Working Poor," *CQ Weekly,* March 13, 1993, pp. 583–87.
5. "A Look at the Highlights of Clinton's Tax Proposals," *CQ Weekly,* February 20, 1993, pp. 362–63.

or less. The lowest-wage working families would see a net decrease in their tax liability, and the average family earning between $20,000 and $30,000 would owe $2 more per month in 1997, when the new taxes phased in.[6] In contrast, families earning more than $30,000 a year would see their taxes rise more significantly because of the energy tax. This marked a major reversal of Clinton's campaign promise to offer tax relief to all working families earning up to $60,000 annually.

Beyond offsetting the new energy tax, Clinton was committed to using the EITC to enable poor working families to escape poverty. To receive the maximum $1,513 in 1993, a family must have had two children and earned between $7,760 and $12,210 a year. Families with incomes below or above that range received a partial credit, although no one making over $23,070 in adjusted gross income was eligible. In 1991 nearly 5 million people worked full-time without earning enough to put them above the federal poverty threshold. A family of four supported by a single worker who earned the $4.25 minimum wage was more than $1,000 below the $15,444 federal poverty line in 1994, even after factoring in the maximum EITC and food stamps.[7] Clinton intended to make the credit generous enough to make up the difference between a low-income family's earnings and the federal poverty level. This was the first time since the credit's enactment in 1975 that any administration had adopted this goal. The emphasis on helping low-income individuals with jobs, rather than those on welfare, was intentional and reflected a conviction often repeated by Clinton that the federal government should "make work pay" for those at the bottom.

The proposed expansion of the EITC would have to be financed through cuts in other programs or increases in revenue. The solution favored by House Democrats included an increase in the top income tax rate. Their plan created a new top bracket of 36 percent, which would apply to taxable income above $140,000 for married couples, $115,000 for single earners, and $127,500 for heads of households.[8] However, their proposal also made substantial budget cuts in entitlement programs (as well as reductions in Clinton's proposed energy tax)—concessions demanded by more conservative Democrats as the price of their support. Ultimately, this omnibus

6. Cloud, "Clinton Looking to Tax Credit."

7. Ibid.

8. David S. Cloud, "Highlights of Revenue Provisions in House Reconciliation Bill," *CQ Weekly*, May 22, 1993, pp. 1280–81.

package of tax increases and spending cuts passed the House by a margin of one vote.[9]

The Senate, which included more fiscal centrists, scaled back the EITC proposal that emerged from the House. Under the House plan, families making up to $28,000 would qualify for the credit; the maximum credit for families with two or more children would rise from $1,384 in 1992 to $2,685 in 1994 and $3,371 thereafter; and low-income earners with no children would receive a maximum credit of $306. Senate Democrats eliminated the proposed credit for single workers or childless couples and reduced the maximum credit for families with two or more children to $3,315, beginning in 1996.[10] The Senate softened the blow for low-income families by replacing the regressive energy tax proposed by the White House with a modest increase in the federal gasoline tax. Nonetheless, the White House fought to restore the House's EITC proposal as part of its efforts to expand incentives for individuals to move from welfare to work.[11] Calling it a "solemn, simple commitment," Clinton claimed the federal government must ensure that "if you work 40 hours a week and you've got a child in the house, you will no longer be in poverty. It is an elemental, powerful, and profound principle. It is not liberal or conservative. It should belong to no party. It ought to become part of the American creed."[12]

Ultimately, the essentials of the president's EITC proposal survived as part of the 1993 Omnibus Budget Reconciliation Act (OBRA), which was adopted without a single Republican vote and only after Vice President Al Gore cast two tie-breaking votes in the Senate. The final agreement increased the rate at which families could claim the credit (from 18.5 percent to 34 percent of earned income for one-child families and from 19.5 percent to 40 percent for two-child families between 1992 and 1996) and raised the income level at which the credit was fully phased out to roughly $25,000 for a one-child family and $28,500 for a two-child family in 1996. As a result, the maximum credit rose to nearly $3,600 for a family with two or more children in 1996. In addition, for the first time,

9. George Hager and David S. Cloud, "Reconciliation: Democrats Pull Off Squeaker in Approving Clinton Plan," *CQ Weekly*, May 29, 1993, pp. 1340–45.

10. David S. Cloud and George Hager, "Deal on Deficit Sets Stage for Senate Floor Fight," *CQ Weekly*, June 19, 1993, pp. 1542–44.

11. David S. Cloud, "Reconciliation: Conferees Must Wrestle with Major Differences," *CQ Weekly*, June 26, 1993, pp. 1636–38.

12. William J. Clinton, "Remarks on the Earned-Income Tax Credit and an Exchange with Reporters, July 29, 1993," *American Presidency Project* (www.presidency.ucsb.edu/ws/?pid=46924).

childless workers earning up to $9,000 became eligible for a maximum credit of $306 in 1994.[13] When fully phased in, the EITC expansion (plus food stamps) would lift families with children and at least one full-time worker above the federal poverty threshold. To finance the EITC expansion, the OBRA created new tax brackets with rates of 36 percent and 39.6 percent and increased the gasoline tax.[14] The BTU tax was defeated.

This package recast the EITC as a policy tool not only to support the lowest-income families but also to provide modest support to moderate-income working parents.[15] President Clinton touted the expansion of the Earned Income Tax Credit as part of a grander scheme to reform the welfare system and to "make work pay" for low-income Americans, and the forging of this agreement was indeed a significant political accomplishment. However, the Clinton White House failed to achieve one other major political goal: the 1993 tax package did nothing to reduce the tax burden on middle-class families. Although families earning less than $30,000 a year would see their taxes fall—and families earning less than $10,000 would see their taxes fall by nearly 15 percent—the federal income tax liability of higher-earning families would rise by amounts ranging from 0.7 percent for families earning between $30,000 and $40,000 to 1.9 percent for families earning between $100,000 and $200,000 and 17.4 percent for families earning $200,000 or more.[16] Republicans charged that Clinton had promised a middle-class tax cut and delivered a tax increase instead. The part of the 1993 tax bill that most directly affected middle-income families was a 4.3-cent-per-gallon boost in the gasoline tax. This provision cost the average family $45 a year.[17]

The Republican Attack on the EITC

The failure to boost the paychecks of middle-income working families played a significant role in the Republican Revolution of 1994, which brought the

13. These numbers come from figure 4-2, which is based on data from the Joint Committee on Taxation, Ways and Means Committee (U.S. House of Representatives 2004).

14. David S. Cloud and George Hager, "With New Budget Deal in Hand, Clinton Faces Longest Yard," *CQ Weekly*, July 31, 1993, pp. 2023–28.

15. "Special Report: 1993 Budget-Reconciliation Summary: Evolution of Tax Proposals from Clinton through Conference," *CQ Weekly*, December 18, 1993, pp. 18–19.

16. Congressional Budget Office (1994, p. 32) .

17. Jodie T. Allen, "The Biggest Tax Increase in History," August 16, 1996 (http://www.slate.com/id/1037).

House of Representatives under Republican control for the first time since 1954 and installed a Republican majority in the Senate after eight years of Democratic dominance. The new Republican majority promised across-the-board income tax relief, attempting to repeat Reagan's political success with the 1981 tax reductions.[18] House Speaker Newt Gingrich (R-Ga.) called the Republicans' package of tax and spending reductions the "crown jewel" of the Contract with America, and House Republicans quickly proposed a range of "family friendly" middle-income tax relief, including a child tax credit and partial repeal of the marriage penalty. They also pledged to combat the "new tax welfare," as exemplified by the EITC.[19]

Efforts to roll back the EITC were driven by two concerns. Many conservative Republicans had come to view the refundable EITC as a form of welfare. They claimed that the original legislative intent of the Earned Income Credit was to offset federal tax liability for low-income, full-time workers. The most recent Clinton expansion, they argued, had transformed the EITC "into more of a welfare program than a tax refund."[20] According to Republicans, "only the remaining 20 percent of the EITC went for income tax relief, or refunds, in the amount of actual federal income tax liability."[21] "The EITC is not a tax cut," one of its most vocal opponents, Senator Don Nickles (R-Okla.), proclaimed. "It is the federal government's fastest growing and most fraud-prone welfare program."[22]

In addition, many Republicans were concerned that the budget outlays for the refundable portion of the EITC were growing at an exponential rate. (See figure 5-2.) The number of workers eligible for the EITC more than tripled between 1975 and 1994, from 6 million to 19 million.[23] In 1994 the total cost of the credit was more than $15 billion. The refundable EITC, which was counted as a budget outlay, accounted for nearly three quarters of the total, at close to $11 billion; the nonrefundable EITC, which was counted as a revenue loss, amounted to roughly $4 billion.

18. Andrew Taylor, "Taxation: Ready Opposition to Tax Overhaul Means No Chance for Quick Fix," *CQ Weekly*, January 24, 1998, pp. 174–77.

19. Institute for Policy Innovation, "Obama's New Welfare Scheme," *Tax Bytes*, 5.35, September 23, 2008 (www.ipi.org/ipi/ipipressreleases.nsf/9e3b904077cd41f3862571e6007821b0?OpenView&Start=1.29).

20. Alissa J. Rubin, "Low-Income Workers' Tax Credit among GOP Budget Targets," *CQ Weekly*, October 7, 1995, pp. 3055–57.

21. Ibid.

22. Collette Fraley, "Senate Finance Outlines GOP Plan," *CQ Weekly*, September 23, 1995, p. 2898.

23. Rubin, "Low-Income Workers' Tax Credit."

Figure 5-2. *Cost of the Nonrefundable (Revenuue Loss) and Refundable (Budget Outlay) EITC, 1976–2014*[a]

Billions of dollars

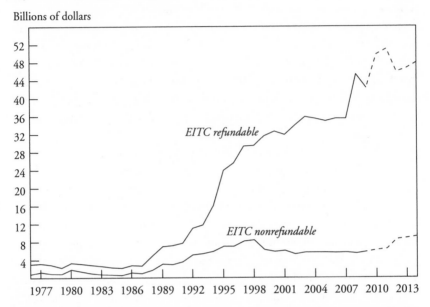

Source: Office of Budget and Management, "Table 5-2. Corporate and Individual Income Tax Estimates of Tax Expenditures," *Analytical Perspectives, Budget of the United States Government,* fiscal years 1976–2003; "Estimates of Tax Expenditures for the Corporate and Individual Income Taxes for Fiscal Years 2008–2014," *Analytical Perspectives, Budget of the United States Government* (www.white house.gov/omb/budget/fy2010/assets/list.pdf).

a. All dollar values are reported in 2009 constant dollars utilizing the latest CPI index as calculated by the Bureau of Labor Statistics. Solid lines denote actual revenue loss–budget outlay. Broken lines denote estimated revenue loss–budget outlay.

As part of their efforts to craft a plan that would balance the federal budget by 2002, House Republicans sought to cut the EITC in three ways. First, Social Security benefits and other forms of earned income would be counted in determining EITC eligibility. This change would significantly affect grandparents caring for young children. Second, childless low-income workers would no longer be eligible for the credit, removing 4 million individuals from the program. Finally, the EITC would be phased out entirely at income levels of $27,126 for a worker with two children and at $23,608 for a worker with one child (rather than $28,500 and $25,000, as they were scheduled to be in 1996). Altogether, House Republicans approved reducing or eliminating the EITC for approximately 14 million of the over 20 million low-income workers eligible to receive it in 1996.[24] Similarly the Senate proposal reduced both the number of people eligible for the credit and the amount that many beneficiaries received.[25] In fact, the Senate went even further than the House, approving cuts in EITC budget outlays by $43.2 billion over seven years, compared to the $23.3 billion in cuts passed by the House.[26]

In conference, agreement was hammered out between House and Senate Republicans on a package that tightened the EITC's eligibility rules, froze the maximum credit for some workers, and eliminated the credit for earners without children.[27] Altogether, the changes, which were written into the massive budget reconciliation bill adopted by both chambers in November 1995, cut EITC benefits by $32.4 billion and were expected to drop 1 million people from the program.[28]

Not surprisingly, the Clinton White House opposed the EITC reductions, particularly since they were coupled with plans to reduce taxes for middle- to upper-income earners by $245 billion over seven years. Leslie Samuels, assistant treasury secretary for tax policy, argued, "You are absolutely raising taxes for [low-income] people."[29] Clinton denounced the Republicans' reductions as "inconsistent with those basic bedrock values this country should be standing for. . . . Don't raise taxes on working people while we're lowering taxes on everybody else in the country."[30] In vetoing the Republican budget reconciliation bill in December 1995, he listed the proposed cuts in the EITC among the reasons for his decision: "While cutting taxes for the well-off, this bill would cut the EITC for almost 13 million working families. It would repeal part of the scheduled 1996 increase for taxpayers with two or more children, and end the credit for workers who do

24. Alissa J. Rubin, "Reconciliation: Panel OKs Plan to Cut Tax Breaks for Businesses, Working Poor," *CQ Weekly Online*, September 23, 1995, pp. 2867–69.

25. Alissa J. Rubin, "Reconciliation: Comparing House, Senate Versions of Republican EITC Proposals," *CQ Weekly Online*, October 7, 1995, pp. 3056–57.

26. George Hager, "Tax Cuts Dominate Agenda," *CQ Weekly*, June 10, 1995, pp. 1619–22); Rubin, "Low-Income Workers' Tax Credit."

27. Alissa J. Rubin, "Special Report: Taxes: Conferees Reach Agreement on $245 Billion in Cuts," *CQ Weekly*, November 18, 1995, pp. 3510–11.

28. "Reconciliation Bill Highlights," *CQ Almanac*, 1995, pp. 2–60.

29. Rubin, "Reconciliation: Panel OKs Plan to Cut Tax Breaks."

30. Todd S. Purdum, "Clinton Defends Income Tax Credit against G.O.P. Cut," *New York Times*, September 19, 1995, p. A1.

not live with qualifying children. Even after accounting for other tax cuts in this bill, about eight million families would face a net tax increase."[31]

In the absence of agreement to roll back the EITC, Republicans believed that improved EITC oversight and compliance was their second-best political goal.[32] Although Republicans and Democrats both agreed that noncompliance with EITC provisions was common, they disagreed on the cause and cure. Republicans claimed that intentional fraud was rampant and that the solution was to ramp up oversight and enforcement.[33] In contrast, Democrats concluded that the source of noncompliance was confusion, and their solution was education and simplification of the EITC.

The Republicans secured new rules to strengthen EITC compliance and enforcement as part of several pieces of legislation, including the 1996 Personal Responsibility and Work Opportunity Reconciliation Act (more widely known as the welfare reform act), the 1997 Taxpayer Relief Act, and the 1997 Balanced Budget Act. At the same time, the White House directed the Internal Revenue Service to develop a "revenue protection" strategy designed to identify returns with questionable claims for the EITC. This effort sought to address the problem of noncompliance and prevent erosion of popular support for the EITC by improving the "targeting and operation" of the credit.[34]

Courting the Middle Class: The Child Tax Credit

At the same time that the White House and Congress were fighting over the EITC, they were also battling to define the terms of middle-class tax relief. Following the Democratic Party defeat in the 1994 midterm elections, the Clinton administration made this goal a top priority, as the Republicans had already done. However, bipartisan unity was far from assured. The parties were still divided, even though both called for middle-class tax relief. Republicans wanted tax relief for all families. Democrats wanted tax relief for everybody but the highest-income families.

---

31. William J. Clinton, "Message Returning without Approval to the House of Representatives Budget Reconciliation Legislation, December 6, 1995," *American Presidency Project* (www.presidency.ucsb.edu/ws/?pid=50858).

32. U.S. House of Representatives (1997).

33. Rubin, "Low-Income Workers' Tax Credit among GOP Budget Targets," p. 3055.

34. U.S. House of Representatives (1997).

A child tax credit was a central element of both the Republican and Democratic plans. However, there was considerable divergence of preferences both between and within the parties over the form such a credit should take. Liberal Democrats were committed to helping the working poor by making a child tax credit fully refundable. Centrist Democrats were less supportive of efforts to target the credit to low-income families, believing that it was critical to provide tax relief for middle-income earners making up to $90,000 a year. Centrist Republicans held similar preferences, believing that the credit should be available to families earning up to $100,000. Conservative House Republicans, who saw a child tax credit as a critical part of their pro-family Contract with America, wanted the income ceiling on eligibility to be as high as $200,000.

The Clinton White House saw a child tax credit as a way to return to the president's 1992 campaign pledge to provide middle-class tax relief. Clinton proclaimed a nonrefundable tax credit of up to $500 for each child under thirteen, available to all families earning up to $75,000, as one of the central elements of his proposed "middle class bill of rights."[35] The message the Democrats sought to deliver with this proposal was simple: the Republican tax relief plan would do more for "the rich and for business," while Democrats would assist working families, with a focus on the middle class. However, congressional Democrats, consigned to minority status, could do little to move Clinton's plan forward. Instead the initiative belonged to the House Republican leadership. They quickly introduced the American Dream Restoration Act, which included a partially refundable $500-per-child tax credit for families earning up to $200,000 a year. (The credit was later made nonrefundable in order to limit its cost, but even then, by claiming a child tax credit, families with income tax liability could increase the amount of their EITC payment.) In addition, the Republican plan provided for a tax credit for two-earner married couples in an effort to help offset the marriage penalty.[36]

House Republicans were initially divided over which families should be eligible for the proposed child tax credit. Nearly half favored limiting it to families earning $95,000 or less. Centrists argued that allowing higher-income families to claim the credit "would make Republicans look like the

35. William J. Clinton, "Address to the Nation on the Middle Class Bill of Rights, December 15, 1994," *American Presidency Project* (www.presidency.ucsb.edu/ws/?pid=49591).

36. "Republican Contract: Middle-Class Tax Cut," *CQ Weekly*, February 25, 1995, pp. 583–85.

party of the 'rich.'"[37] House Speaker Gingrich decisively rebutted this argument, declaring, "Our bill categorically rejects the class warfare that has made Democratic tax policy so destructive to economic growth, rationality, justice and fairness. . . . We believe that just as all Americans are equal in the eyes of God and the eyes of the law, so too should they be equal in the eyes of the Internal Revenue Service."[38] However, when the bill entered conference, Senate Republicans insisted on lowering the eligibility ceiling to $110,000.

President Clinton vetoed this measure in December 1995 together with the rest of the Republican package to cut federal spending and balance the budget over seven years. A tense period of stalemate followed, punctuated by a partial shutdown of the federal government. But in the end, the Republicans were forced to back down. Centrist Republicans worried that Democrats would inflict political damage on them by insisting that the Republicans had cut popular programs, including Medicare, to finance tax relief for higher-income earners. (Nearly half of the tax benefits in the Republican plan would go to families with incomes over $100,000.) They also feared that the failure to target more relief to middle-income families would allow Democrats to paint Republicans as favoring higher-income families. In April 1996, Congress and the White House finally reached agreement on a budget for fiscal year 1996. The legislation did not include any important new tax provisions.

Progress on Middle-Class Tax Relief: The Taxpayer Relief Act of 1997

Following the 1996 election, which cut the Republican margin in the House from 38 seats to 22, increased it in the Senate from 6 seats to 10, and decisively returned President Clinton to office, both parties were determined to cooperate on family-oriented income tax relief. In the budget plan introduced in February 1997, the White House proposed a $500 tax credit for each child under thirteen for families earning up to $60,000 a year; families earning between $60,000 and $75,000 would receive a partial credit. In addition, the White House plan offered postsecondary education and training tax cuts and deductions to families earning up to $100,000 a

37. Alissa J. Rubin, "Finishing the 'Contract' in Style, House Passes Tax-Cut Bill," *CQ Weekly,* April 8, 1995, pp. 1010–14.

38. "Taxes: 'The Crowning Jewel,'" *CQ Weekly,* March 25, 1995, p. 858.

year.[39] In this way, the White House hoped to help Democrats solidify their position with middle-class voters.

Republicans also favored a child tax credit, in addition to capital gains and estate tax relief. However, debate quickly erupted over who should get this credit. Republicans wanted to make it available to families earning up to $110,000 a year. They also opposed efforts by Democratic leaders, such as Charles Rangel (D-N.Y.), the ranking Democrat on the House Ways and Means Committee, to make the proposed child tax credit fully refundable. According to Ways and Means Committee Chair Bill Archer (R-Tex.), "This is a bill for people who pay income taxes. It will be very hard for the American people to accept the president's proposal to increase welfare spending by providing tax relief to people who pay no taxes."[40] House Minority Leader Richard A. Gephardt (D-Mo.) countered by arguing, "It is, to me, a breathtaking conclusion to say that people that work hard every day and are out there trying to support their family are somehow welfare recipients because they get the earned-income credit."[41]

Ultimately, the White House and the Republican majority in Congress came to a compromise as part of the 1997 Taxpayer Relief Act, the first major bipartisan agreement to provide broad-based income tax relief in sixteen years. In addition to Republican-initiated reductions in the capital gains rate, a tax exemption for profits from personal home sales, and an increase in the estate tax exemption, the 1997 act included a variety of tax benefits aimed to help working families meet the cost of postsecondary education, as demanded by the Clinton administration. In addition, it provided a child tax credit for each child under seventeen. The Child Tax Credit (CTC), which started at $400 and increased to $500 by 1999, was available to single earners making up to $75,000 annually and couples making up to $130,000, but it began to phase out once couples reached $110,000 in annual income. At the other end of the spectrum, families earning $30,000 or less could claim the CTC before taking the EITC. Thus in practice, the credit was at least partially refundable for families with income tax liability. In addition, families with three or more children and too

39. Clay Chandler, "Budget Deal May Stall on Tax Differences," *Washington Post,* February 7, 1997; Alissa J. Rubin, "Taxes," *CQ Weekly,* February 8, 1997, pp. 332–33.

40. Alissa J. Rubin and David Hosansky. "Taxes: Democrats Steamrolled in House but Find Senate GOP Obliging," *CQ Weekly,* June 28, 1997, pp. 1495–97.

41. Ibid.

little income to pay federal income tax could use the CTC to offset any federal payroll tax liability that was not covered by the EITC.[42]

Back to Partisan Stalemate

With the CTC in place, Clinton and the Democrats turned to other working family–friendly priorities, such as helping low- to moderate-income working families pay for child care. In early 1998, President Clinton announced that he was proposing "the single largest national commitment to child care in the history of the United States." As part of his effort to help low-income earners enter and remain in the labor force, he called for increased block grants to the states to pay for child care subsidies, tax credits to encourage employers to provide child care for their employees, and a dramatic expansion of the child care tax credit. "These tax credits," he claimed, "will mean that a family of four making $35,000 and saddled with high child care bills will no longer pay one penny in federal income taxes."[43]

Clinton's expansion of the child care tax credit was a strategic effort to address rising out-of-pocket child care expenses for low-income working families without proposing new discretionary spending. As William Gale, a senior fellow with the Brookings Institution, explained, "Given the president's preference for health care, education, et cetera, and given the Republican Congress' opposition to new spending programs, the president is being forced to run these through the income tax code. . . . It's not the first best policy; it's probably not the second best policy, but it might be the best the two sides can do."[44]

Specifically, Clinton proposed to increase the Child and Dependent Care Tax Credit from 30 percent to 50 percent of a family's qualifying child and dependent care expenses, providing an additional credit of $358 a year, on average.[45] To help working parents, the Clinton plan would award $5.6 billion in tax relief over five years for child care. The plan would also give em-

42. Ibid.

43. Alissa J. Rubin, "Key Cuts and Revenue Raisers in Tax Cut Package," *CQ Weekly,* August 2, 1997, pp. 1840–41; Rubin, "Provisions: Inside the Tax-Cutting Bill," *CQ Weekly,* September 27, 1997, pp. 2331–38.

44. William J. Clinton, "Remarks Announcing Proposed Legislation on Child Care, January 7, 1998," *American Presidency Project* (www.presidency.ucsb.edu/ws/?pid=55514).

45. David Hosansky, "Abundant Foes Say 'No Chance' to Clinton's Chosen Tax Breaks," *CQ Weekly,* February 7, 1998, pp. 292–93.

ployers incentives to create child care facilities or provide child care services to employees. However, Clinton's proposal opened up a partisan divide over whether to offer support only to women in the labor market or to include stay-at-home mothers as well.[46] Democrats were particularly concerned with helping low-income, female-headed working families. In contrast, Republicans believed that the priority should be helping women stay at home with their children.

A similar disagreement was spurred by Republican efforts to reduce the marriage penalty, which resulted in about 21 million couples paying more in taxes than they would if they were single and filed separate returns. The marriage penalty was a result of the progressive nature of the federal income tax code. As income rose, it was taxed at higher rates. When two workers married, their incomes were added together, so for example, instead of two single filers in the 15 percent bracket, they became a married couple partly in the 15 percent bracket and partly in the 28 percent bracket. Conservative Republicans blamed the federal income tax code for "discouraging marriage," and made repeal of the penalty a top priority.[47] The average marriage penalty was about $1,400 annually, but it did not affect all married couples; in fact, slightly more than half received a marriage "bonus."[48] President Clinton supported reducing the marriage penalty on couples with incomes under $50,000.[49] In contrast, many Republicans wanted to abolish the marriage penalty altogether, despite the consequent revenue loss.[50]

Agreement was not reached on either issue. In 1998 the common ground shared by Congress and the White House was limited to a modest measure to provide tax relief for middle-income earners. The two sides agreed to allow nonrefundable tax credits (such as the Child and Dependent Care Tax Credit, the CTC, and the adoption credit) to offset an individual's alternative minimum tax (AMT) liability, but only for 1999. The goal was to shield some middle-income earners from liability for the AMT, which was originally aimed at ensuring high-income earners did not eliminate their income

46. Sue Kirchhoff, "Human Services: Child Care Proposal Sparks Debate over Working, at-Home Mothers." *CQ Weekly*, January 17, 1998, pp. 129–30.

47. Ibid.

48. David Hosansky, "Taxes: Resounding Votes for a Tax Cut May Amount to Little This Year," *CQ Weekly*, June 20, 1998, pp. 1682–83.

49. Lori Nitschke, "Taxes: GOP Tax Cut Plans Yield to Political Reality: Not Much and Not Now," *CQ Weekly*, February 27, 1999, pp. 477–78.

50. William J. Clinton, "Remarks prior to a Meeting with the Economic Team and an Exchange with Reporters, June 19, 1998," *American Presidency Project* (www.presidency.ucsb.edu/ws/?pid=56162).

tax liability through deductions and credits.[51] The AMT operates in effect as a parallel tax system, with its own definition of taxable income, exemptions, and tax rates. Earners compute tax owed under the "regular" and AMT systems and are liable for whichever is higher.

The struggle resumed after the 1998 midterm elections, which left the Republicans in control of both chambers of Congress despite the loss of five seats in the House. Clinton's proposals, which included tax credits to help parents pay for child or elder care, continued to target relief toward low- to moderate-income families.[52] However, in response to Republican criticism that his original child care proposal did not extend to stay-at-home parents, Clinton also offered all families a $250-per-child tax credit for children one and younger.[53] A new stalemate ensued, leading the president to veto the tax package adopted by Republicans in 1999.

In 2000, calculating that Clinton would be hard-pressed to veto tax relief in an election year, the Republicans made one more effort to eliminate the marriage penalty. Although Democrats shared this goal, the two parties remained divided over who should benefit from such relief. The Republicans sought to provide tax relief to all married couples—those affected by the penalty as well as those who received a bonus. Charging that the Republican plan would provide more than half of its tax relief to couples unaffected by the marriage penalty, Democrats supported an alternative that would permit married couples to file their taxes as though they were single.[54] The Republican proposal, they argued, offered "too small a share of benefits to lower-income and middle-income earners, and too large a share devoted to couples who do not suffer marriage penalties."[55] Ignoring the Democrats, the Republican majority carried its plan forward, but it was vetoed by President Clinton, leaving the marriage penalty in place.[56]

51. Hosansky, "Taxes: Resounding Votes."

52. Heather A. Hope and David Hosansky, "Provisions: Tax Provisions," *CQ Weekly*, October 24, 1998, pp. 2922–23.

53. Lori Nitschke, "Tax Cuts Are in the Air, but Consensus May Be Elusive," *CQ Weekly*, January 16, 1999, pp. 148–49.

54. Lori Nitschke, "Taxes: Clinton Pushes Limited Cuts," *CQ Weekly*, February 6, 1999, pp. 299–300.

55. Andrew Taylor, "Marriage Penalty Tax Bill Is Stalled by Senate Leaders' Impasse over Amendments," *CQ Weekly*, April 15, 2000, pp. 887–89.

56. Lori Nitschke and Mary Dalrymple. "GOP Leaders' Tax Strategy Streamlines the Path for Marriage Penalty Relief Bill," *CQ Weekly*, June 17, 2000, p. 1450.

Increasing the Minimum Wage

Despite the stalemate over how to define middle-income tax relief, an unlikely agreement was struck between Clinton and the Republican Congress on increasing the minimum wage in 1996. As a candidate for president, Bill Clinton positioned himself as a moderate Democrat who promised to "end welfare as we know it" and to make work pay. Polls showed that the public favored work over welfare by huge margins. Although Clinton had promised to increase the minimum wage during his first year in office, he delayed proposing an increase because of concerns about undermining job growth and antagonizing moderate-to-conservative Democrats who were needed to help pass the 1993 budget and tax package. But after Republicans took control of Congress in the historic 1994 midterm elections, Clinton proposed a two-step increase that would raise the minimum wage from $4.25 to $5.15 over two years. In support of his proposal, he argued,

> I believe if we really honor work, anyone who takes responsibility to work full time should be able to support a family and live in dignity. . . . The only way to grow the middle class and shrink the under class is to make work pay. In addition, in terms of real buying power, the minimum wage will be at a 40-year low next year if we do not raise it above $4.25 an hour.[57]

Republican House leaders opposed any increase. Moderate House Republicans, in contrast, supported a modest increase. As one moderate Republican claimed, "It will be difficult to present oneself as an advocate of working men or women if you have opposed a modest increase to the minimum wage . . . the message of this vote says a great deal about a candidate."[58] Thus a new intraparty conflict emerged between conservative House leaders, primarily from the South, and a small group of moderate Republicans from the Northeast and Midwest who feared that a vote against an increase would hurt them in the 1996 election.

The Republican leadership responded to these concerns by packaging a modest minimum wage increase with a small business tax relief package that was pending before the House Ways and Means Committee. Although many

57. "2000 Legislative Summary: 'Marriage Penalty,'" *CQ Weekly*, December 16, 2000, p. 2920.

58. William J. Clinton, "Remarks on the Minimum Wage, February 3, 1995," *American Presidency Project* (www.presidency.ucsb.edu/ws/?pid=50731).

small businesses—that is, most businesses with under $500,000 in annual sales—were already exempt from the federal minimum wage, lawmakers feared that they would be negatively affected by a general increase in wage levels.[59] Therefore, House Speaker Gingrich (R-Ga.) argued, "Since we know that a minimum wage increase kills jobs, there ought to be a package that includes other things that create more jobs to make up [for it]."[60] The $7 billion small business tax relief package included provisions to increase equipment write-offs; to create a new, simpler pension plan for companies with 100 or fewer employees; and to loosen tax rules that governed certain types of corporations.[61] The Republican leadership also demanded a three-month, $4.25-an-hour training wage for teenage workers but failed in efforts to exempt even more small businesses from the federal minimum wage.[62]

Agreement on a similar measure was forged in the Senate, where centrist northeastern Republicans (who tended to be responsive to the demands of labor groups) and more liberal northwestern Republicans (who traditionally supported minimum wage increases) provided the winning margins. Although initially designed to target only small business, the final package included business tax relief for some of the largest U.S. companies, amounting in total to $16.2 billion in reductions over ten years.[63] Ultimately, as part of the Small Business Job Protection Act of 1996, the White House and the Republican majority in Congress approved a two-step increase in the minimum wage (from $4.25 to $4.75 and then to $5.15 by September 1997) and froze the minimum cash wage at $2.13 an hour for tipped workers. (If tips did not bring a worker's hourly pay from the minimum cash wage up to the federal minimum wage, employers were required to make up the difference.)

According to the Clinton administration, nearly 10 million working Americans would get a pay raise when the minimum wage was increased to

59. Jonathan Weisman, "Labor: House Wage Increase Foes Showing Battle Fatigue," *CQ Weekly*, May 4, 1996, p. 1225.

60. Employees of noncovered firms are still covered by the provisions of the Fair Labor Standards Act during workweeks in which they engage in activities related to interstate commerce; in addition, many smaller firms are covered by state minimum wage laws.

61. Jackie Koszczuk and Jonathan Weisman, "GOP Bending on Raise in Minimum Wage," *CQ Weekly Report*, April 20, 1996, pp. 1047–48. See also Alissa J. Rubin and Jonathan Weisman, "Provisions: Tax Cut, Minimum Wage Law," *CQ Weekly*, September 21, 1996, pp. 2705–08, and "A Minimum Wage but a Maximum Impact" *National Journal*, June 1, 1996, p. 1217.

62. Jonathan Weisman and Alissa Rubin, "Tax Cut, Minimum Wage Law," *CQ Weekly Report*, September 21, 1996, pp. 2705-8. See also Alissa Rubin, "Bipartisan Tax Cut Plan May Break the Stalemate," *CQ Weekly Report*, May 18, 1996, pp. 1375–77.

63. "Social Policy: Minimum Wage," *CQ Weekly*, November 2, 1996, p. 3150.

$5.15 an hour.[64] In states that already had a minimum wage above the federal minimum wage, low-wage workers would see a less dramatic boost in their paychecks.[65] Liberal Democrats viewed the increase as "an enormous victory." President Clinton claimed, "This is important and long overdue legislation that provides a badly needed pay raise for millions of Americans and their families who struggle to make ends meet while working at the minimum wage."[66] Republicans expressed disappointment over the increase but hoped that it would allow their party to refocus on issues where they had an electoral advantage. As House Majority Leader Dick Armey (R-Tex.) said, "My mama told me you gotta take the bad with the good."[67]

The 1996 agreement represented the first minimum wage increase to be adopted when the Republicans were control of at least one chamber of Congress. It reflected a new bargain: conservative southern House Republicans allowed a coalition of centrist northeastern Republicans and liberal Democrats to enact an increase in the minimum wage, but only if it was coupled with tax relief for small business. Later in the decade, many Republicans were again ready to make a similar deal. Although many remained strongly opposed to the minimum wage on ideological grounds, they recognized it as an issue that was important to moderate Republicans' electoral fortunes and to their own control of Congress. Some supported a minimum wage increase because they hoped to remove the issue from the Democrats' political arsenal, especially before the 1998 and 2000 elections. In addition, an increase in the minimum wage offered Republicans a vehicle for passing a variety of provisions that would achieve partisan distributional goals.[68] In the end, however, with the Clinton White House and Republicans differing on the timing and amount of an increase, the House refused to consider it in 1999.[69]

Clinton again pushed for a minimum wage increase in 2000 as both parties prepared for the upcoming election.[70] His position was strengthened by

64. For a summary of the final tax provisions, see "Congress Clears Wage Increase with Tax Breaks for Business," *CQ Almanac*, 1996, LII, pp. 7-3–7-9.

65. U.S. Department of Labor (1996).

66. Alissa J. Rubin, "Popular Minimum Wage Hike Gets Solid Senate Approval," *CQ Weekly*, July 13, 1996, pp. 1964–68.

67. Jonathan Weisman, "Republican Defectors Help Propel Minimum Wage Bill to Passage," *CQ Weekly*, May 25, 1996, p. 1461; Clinton (1996, p. 1475).

68. Weisman, "Republican Defectors Help Propel Minimum Wage Bill," p. 1461.

69. Lori Nitschke, "Labor and Employment: GOP Hopes Minimum Wage Bill with Tax Benefits Will Lure Votes and Disarm Democrats," *CQ Weekly*, September 25, 1999, pp. 2227–28.

70. "Proposals and Prospects," *CQ Weekly*, January 29, 2000, p. 179; "Legislative Summary: Employment and Labor: Minimum Wage," *CQ Weekly*, November 27, 1999, p. 2869.

the House Republicans' determination to protect their narrow majority by keeping a potentially explosive electoral issue out of the Democrats' hands. By packaging a minimum wage increase with additional tax relief for small businesses, they hoped to replicate their success in 1996, when they were able to neutralize the issue and help a small but key group of moderate Republicans from districts where labor groups were strong. Thus in 2000 House Republicans approved a $1 increase in the minimum wage to $6.15 an hour over two years and linked it to a broader package of tax relief for businesses, pensioners, and those receiving inheritances.

Clinton's response to the House proposal did not suggest a spirit of compromise. In remarks announcing an unrelated initiative, he declared, "The American people question why Congress can't do something as simple as raising the minimum wage without loading it up with special favors, and I think it's a good question. . . . The right answer is to send me a clean bill, a bill simple and clear that could fit on [one] side of one piece of paper."[71] Other Democrats argued that Republicans were trying to pass tax provisions that Clinton had previously vetoed on the back of an increase in the minimum wage.[72]

In the end, both houses of Congress approved a $1 increase, but they were unable to secure agreement in conference. The House wanted the increase phased in over two years whereas the Senate insisted on three. In addition, the Senate had linked the minimum wage increase to bankruptcy reform legislation. After separating the two measures, the Senate adopted the bankruptcy reform but took no further action on the minimum wage. Back in the House, Republicans tried to reach agreement with the White House by proposing an increase by $1 over two years, accompanied by a scaled-back package of tax relief.[73] However, the effort came unglued after conservative House Republicans produced a broader package to reduce federal income taxes over ten years.[74] Once again, Clinton and the Republican Congress had reached an impasse.

71. "Proposals and Prospects," *CQ Weekly*, January 29, 2000, p. 179.

72. William J. Clinton, "Remarks Announcing the Initiative to Reduce Air Travel Delays, March 10, 2000," *American Presidency Project* (www.presidency.ucsb.edu/ws/?pid=58234).

73. James C. Benton and Lori Nitschke, "Labor Employment: House-Passed Wage and Tax Bill Heads toward Another Thicket," *CQ Weekly*, March 11, 2000, pp. 531–36.

74. Andrew Taylor, "Conciliatory Congress Faces a Noncommittal Clinton," *CQ Weekly*, September 2, 2000, pp. 2021–24.

The Impact of Partisan Distributional Goals

The contrast between the distributive consequences of the bargains on tax relief made in 1993 and 1997 illustrates the importance of partisan control. In 1993, one year before the "Republican Revolution," the Democratic approach to family-oriented tax relief prevailed in the form of the expansion of the EITC. Through this measure, Democrats sought to reward work, reduce welfare dependence, and help a core constituency—lower-income working families. This strategy worked to a significant degree. In 1993 a worker who had two children and earned the minimum wage made $10,559 (in 1998 dollars), including the EITC—well below the poverty threshold for a household of three. After the 1993 increase in the EITC and the 90-cent increase in the minimum wage in 1996 and 1997, the same family made $13,268 in 1998, representing a 26 percent increase in its standard of living that raised its income above the poverty level.[75] Moreover, the EITC's effectiveness in alleviating poverty may have been even greater than this example suggests given the evidence that the EITC provides a powerful incentive to work. Thus, in size and scope, the EITC became one of the most important elements of a policy regime to support low-income working families.[76]

In contrast, the CTC that was adopted in 1997 by a Republican-dominated Congress and signed into law by President Clinton benefited very few low-income working families. Only families with three or more eligible children could receive a refund if their total child tax credit exceeded their income tax, and even then the refund was limited to the amount by which their payroll taxes exceeded their EITC. Thus families with no income tax liability and fewer than three children received no benefit from the child tax credit, while families with low income tax liability receive only a partial benefit. In 1998 only about two-thirds (25 million) of families that filed a tax return claimed full or partial child credits. Of the approximately one-third of families with children that received no credit, most (11.5 million) were low-income families who had no income tax liability. Only about 700,000 families benefited from the credit's refundability provision.[77]

---

75. Lori Nitschke and Julie R. Hirschfeld, "Tax, Wage Bill Hurtles toward Veto after GOP Adds Disputed Policy Riders," *CQ Weekly*, October 28, 2000, pp. 2532–34.

76. National Economic Council with the Assistance of the Council of Economic Advisers and the Office of the Chief Economist, U.S. Department of Labor, "The Minimum Wage: Increasing the Reward for Work," March 2000 (http://clinton4.nara.gov/textonly/WH/EOP/nec/html/doc030800. html).

77. "Provisions: 1993 Budget-Reconciliation Act," *CQ Weekly*, September 18, 1993, pp. 2482–97.

Conclusion

Both the EITC expansion in 1993 and the CTC in 1997 enabled Democrats and Republicans to claim credit for boosting the paychecks of low- to middle-income working families. However, tax relief for the middle class remained a popular and potent theme in the 2000 election. In setting out their campaign agendas, Vice President Al Gore and Texas governor George W. Bush both counted on a projected federal budget surplus of nearly $4.6 trillion over ten years.[78] However, each candidate proposed to spend the anticipated surplus with different distributional goals in mind.

Bush favored using the projected federal surplus to finance a five-year, $460 billion tax cut, including a simplification of income tax rates. In place of the existing system of five brackets, with rates ranging from 15 percent to 39.6 percent, he proposed four brackets with a bottom rate of 10 percent and a top rate of 33 percent. His tax plan also included the reduction of the marriage penalty, the doubling of the CTC to $1,000 per child, and the repeal of estate taxation. The Bush tax plan was presented as "providing benefits to earners across the income spectrum" and "putting money back in the hands of taxpayers to keep Washington from spending it on ever-larger government programs."[79] Supporters argued that it would "raise the standard of living of every earner and prevent the increases in revenue that would simply finance more federal government spending."[80] Altogether, the Bush proposals were expected to soak up almost $1.7 trillion of the budget surplus over ten years.

Gore also called for ambitious tax cuts, amounting to more than $500 billion over five years, but his plan differed sharply in focus. Although most of the tax relief provided under the Bush plan would go to workers making more than $100,000, almost all of the tax relief Gore proposed was intended to benefit people earning less than that amount. Declaring that the "right kind of tax cuts are good for our economy," the Democratic candidate pledged to raise the income ceiling on eligibility for the EITC to allow more moderate-income families to take advantage of the credit. He also favored making the Child and Dependent Care Tax Credit refundable and

---

78. Sammartino (2001).

79. Kliesen and Thornton (2001, pp. 1–14).

80. Richard W. Stevenson, "Candidates Offer a Variety of Ways to Spend Surplus," *New York Times*, December 27, 1999, pp. 1–3. See also Lori Nitschke, "Compromising on Tax Cuts," *CQ Weekly*, April 14, 2001, pp. 830–31.

proposed a new refundable after-school tax credit to help working families pay for after-school programs.[81] The Gore campaign estimated that its key tax and spending proposals would cost about $1.5 trillion over the decade.[82]

However, the candidates also found some common ground. In order to help upper-middle-class families, both candidates proposed raising the threshold at which the CTC began to be phased out from $110,000 to $200,000 for married couples and from $75,000 to $200,000 for single parents. They both supported a proposal to reduce the marriage penalty by reinstating the 10 percent deduction for families with two earners.[83] This measure would allow a couple to deduct 10 percent of the income of the lower-earning spouse—up to a maximum of $3,000. For a husband and wife who each earned $35,000 a year, it would cut their marriage penalty by roughly 36 percent. In addition, Gore proposed to increase the standard deduction for married couples to reduce or eliminate the "marriage penalty" for millions of families.

Summing up the differences between the candidates, Robert S. McIntyre, director of Citizens for Tax Justice, claimed:

> On one side, we have a moderate Democrat offering something close to fiscal prudence and tax relief limited to middle- and low-income Americans—albeit tarnished by far more complexity than necessary. On the other side, we have a Republican who wants to sound moderate, but offers huge tax cuts targeted to the rich and an overall fiscal program that would undermine our economic and fiscal health. One hopes the public can tell the difference.[84]

These differing partisan distributional goals foreshadowed the politics that would emerge after the Republicans took control of both the White House and Congress in 2001.[85]

81. Martin Feldstein and Kathleen Feldstein, "A Clear Choice on Tax Policy," *Boston Globe*, October 10, 2000.

82. On the Issues, "After-School Care for 10 Million Kids," Press release, May 25, 2000 (www.issues2000.org/Celeb/Al_Gore_Families_+_Children.htm).

83. Citizens for Tax Justice, "Preliminary Summary of the Gore Tax Plan," August 30, 2000 (http://ctj.org/html/gore0800.htm); see also Katherine Q. Seelye, "Gore Proposing Ways to Improve Child Care," *New York Times,* June 7, 2000, p. 1.

84. CNNfyi.com, "Where They Stand: Al Gore and George Bush" (http://archives.cnn.com/2000/fyi/teachers.ednews/08/31/where.they.stand/index.html [August 2009]).

85. McIntyre (2000).

6 George W. Bush and the Return of Across-the-Board Tax Relief

The opening decade of the twenty-first century brought much more modest gains to low-income workers and their families. The 2000 election gave the Republicans control of the White House and both chambers of Congress for the first time since 1954. Encouraged by projections that put the federal budget surplus at $5.6 trillion over the next decade, the new president, George W. Bush, and Republican leaders in the House seized this opportunity to push for what they would later tout as the largest package of across-the-board tax relief since the 1981 tax reform masterminded by Ronald Reagan. This strategy was driven by both ideological preferences and electoral goals, notably the desire to rally conservative Democratic voters to the Republican side. It met with resistance from both Democrats and moderate Republicans, principally in the Senate, which swung back to the Democrats in June 2001 when Jim Jeffords of Vermont left the Republicans to become an independent. In 2001 a bipartisan group of Senate centrists succeeded in securing agreement on provisions that targeted some tax relief to low- and moderate-income families. However, most of their later efforts produced more modest gains. Most of the tax relief delivered under the Bush administration benefited higher-income earners.

In another blow for low-income workers, between 2001 and 2006, President Bush, backed by Republican leaders in Congress, refused to act on a minimum wage increase. After regaining control of Congress in 2006, the Democrats secured an increase as part of a supplemental defense appropriations bill that provided emergency funds for the war in Iraq. The compromise package provided for a three-step increase from $5.15 to $7.25 by 2009. It also distributed nearly $5 billion in additional tax relief for small businesses, some in the form of an expanded Work Opportunity Tax Credit. However, even this measure did little to restore the real value of the minimum wage, which by 2006 was at its lowest level since 1955.

Republican Control and Across-the-Board Tax Relief in 2001

Following the 2000 elections, the Republicans held a six-vote margin in the House, and the Senate was divided 50-50, with Vice President Dick Cheney holding the tie-breaking vote. Despite this slim margin of control, the Republicans were determined to press ahead with their tax cut agenda. They had potential allies in the Blue Dog Coalition, a group of thirty fiscally conservative House Democrats who had voted with Republicans on tax and budget issues throughout the 1990s. However, they faced potential opponents among the centrist Republicans and Democrats who made up a small but pivotal subgroup on the Senate Finance Committee, as well as in the sixty-two-member Republican Main Street Partnership. This group, which included centrists from the House and Senate, was dedicated to forging a bipartisan agreement. They warned that House Republican leaders "will have to rule from the center, not from the right, or risk losing those of us in the middle."[1]

The Bush White House's first tax plan, which was presented in early 2001, called for reducing income tax rates across the board, reducing the marriage penalty, doubling the Child Tax Credit (CTC) to $1,000 per child, and repealing the estate tax.[2] Republican leaders argued that this proposal would stimulate the economy and boost paychecks for working families in all income categories. Its primary goal was to reduce taxes for the highest-income earners and thereby stimulate investment and economic growth.[3]

1. David Nather and Adriel Bettelheim, "2000 Vote Studies: Moderates and Mavericks Hold Key to 107th Congress," *CQ Weekly*, January 6, 2001, pp. 49–51. As a group, moderate Republicans were similar to the Democratic Blue Dogs, but their members tended to be more diverse and included conservatives with a reputation for reaching across party lines.

2. Brownlee (2004, p. 220).

3. Jill Barshay, "'Progressive' Tax Debate: Rich vs. Poor," *CQ Weekly*, February 7, 2005, pp. 294–96.

However, to provide political cover and reach out to moderates in their own party, the Republican plan also included some tax relief for lower-income working families. For example, the rate in the lowest tax bracket would be reduced from 15 percent to 10 percent by 2006.

To support the White House plan, the Treasury Department produced distributional tables—analyses of how the proposal would affect different income groups—showing that the Republican plan was "progressive because high-income taxpayers would receive a tax cut that is less than proportional to their income tax liability."[4] According to the Treasury, under the Bush proposal, families with incomes under $100,000 would pay a smaller share of the total income tax burden than they did under the system it would replace. Conversely, families with incomes of $100,000 or more would see their share of the total income tax burden rise.

The Democratic leadership countered that the Treasury tables omitted critical information—notably the fact that the president's proposals would have no effect on regressive payroll and excise taxes.[5] Individual income taxes accounted for less than half of all federal tax collections in 2000, and most earners paid more in federal payroll taxes than individual income taxes. Reducing individual income taxes without reducing the federal payroll tax, Democrats argued, would increase "the relative reliance on regressive taxes, and thus make the overall federal income tax code less progressive."[6] They denounced the White House plan as "too heavily tilted to the benefit of those [in] the top-rate brackets, who pay the most in income taxes, while doing little for those in the lower brackets, who pay more in payroll taxes than in income taxes."[7]

Democratic lawmakers pushed to make Bush's proposal more favorable to lower-income working families. Their alternatives included proposals to limit tax credits to low-income earners and to cut the marginal tax rate only in the lowest bracket, rather than across the board. This approach, they argued, would still benefit higher-income households because their first

4. OMB Watch, "Disturbing Pattern Emerging on Government Budget Analysis," August 8, 2003 (www.ombwatch.org/node/1519).

5. See U.S. Department of the Treasury, Office of Tax Analysis, "Table 1: Major Individual Income Tax Provisions of the President's Tax Proposal," March 8, 2001 (www.ustreas.gov/offices/tax-policy/library/distributionrel.pdf).

6. Burman (2001, p. 6, table 1).

7. Lori Nitschke, "Tax Plan Destined for Revision," *CQ Weekly*, February 10, 2001, pp. 318–21.

$26,250 in earned income would be taxed at a lower rate.[8] However, the party was not united around these proposals. As concern about a recession grew in 2001, fiscally conservative Democrats endorsed the Bush income tax reduction package.[9]

As the debate progressed, a small group of fiscal moderates in the evenly divided Senate came to wield significant political influence over the negotiations between the parties and between the two houses of Congress. The bipartisan Centrist Coalition, cochaired by Olympia J. Snowe (R-Maine) and John B. Breaux (D-La.), negotiated a compromise that provided more benefits for low-income working families and limited the overall cost of the tax package. The bipartisan group proposed to block the phasing in of across-the-board tax relief if annual budget surpluses came in lower than expected. In a departure from the Bush proposal, they also required that the tax proposal expire in ten years, after which all tax rates and provisions would automatically revert to their 2001 levels.[10]

In addition, the Senate centrists insisted on more tax relief for those at the lower end of the income distribution. For example, they won agreement on a refundable Child Tax Credit (CTC) for working poor households earning at least $10,000 in 2001. The income threshold for eligibility was set to satisfy Republicans who opposed earning subsidies for nonworking poor families. Since the 1990s, conservatives, particularly in the House, had portrayed refundable credits as welfare programs, arguing that refund payments amounted to federal cash assistance for those who had little or no federal income tax liability. With a typical minimum wage worker earning a little more than $10,500 in 2001, the income eligibility threshold allowed Republicans to claim that only families with the equivalent of a full-time, working parent would benefit from the refundable CTC.[11] Single parents who worked less than full time and two-parent families with very limited earnings would not qualify for the credit. (See figure 6-1.)

Describing the Senate package as a whole, Majority Whip Don Nickles (R-Okla.) claimed, "This is loaded towards low-income people. . . . We've

8. Lori Nitschke, "Tax Cut Momentum Builds," *CQ Weekly*, January 13, 2001, pp. 100–01.

9. Hall and others (2003, pp. 1–6).

10. Lori Nitschke and Wendy Boudreau, "Provisions of the Tax Law," *CQ Weekly*, June 9, 2001, pp. 1390–94.

11. Lori Nitschke and Bill Swindell, "Grassley–Baucus Tax Blueprint Heads for Rough-and-Tumble Markup," *CQ Weekly*, May 12, 2001, pp. 1069–70.

Figure 6-1. *Minimum Annual Income Threshold for Child Tax Credit Refundability, 2001–09*

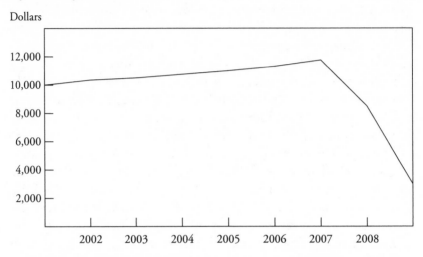

Dollars

Sources: Internal Revenue Service Form 1040, Form 2441, and Form 8812 instructions, various years; Internal Revenue Service, "Revenue Procedure 2007-66" (www.irs.gov/pub/irs-drop/rp-07-66.pdf) and "Revenue Procedure 2008-66" (www.irs.gov/pub/irs-drop/rp-08-66.pdf); H.R. 1, American Recovery and Reinvestment Act of 2009.

done a whole heck of a lot both in size and composition to accommodate many of the moderate political influences that we now have in the Senate."[12] In conference, House Republicans accepted much of the Senate proposal targeting low-income working families, despite reservations, in order to secure the larger political goal of across-the-board tax relief. The package cleared Congress less than two weeks before Democrats regained control of the Senate in June 2001, when Vermont Senator Jim Jeffords defected from the Republican Party.

In its final form, the 2001 Economic Growth and Tax Relief Reconciliation Act provided major across-the-board income tax reductions and targeted some tax relief for low- and moderate-income working families.[13] Tax rates were cut in all five existing tax brackets, with the top rate slated to fall from 39.6 percent to 35 percent by 2006, and a new bottom bracket was created that taxed income at 10 percent for single earners earning up

12. Ibid.
13. For a summary of the major provisions of the 2001 Economic Growth and Tax Relief Reconciliation Act, see Nitschke and Boudreau, "Provisions of the Tax Law."

to $6,000, married couples earning up to $12,000, and heads of households earning up to $10,000.[14] The two bottom brackets were defined to be twice as wide for married couples as for single filers, and the standard deduction for married couples was set to twice the amount for single earners. Both measures alleviated the marriage penalty, particularly for low- and moderate-income families. In addition, Congress provided a one-time rebate of $300 for single earners, $500 for heads of households, and $600 for married couples. This one-time boost in after-tax income could not be greater than a worker's federal tax liability.

The legislation also doubled the existing CTC from $500 to $1,000 over ten years and increased the dependent care tax credit, which helped offset out-of-pocket child care expenses of working families, beginning in 2003.[15] The maximum dependent care tax credit would rise from $720 to $1,050 for one dependent and from $1,440 to $2,100 for two or more. The credit would begin to phase out once a family's adjusted gross income reached $15,000.

These provisions were principally targeted at moderate- and middle-income families. The full CTC, for example, was offered to couples earning up to $110,000 a year and single parents earning up to $75,000; above those income levels, it was phased out. However, lower-income families benefited from the expanded refundability of the new CTC (as well as another expansion in eligibility for the EITC). Under the old law, only families with three children could take the CTC as a refundable credit, and the refund such a family could receive was capped by the lesser of the maximum CTC ($500) and the gap between its federal payroll tax liability and its EITC. Under the new law, all families with children could take up to 10 percent of their income above a threshold (up to the maximum value of the credit) as a refund in excess of their tax liability. In 2005 the rate at which the credit could be claimed would rise to 15 percent. The threshold, which was initially set at $10,000, was indexed for inflation, requiring families to earn more each year to remain eligible for this benefit. For low-income parents, any resulting boost in their income would not be counted as earned income when determining their eligibility for other federal safety net programs or state or local programs financed with federal funding.

14. Beginning in 2008, the 10 percent bracket would apply to the first $7,000 of income for individuals, $10,000 for single parents, and $14,000 for married couples. Those amounts would be indexed for inflation beginning in 2009.

15. Nitschke and Boudreau, "Provisions of the Tax Law."

Figure 6-2. *Share of the Income Tax Relief Going to Families at*
Different Strata of the Income Distribution, 2001–10[a]

Percent of tax cut

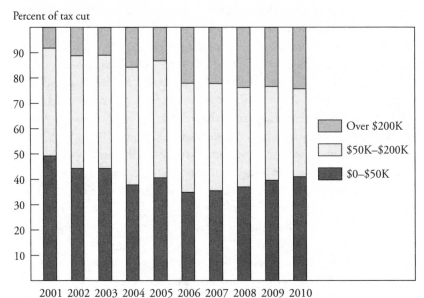

Source: Urban-Brookings Tax Policy Center Microsimulation Model; Burman, Maag, and Rohaly (2002).

a. Includes provisions affecting marginal tax rates, the 10 percent bracket, the CTC, the Child and Dependent Care Tax Credit, the limitation of itemized deductions, the personal exemption phaseout, and the Alternative Minimum Tax.

These provisions did not alter the fact that the CTC primarily helped middle- and upper-income families. According to the Tax Policy Center, a joint project of the Urban Institute and the Brookings Institution, by 2005 "nearly 60 percent of its benefits . . . went to families in the top 40 percent of the income distribution, and less than 1 percent went to those in the lowest income quintile [income below $14,000]."[16] Nonetheless, taken as a whole, the 2001 Economic Growth and Tax Relief Reconciliation Act was considerably more balanced in its distributional impact than the tax package originally proposed by the White House. Although the largest increases in after-tax income went to high-income earners, most working

16. Tax Policy Center, "Taxation and the Family: What Is the Child Tax Credit?" *Tax Policy Briefing Book: A Citizens' Guide for the 2008 Election and Beyond*, May 20, 2009 (www.taxpolicycenter.org/briefing-book/key-elements/family/ctc.cfm).

low- and moderate-income earners could expect a modest increase in their annual paychecks. (See figure 6-2.)

To appease fiscal centrists, who were concerned about the cost of these measures (calculated as revenue loss), Congress approved sunsets—binding expiration dates—for each reduction. Most of the 2001 reductions were originally set to expire in January 2011. However, the Republican Congress and President Bush extended some expiring provisions on a case-by-case basis between 2001 and 2006.

Partisan Stalemate over Increased Support for the Lowest-Income Families

After adoption of the 2001 package, the White House and House Republicans pushed to make the temporary reductions, which also included retirement savings incentives and the repeal of the estate tax, permanent features of the federal income tax code. However, by 2002 the Congressional Budget Office (CBO) and the Office of Management and Budget were predicting major budget deficits because of the collapse of a stock market bubble, the recession, and the war in Afghanistan. This led Senate Democrats to oppose any proposal to make tax reductions permanent. Democrats argued that the return of large budget deficits proved that the prior year's $1.35 trillion tax reduction was a huge mistake.[17]

However, that fall the Democrats lost two Senate seats in the midterm elections, as well as five seats in the House, returning the country to unified Republican government. The Republicans took this opportunity to press for further short-term cuts. Their strategy was to accelerate the tax reductions that were scheduled to take effect in 2004 and 2006. President Bush proposed to make the rate reductions and the scheduled doubling of the CTC effective immediately, as well as to eliminate income taxes on dividends. However, fiscally conservative House Democrats, who had been instrumental in securing the 2001 package, opposed the size and distributional consequences of the new tax package.[18] By 2003 most of the income tax relief distributed to low- and moderate-income working families had already been phased in. Therefore, Democrats claimed that accelerating

---

17. Alan K. Ota, "Tax Cut Becomes Top Priority," *CQ Weekly*, November 9, 2002, p. 2895.

18. Jill Barshay, "Democrats Splinter on Stimulus Alternative as Daschle's Plan Fails to Unite Caucus," *CQ Weekly* January 25, 2003, pp. 199–201.

the tax rate reductions would only benefit upper-income earners and would not be an effective stimulus for the economy.

Once again, the bipartisan Centrist Coalition occupied the middle ground. Its members supported a more limited proposal to accelerate the provisions that would provide tax relief for married couples (originally intended to be phased in through 2009) and to increase temporarily the CTC to $1,000. (The original schedule called for it to rise from $600 in 2001 to $700 in 2005, $800 in 2009, and $1,000 in 2010, before reverting to $500 in 2011.) Under the new plan, the credit would be $1,000 in 2003 and 2004 and then return to its original path.[19] They argued that this approach would provide a more effective economic stimulus, in comparison to acceleration of across-the-board rate reductions, because it was aimed at low- to moderate-income earners and their families—that is, those who were most likely to spend any increase in their take-home pay. In addition, the bipartisan package had the advantage of offering something to partisans on both sides. Both middle-class tax relief for married couples and the CTC enjoyed support among Democrats as well as Republicans.[20] Centrist Republicans, meanwhile, hoped that by adopting this proposal, they could avoid handing Democrats a major electoral issue in the form of large tax cuts that largely benefited upper-income families and would push the budget deficit to record levels.[21]

Under a bipartisan Senate agreement, parents who claimed the CTC in 2002 would receive an advance cash payment reflecting the increase in the credit to $1,000 in 2003. The maximum advance would be $400; the remainder would be applied to their 2003 tax return. However, the Senate rejected an effort by some Democrats to make the partially refundable CTC more helpful to low-income working families by lowering or eliminating the earnings threshold families needed to meet before claiming the credit. Instead, Senate centrists agreed to increase the value of the credit for families that already qualified. Under the 2001 law, in 2003 parents could take up to 10 percent of their income above the qualifying threshold (but no more than $600) as a refundable credit; under the Senate plan, they would be allowed to claim up to 15 percent of their qualifying income (but no more than $1,000). (The increase from 10 percent to

19. "Details of Expiring Tax Cuts," *CQ Weekly,* July 10, 2004, p. 1675.
20. Ibid.
21. Alan K. Ota, "For Business, Tax Conference Will Be All Damage Control," *CQ Weekly*, May 17, 2003, pp. 1168–75.

15 percent was part of the 2001 law, but it was originally scheduled to take place in 2005.)

The final version of the Jobs and Growth Tax Reconciliation Act, which emerged from the House–Senate conference in May 2003, dropped this provision, reducing the package's cost by $350 million. The Bush White House argued that other parts of the tax package would still benefit low-income working families. However, Democrats complained that 7 million low-income working families had been denied the most modest boost in their after-tax income. On the Republican side, a major intraparty conflict emerged between conservatives and moderates over whether to introduce a stand-alone amendment to restore the deleted provision. Ultimately, the conservatives' opposition prevailed, with the White House making the argument that the agreement "was intended to help people who pay taxes, not those who are too poor to pay."[22]

However, the conflict quickly reemerged. That summer both the House and the Senate passed bills that that would allow families to claim up to 15 percent of qualifying income as a refundable CTC in 2004, rather than in 2005. The Senate's measure went even further by providing for families to receive the increase as a cash advance in 2003. In contrast, the House made the increase available only in 2004.[23] In addition, the House raised the ceiling on eligibility from $110,000 to $150,000 in annual income, further tilting the distributional profile of the CTC toward the upper end of the income distribution.[24] At the same time, the House approved keeping the child credit at $1,000 through 2010, rather than letting it drop down to $700 in 2005 as provided for in the 2003 Jobs and Growth Tax Reconciliation Act. The more fiscally conservative Senate did not adopt this increase.

In conference, the Bush White House urged House Republican leaders to accept the Senate version, but House negotiators dug in their heels in opposition to the Senate's plan for advance payment. Democrats used the stalemate to highlight their support for efforts to help low-income working families, calling 15 (procedural) votes to instruct the House to accept the Senate's version. However, the impasse continued into 2005, when the

22. David Firestone, "Battle on Child Tax Credit Intensifies in the Capital," *New York Times*, May 30, 2003.
23. Alan K. Ota and Jill Barshay, "Flap over Child Tax Credit Heats Debate on 'Sunsets.'" *CQ Weekly*, June 14, 2003, pp. 1449–52.
24. Ibid.

issue became moot as the enhanced refundability provision went into effect in 2005 under the original schedule.

Democrats viewed the stalemate over accelerating the refundability of the CTC as an opportunity to focus on the theme of tax fairness for working families in the run-up to the 2004 election.[25] They set the stage for renewed battle over partisan distributional goals by focusing on whom and what the Republicans had left out in their distribution of tax relief. Democrats argued that Republicans were indifferent to the tax burden of ordinary low- and moderate-income working families. In reply, Republicans claimed that 10 million lower-income earners had seen their federal income tax liability fall to zero during President Bush's first term.[26]

The issue of tax fairness had the potential to become a potent political theme. According to a comprehensive analysis carried out by the CBO, many of the tax reforms that were adopted from 2001 to 2003 disproportionately benefited higher-income earners, including reductions in the top rate, reductions in taxes on dividends and capital gains, and a gradual elimination of the estate tax. The CBO also concluded that the 20 percent of Americans at the bottom of the earnings distribution would see their after-tax incomes increase by an average of 1.5 percent due to the Bush tax reductions, while the middle 60 percent would see an increase of about 2 percent (on average), and the top 1 percent would gain by an average of 5.3 percent. Thus the tax reductions were likely to lead to a greater concentration of income among those at the top and to decrease correspondingly the share of after-tax income received by low- and middle-income households.[27]

However, public opinion polls suggested that many Americans had little knowledge of the income tax policies under consideration or actually adopted and were unclear about their distributional consequences. When asked in a 2003 poll whether the 2001 tax reductions should be made permanent, rather than being allowed to expire in 2011, 60 percent said they did not know. Asked whether speeding up the tax cuts and making them permanent would mainly help high-, middle-, or low-income earners, 41 percent of respondents did not know.[28] This lack of attention to the

25. Alan K. Ota, "Republicans of Two Minds on Refundable Tax Credits," *CQ Weekly*, June 28, 2003, pp. 1599–1601.

26. Scott A. Hodge, "40 Million Filers Pay No Income Taxes, Many Get Generous Refunds," *Fiscal Facts*, June 5, 2003 (www.taxfoundation.org/news/show/207.html).

27. Congressional Budget Office (2004).

28. Bartels (2005, p. 20).

issue made it difficult for Democrats to use their call for greater tax fairness to their political advantage.

Election Year Tax and Paycheck Politics

Meanwhile, the Republicans pushed ahead with efforts to make some of their more popular income tax reductions permanent. The Republicans' "family friendly" tax agenda, which included retaining the CTC at $1,000 per child, extending marriage penalty relief, and maintaining the 10 percent tax bracket at current income levels, enjoyed bipartisan political support. However, the CTC once again became part of a larger partisan battle over tax equity. Democrats preferred to extend the benefits of the CTC to more low-income families. House Republicans again hoped to extend it to higher-income families by raising the income ceiling on eligibility. The centrist coalition in the Senate acted as a brake on both sides by demanding that any income tax reductions, including those caused by the extension of time-limited provisions, be offset with revenue increases.

As part of an election-year Working Families Tax Relief Act, Congress did agree to a short-term extension of several popular provisions that were soon to expire. The $1,000 CTC was extended until 2009; the 10 percent income tax bracket was extended until 2007; the upper limit of the 15 percent bracket for married couples was kept at twice its value for single earners until 2007; and the doubling of the single standard deduction for married couples was extended until 2008. Congress also increased the value of the child credit and earned income credit to military families by expanding the definition of earned income to include combat pay. However, Democrats failed in their efforts to expand the EITC and the CTC. Republicans rejected their proposals to lower the eligibility threshold for the refundable CTC and to end the indexing of the threshold for inflation. Consequently, Democrats attacked the agreement as "a budget deficit maker that failed to include proposals to distribute any additional tax relief for very low-income workers and their families."[29] However, centrist Republicans claimed that this package distributed some tax relief to low-income earners.

The fairness of the Republican approach to income tax relief emerged as a major issue in President Bush's 2004 reelection campaign. Democratic

29. Alan K. Ota, "GOP Faces Tough Tax Choices after Easy Renewal of Some Cuts," *CQ Weekly*, September 25, 2004, pp. 2250–53.

nominee John Kerry proposed to assist middle-income families through a tax credit to defray the cost of health insurance.[30] Democrats also continued to promise to increase tax rates on higher-income earners, in part, to finance additional income tax relief for low-income and moderate-income families. However, the party again lost ground, failing to regain the White House and losing four House and four Senate seats. Notably, Republicans secured gains in the Senate by winning the seats of southern Democrats who had voted with the Republicans.

Following his reelection, President Bush called for making the tax system "simpler and fairer" and appointed a bipartisan advisory group, the President's Advisory Panel on Federal Tax Reform, to examine options for reforming the federal tax system. However, the burgeoning federal deficit made it difficult for the administration to push openly for more broad-based or permanent tax relief. Instead, in the 2006 midterm elections, Republicans campaigned on the general idea of reforming an income tax that was "too complex, inherently unfair and, of course, took too much money out of Americans' take-home pay."[31] Citing figures from the Joint Committee on Taxation, they also argued that targeted proposals, such as a reduction in the capital gains tax, would benefit both middle-income earners and the economy as a whole.[32] Characterizing the proposed capital gains tax cut as "a windfall for the highest earners, which was fiscally irresponsible and would not do enough for the middle class," Democrats countered that this approach would increase the share of the tax burden borne by working poor and low-income earners, who relied almost entirely on salaries and wages.[33] According to data from the Tax Policy Center, 22.6 million households would benefit from the capital gains tax break in 2005, but those with incomes below $100,000 would receive only 10 percent of the tax savings.[34] However, the more potent argument against it was growing concern about the cost of further tax relief and the size of the federal budget deficit. By the end of 2006, these concerns were shared by more

30. Alan K. Ota, "It's All about Sunsets and Offsets as Parties Sell Their Tax Plans," *CQ Weekly*, July 10, 2004, pp. 1673–75.

31. Joseph J. Schatz, "Tax Break Tries on 'Middle Class' Label," *CQ Weekly*, February 20, 2006, pp. 468–70.

32. Ibid.

33. Rachel Van Dongen, "Tax Package Clears Congress," *CQ Weekly*, May 15, (2006, pp. 1326–27).

34. Tax Policy Center, "Distribution of Qualifying Dividends and Capital Gains, 2005" (www.tax policycenter.org/numbers/displayatab.cfm?Simid=52).

and more centrists in both parties. No additional tax relief was secured by Republicans between 2005 and 2007.

Increasing the Minimum Wage

Another important issue in the 2006 midterm elections was the Republicans' opposition to an increase in the federal minimum wage, which had remained stuck at $5.15 an hour for a decade. In the absence of federal action, twenty-three states had set their state minimum wage above the federal level.[35] National polls showed broad bipartisan support among Americans for a minimum wage increase.[36]

Democrats seized the opportunity to target centrist Republicans who had voted against prior minimum wage increases. Democrats blamed Republicans for the stagnation of the federal minimum wage: "A full-time minimum wage worker in 2006 earned only $10,712, which [was] $5,888 less than the $16,600 needed to lift a family of three out of poverty."[37] They asserted that due to Republican inaction, the buying power of the minimum wage was at its lowest level in more than fifty years when adjusted for inflation. In fact, at 75 cents an hour, the minimum wage had had more purchasing power in 1950 than it had at $5.15 an hour in 2006.

Buoyed by concern over the economy and unease with the war in Iraq, Democrats emerged from the election with a majority in both chambers of Congress. However, that majority had shifted somewhat to the right. Of the twenty-nine seats that Democrats gained to win political control of the House, eighteen were won by challengers who identified with the pro-business New Democrat Coalition, the fiscally conservative Blue Dogs, or both.[38] (The Blue Dogs got their name when one member quipped that moderate Democrats, traditionally known as "Yellow Dogs," had been

35. Christine Vestal, "Minimum-Wage Hikes Sweep States," September 22, 2006 (www.stateline. org/live/details/story?contentId=143470).

36. Ibid.

37. U.S. House of Representatives, Committee on Education and Labor, "Minimum Wage Increase: Value Was at a 51-Year Low" (http://edlabor.house.gov/minimum-wage-increase-value-was-at-a-51-year-low/index.shtml).

38. Gregory L. Giroux, "Voter Discontent Fuels Democrats' Day," *CQ Weekly*, November 13, 2006, pp. 2983–87.

"choked blue" on spending by the demands of more liberal party members.)[39] With Democrats holding a thirty-one-seat advantage over the Republicans, the forty-three-member Blue Dog Coalition asserted major political influence within the House, somewhat like the conservative Boll Weevil Democrats of the Reagan era. This development posed new challenges for Democratic leaders as they attempted to forge agreement on the federal minimum wage and other key issues in the face of White House political opposition.

In early 2007, House Democratic leaders proposed increasing the minimum wage to $7.25 an hour, either immediately or over two years. Democrats claimed that the increase for "hard-pressed employees would offer a sharp contrast to tax cuts for the affluent approved under Republican rule."[40] House Majority Leader Steny H. Hoyer (D-Md.) remarked, "In the United States of America, the richest nation on earth, workers should not be relegated to poverty if they work hard and play by the rules."[41] The new House Democratic leaders also pledged to block the annual cost-of-living increases in congressional salaries, which were set automatically to keep pace with inflation, until a federal minimum wage increase was adopted.

For the first time in his presidency, Bush endorsed a modest minimum wage increase, but he indicated that his political support was contingent on small business tax relief to help offset any costs arising from the increase: "I support pairing it with targeted tax and regulatory relief to help these small businesses stay competitive and to help keep our economy growing."[42] In taking this stand, Bush parted company with conservative House Republicans, who held that any increase would hurt business and ultimately harm the economy. However, he found support among Senate centrists—Republicans and Democrats—who shared his belief that a federal minimum wage increase coupled with a package of small business tax relief could provide the basis for a filibuster-proof majority.[43]

39. Shailagh Murray, "Looking Ahead, Obama Builds Ties with 'Blue Dogs,'" *Washington Post*, October 14, 2008, p. A04.

40. "First 100 Hours: Democratic Leaders in the House of Representatives Have Pushed through Six Major Bills since the Start of Their 100-Hour Legislative Drive on Jan. 9," *New York Times*, January 18, 2005, p. 1.

41. Carl Hulse, "House Votes to Raise Minimum Wage," *New York Times*, January 10, 2007, p. 1.

42. George W. Bush, "Statement of Administration Policy: H.R. 2—Fair Minimum Wage Act of 2007, January 10, 2007," *American Presidency Project* (www.presidency.ucsb.edu/ws/?pid=24981).

43. John Arensmyer, "Small Business Review: The Minimum Wage Bill," March 23, 2007 (www.businessforsharedprosperity.org/node/18).

Despite this warning, House Ways and Means Committee Chair Charles B. Rangel (D-N.Y.) opposed efforts to couple small business tax relief with the minimum wage increase. Although small business tax relief had bipartisan support, Rangel and more liberal House Democratic leaders sought a showdown on a "stand-alone" minimum wage increase. With the support of eighty-two centrist Republicans, House Democrats passed a three-step increase in the minimum wage to $7.25 an hour. Separately, the House passed a $1.3 billion package of small business tax relief.[44]

Senator Charles E. Grassley (R-Iowa), the Finance Committee's top Republican, criticized House Democrats for trying to promote a showdown: "It's one thing to live in political and ideological fantasy land, and it's quite another to make law."[45] Several top Democrats agreed. Senate Majority Leader Harry Reid (D-Nev.) concluded that small business tax relief was needed to build an enacting coalition that would include centrist Republicans and Democrats. Similarly, Senate Finance Committee Chair Max Baucus (D-Mont.) noted, "The 110th Congress is going to do the right thing and finally [deliver] a minimum wage increase. . . . At the same time, we should help keep jobs available to America's workers by helping small businesses absorb this wage hike."[46]

Working together, Democrats and Republicans on the Senate Finance Committee produced an $8.3 billion package that included a three-step increase in the minimum wage to $7.25 by 2009, small business tax relief, and revenue-raising offsets to pay for the tax cuts.[47] Senate Democrats embraced the package of small business tax relief to lessen the impact of the minimum wage increase on businesses that employed low-wage workers and to win Republican support.[48] All but three Senate Republicans voted for the package.

The final agreement that emerged as the 2007 Small Business and Work Opportunity Tax Act combined a minimum wage increase to $7.25 an hour by 2009 and $4.84 billion in small business tax relief and offsetting revenue increases. Among other measures, the bill extended the Work Opportunity Tax Credit through August 2011 and expanded it to cover

44. Alan K. Ota, "Comparing the Tax Break Plans," *CQ Weekly*, February 19, 2007, p. 546; Ota, "Senate Backs Small-Business Tax Cuts," *CQ Weekly*, January 22, 2007, pp. 256–57.

45. Ibid.

46. Hulse, "House Votes to Raise Minimum Wage."

47. Michael Sandler and Alan K. Ota, "Provisions of the Senate Wage Bill," *CQ Weekly*, February 5, 2007, p. 399.

48. Michael Sandler, "$2.10 Wage Increase Passes House," *CQ Weekly*, January 15, 2007, p. 182.

rural counties that were losing population.[49] (The tax credit, which was introduced in 1996 as part of the Clinton administration's welfare-to-work agenda, offered subsidies to businesses hiring disadvantaged workers.) This package was incorporated into the 2007 fiscal year supplemental defense appropriations bill, which provided almost $100 billion in funding for military operations in Iraq and Afghanistan.[50] The maneuver was designed to guarantee the president's approval, and it did. One observer described the bargain as "the intersection of war and domestic policy."[51]

In addition to increasing the minimum wage, the new Democratic majority sought to reduce the federal income tax liability of low- to moderate-income families by expanding the bottom 10 percent tax bracket, the standard deduction, the EITC, and the refundable CTC.[52] However, the Democrats were stymied by the contending claims of tax relief for lower-income families, tax relief for middle-income families, and newly approved pay-as-you-go rules, which required revenue offsets for any new tax relief or entitlement spending.[53] In the end, Democratic lawmakers chose to give immediate priority to boosting the after-tax income of middle-class taxpayers by approving a one-year patch for the Alternative Minimum Tax (AMT) that allowed up to 21 million earners to avoid liability for the AMT in 2007. Enacted in 1969, the AMT was intended to ensure that high-income earners paid at least some income tax, even if they claimed many itemized deductions. However, by 2008 more than half of AMT payers were expected to have incomes of less than $125,000, and about 3.5 million were expected to have incomes of less than $75,000.[54] By helping such taxpayers, Democrats hoped to boost their electoral fortunes in 2008.

49. Richard Rubin, "Democrats Cut Deal on Tax Break Package," *CQ Weekly*, April 23, 2007, p. 1193; Rubin, "Democrats Victorious on Wage Hike, Tax Breaks," *CQ Weekly*, May 28, 2007, p. 1600.

50. U.S. Congress (2007, pp. 1–2).

51. Richard Rubin, "The Intersection of War and Domestic Policy," *CQ Weekly*, April 30, 2007, p. 1268.

52. Richard Rubin, "Fall Agenda: Alternative Minimum Tax," *CQ Weekly*, September 3, 2007, pp. 2558.

53. Jeffrey H. Birnbaum, "Democrat Proposes Overhaul of Taxes: Range Would Annul AMT, Shift Burden," *Washington Post*, October 26, 2007, p. D1.

54. Burman and others (2002).

The 2008 Stimulus and One-Time Boosts in Paychecks

As the election year opened, Congress faced the political challenge of responding to an economic crisis triggered by the collapse of the housing market in 2007. President Bush outlined plans for a stimulus package, including one-time tax rebates for many Americans and business investment incentives. The House announced a plan similar to the White House proposal, while the Senate developed its own version that included extended unemployment benefits.

One-time tax rebates were considered one of the fastest ways to lift consumer spending, especially if they targeted low- and moderate-income earners. Thus Democrats pushed for one-time cash rebates to 35 million working poor families that earned too little to pay federal income tax, a proposal that Republicans accepted in exchange for faster tax write-offs for corporate investment and tax deductions for small business investment in plants and equipment.[55] Senate Democrats succeeded in extending eligibility for rebates to low-income senior citizens, disabled veterans, and survivors of veterans, benefiting an estimated 20 million senior citizens and 250,000 disabled veterans. However, House Democrats were less successful in obtaining their distributional goals; in the face of Republican opposition, they abandoned a number of provisions intended to assist low-income families, including extension of unemployment and food stamp benefits, funding increases for low-income heating assistance, and aid to state and local governments to help fund Medicaid or infrastructure spending.[56]

Under the final package approved by the Democratic Congress and the Republican White House, most workers would receive rebates of $600 for an individual or $1,200 for a couple. Workers who earned at least $3,000 during 2007 but did not owe income tax would qualify for a rebate of $300 for individuals or $600 for couples filing jointly. The income ceiling on eligibility for a rebate was $75,000 for single earners and $150,000 for married couples. Any worker qualifying for a rebate would also receive an

55. Jonathan Weisman and Peter Baker, "Bush, House Hammer out $150 Billion Stimulus Plan: Tax Breaks a Central Element in Bipartisan Compromise," *Washington Post*, January 25, 2008; Richard Rubin, "Highlights of the Stimulus Legislation," *CQ Weekly*, February 11, 2008, p. 391.

56. Weisman and Baker, "Bush, House Hammer out $150 Billion Stimulus Plan."

additional $300 for each dependent child under age 17.[57] The $152 billion stimulus package was signed into law in early February 2008.

The Decade's Distributive Consequences for Lower-Income Working Families

It is not surprising that the two parties disagreed sharply on how the federal tax policies implemented under the Bush administration affected the distribution of the tax burden as a whole. Republicans concluded that the income tax became more progressive because many low-income earners were taken off the tax rolls altogether and because higher-income earners, by and large, received smaller tax reductions—as a percentage of what they were previously paying in taxes—than lower-income earners. Democrats contended that the income tax code became more regressive because higher-income earners got such a large share of the tax relief—in absolute and percentage terms—and because the after-tax distribution of income was more unequal than when the decade began.

Republicans generally argued that the changes to the tax code in 2001–03 left higher-income earners paying a larger share of the much smaller amount of federal income taxes being collected. They also noted that many working poor families no longer had a federal tax liability. Based on the latest Internal Revenue Service statistics, some 45.6 million earners—one-third of all earners—had no tax liability after taking their income tax credits and deductions in 2006. This was a dramatic 57 percent increase since 2000 in the number of Americans who paid no personal income taxes.[58] The conservative Tax Foundation cited the increase as evidence that "over the past two decades, lawmakers have increasingly turned to the tax system rather than direct spending programs to funnel money to targeted groups of Americans, furthering some social or political goal."[59]

In contrast, Democrats concluded that across-the-board tax relief benefited higher-income families far more than lower-income families. They relied on analysis that concluded that after-tax income—not income tax paid—was a better measure of the distributional impact of changes in the

---

57. Jonathan Weisman, "Congress Approves Stimulus Package: Payments Added for Disabled Vets and Poor Seniors," *Washington Post*, February 8, 2008, p. A01.

58. Scott Hodge, "Both Candidates' Tax Plans Will Reduce Millions of Taxpayers' Liability to Zero (or Less)," *Fiscal Facts*, September 19, 2008 (www.taxfoundation.org/publications/show/23631.html).

59. Ibid.

tax code. Democrats argued that focusing solely on the percentage decrease in a household's federal income tax liability led to misleading conclusions. Since low-income families paid so little federal income tax in the first place, it would take only a small cut in dollar terms to give them a high percentage reduction in their income tax liability. However, such small cuts would have little impact on their after-tax income.[60]

In addition, analyses that looked only at the income tax omitted other federal taxes, such as the payroll tax, that were highly regressive. The CBO reported that three-fourths of all tax filers paid more in payroll taxes than in income taxes. Thus, reducing or eliminating income tax liability had very limited effect on the federal tax burdens of low- and moderate-income earners. When state and local tax liabilities were added into the mix, the reductions in federal income taxes became even less significant to low-income working families.[61]

According to the Tax Policy Center, on average, those at the lower end of the income distribution received a much larger reduction in federal tax liability under the Bush tax reductions in percentage terms than those at the top. However, although virtually every earner with income above $100,000 saw his or her after-tax income rise, this was true for only half of earners with incomes between $10,000 and $20,000 and for only three-fourths of earners with incomes between $20,000 and $30,000. In terms of an actual boost in after-tax income, the average increase was more than $3,700 for an earner between $100,000 and $200,000; however, for a minimum wage worker earning between $10,000 and $20,000, the average increase in after-tax income was only $165.[62]

Moreover, minimum wage workers saw their real pretax earnings decline sharply over this period. The federal minimum wage stagnated at $5.15 an hour from 1997 to 2007 even as the cost of living rose by 32 percent. As a result, even after increasing to $6.55 in mid-2008, the inflation-adjusted value of the minimum wage was 19 percent lower in 2008 than in 1979.[63] It was also only 37 percent of the average hourly wage of production and nonsupervisory workers, well below the ratio of the 1950s,

60. John Cranford, "Deficit Worries Push Tax Talk," *CQ Weekly Online*, February 5, 2007, pp. 381–84.

61. Retail sales taxes, in particular, make up about half of state tax revenues and place significant burdens on low-income families. U.S. Congress (2003).

62. Cranford, "Deficit Worries Push Tax Talk."

63. Bernstein and Shapiro (2006, pp. 1–6).

1960s, and 1970s. Not surprisingly, the annual earnings of a full-time minimum wage worker fell far below the federal poverty threshold for a family of three.[64]

An estimated 4.5 million workers (less than 4 percent of the workforce) were expected to receive an increase in their take-home pay when the minimum wage was raised to $7.25 in 2009. Of these workers, 2.8 million earned less than $7.25 and would be directly affected by the increase.[65] Adults made up the largest share—79 percent—of workers expected to benefit from the increase.[66] Of the expected beneficiaries, 59 percent were women and 26 percent were single parents with children under 18.[67] However, workers in states with minimum wages above the federal level were far less likely to benefit from the increase. As of mid-2008, twenty-three states and the District of Columbia, representing more than half of the country's population, had enacted higher minimum wages than the federal government.[68] In addition, ten states adjusted their minimum wages annually for inflation.

Thus, as the 2008 election approached, the stage was set for a major debate over the economic plight of low- and middle-income families against the backdrop of an economic crisis that many analysts were calling the country's worst since the Great Depression.

64. Ibid., figure 4.
65. Kai Filion, "EPI's Minimum Wage Issue Guide," updated July 21, 2009 (www.epi.org/publications/entry/issue_guide_on_minimum_wage)
66. Ibid.
67. Ibid.
68. U.S. Department of Labor, Employment Standards Division, "Minimum Wage Laws in the States: January 1, 2009," interactive map (www.dol.gov/esa/minwage/america.htm).

7 | Toward a New Bargain?

E ntering the 2008 election season, Republican leaders claimed that they had succeeded in reducing income taxes across the board for all Americans, while Democratic leaders argued that increases in the after-tax income of low- and moderate-income families had been achieved only because they had demanded that additional tax relief be distributed to working poor and moderate-income families. The Republican and Democratic candidates for president in 2008 faced the political challenge of trying to translate these tax policy stories into a narrative about the future of paycheck politics.[1]

Almost all of the tax relief enacted since 2000 was set to expire at the end of 2010. This meant that in 2011 the 10 percent tax bracket would disappear; the top rates would increase from 28, 33, and 35 percent to 31, 36, and 39.6 percent; the Child Tax Credit (CTC) would decrease to $500 per child and revert to being nonrefundable for most earners; and for married couples, the standard deduction and the top boundary of the 15 percent tax bracket would fall to below twice their level for single filers. Both candidates agreed that some of the Bush administration's tax reforms should be retained, such as the expanded CTC and provisions that reduced

1. David Nather, "Democrats Take Small Steps with the Middle Class' Big Problems," *CQ Weekly*, March 12, 2007, pp. 716–23.

the marriage penalty.[2] However, the issues on which they agreed were dwarfed by the questions over which they clashed. The Republican nominee, Senator John McCain of Arizona, sought to capitalize on the popularity of tax relief by promising to make all of the Bush rate cuts permanent. He also pledged to allow American families to keep more of their income by proposing to double the dependent exemption from $3,500 to $7,000. McCain argued that his plan would lift after-tax incomes an average of about 3 percent, or $1,400 annually, for middle-income earners by 2012. However, according to a Tax Policy Center analysis of the candidates' tax plans, most of McCain's proposals primarily benefited those with very high incomes. In 2009,

> Households in the bottom quintile of the cash income distribution would receive an average tax cut of just 0.2 percent of income ($21) and those in the middle fifth of the income distribution would receive an average cut equal to 0.8 percent of income ($325). Households in the top quintile, however, would get an average tax cut of 3.2 percent of income ($6,498). . . . Taxpayers in the top 1 percent of the population would see their taxes fall by an average of 3.7 percent of income or almost $50,000 and the richest 1 in 1,000 would see an average tax cut of more than $290,000 or 4.7 percent of income.[3]

In sum, the McCain tax plan would make the income tax code more regressive.

In contrast, the Democratic candidate, Senator Barack Obama, proposed to extend the Bush rate cuts for the bottom four tax brackets, which included single taxpayers earning up to roughly $165,000 and married couples earning up to roughly $200,000. However, his plan would increase tax rates in the top two brackets and adjust the brackets upward to exclude families making less than $250,000 and single workers earning less than $200,000. In addition, he proposed to make the tax code more progressive by creating a series of refundable tax credits aimed largely at the middle class. The Making Work Pay (MWP) credit, worth $500 for single workers and $1,000 for families, would be made available to 95 percent of the coun-

2. Beach and others (2008); Urban–Brookings Tax Policy Center, "Dueling Tax Plans: What Would McCain and Obama Do? A Conversation with the Candidates' Top Economic Advisers," July 23, 2008 (www.taxpolicycenter.org/events/events_071008.cfm).
3. Burman and others (2008, p. 32).

try's workers and their families, eliminating the income tax liability of 10 million low-income Americans.[4] College students who agreed to perform 100 hours of community service would be eligible for a $4,000 American Opportunity Tax Credit, regardless of whether they paid income taxes. Obama also pledged to help low- and moderate-income families by increasing the minimum wage from $7.25 to $9.50 by 2011 and indexing it to inflation, by expanding the Earned Income Tax Credit (EITC), and by making the Child and Dependent Care Tax Credit refundable for the first time in its history. Under his plan, low-income working families would be able to take up to a 50 percent credit on the first $6,000 of child care expenses. The Obama campaign estimated that this provision would help 7.5 million working mothers.[5] In addition, a 10 percent tax credit for mortgage interest would help nonitemizing taxpayers offset the cost of home ownership.

According to the Tax Policy Center analysis, the Obama plan would make the tax system significantly more progressive:

> Households in the bottom quintile of the cash income distribution (the 20 percent of the population with the lowest incomes) would receive an average tax cut of 5.5 percent of income ($567) and those in the middle fifth of the income distribution would receive an average cut equal to 2.6 percent of income ($1,118). In contrast, taxes would rise by an average of 1.5 percent of income ($3,017) for households in the top quintile. . . . Taxpayers in the top 1 percent would see their taxes rise by an average of 7.0 percent of income or about $94,000. The top 0.1 percent—the richest 1 in 1,000—would face an average tax increase of nearly $550,000, or 8.9 percent of income.[6]

In 2007 households in the bottom quintile of the income distribution had less than $21,000 in income, those in the middle quintile earned between $39,000 and $62,000, and those in the top 20 percent had more than $100,000 in income. The distribution for families skewed somewhat higher. (Households include all residents of a housing unit, whether or not they are related, and can consist of individuals; families include only related

4. BarackObama.com, "Barack Obama: Tax Fairness for the Middle Class" (http://obama.3cdn.net/b7be3b7cd08e587dca_v852mv8ja.pdf [January 2, 2009]).
5. BarackObama.com, "Barack Obama's Comprehensive Tax Plan" (www.barackobama.com/pdf/taxes/Factsheet_Tax_Plan_FINAL.pdf [January 2, 2009]).
6. Burman and others (2008, p. 29).

members and must have two or more members.) Families in the bottom quintile had up to roughly $28,000 in income in 2007; families in the middle quintile earned between $50,000 and $75,000; and families in the top 20 percent had more than $112,000 in income.[7]

McCain called Obama's tax plan "socialist" because it would give tax relief to people who paid no income taxes.[8] In 2006 some 45.6 million tax filers—one-third of all filers—had no tax liability after taking their credits and deductions. According to the Tax Foundation, the number of such "nonpayers" was expected to rise by 16 million under the Obama plan and by 15 million under the McCain plan.[9] The argument that the tax code should not be used to deliver benefits to nonpayers was a frequent theme in conservative venues such as the editorial page of the *Wall Street Journal:*

> Refundable credits are not tax cuts. Indeed, they should be called The New Tax Welfare. In effect, Mr. Obama is proposing to create or expand a slew of government spending programs that are disguised as tax credits. The spending on these programs is then subtracted from the total tax burden, in order to make the claim that his tax plan is a net tax cut overall. In short, welfare spending is to be increased by paying more money out to low-income income tax filers.[10]

However, Obama rejected the Republicans' characterization of his tax plan as "welfare," saying that the proposed credits would go to working Americans: "I'm not giving tax cuts to folks who don't work; I'm giving tax cuts to people who do work. John McCain . . . must be the first politician in history to call a tax cut for working people 'welfare.'" Obama also took issue with claims that refundable credits would go to people who did not pay taxes. As his supporters argued, "Those who don't pay income taxes

7. U.S. Census Bureau, "Historical Income Data, Table H-1. Income Limits for Each Fifth and Top 5 Percent of Households All Races: 1967 to 2007" (www.census.gov/hhes/www/income/histinc/h01AR.html); "Historical Income Data, Table F-1. Income Limits for Each Fifth and Top 5 Percent of Families (All Races): 1947 to 2007" (www.census.gov/hhes/www/income/histinc/f01AR.html).

8. Nick Timiraos and Laura Meckler, "Use of Refundable Tax Credits Has Grown in Recent Years," *Wall Street Journal*, October 21, 2008, p. 1.

9. Scott A. Hodge, "Both Candidates' Tax Plans Will Reduce Millions of Taxpayers' Liability to Zero (or Less)," *Fiscal Facts,* September 19, 2008 (www.taxfoundation.org/publications/show/23631.html).

10. Peter Ferrara, "Obama's Tax Plan Is Really a Welfare Plan," *Wall Street Journal*, August 19, 2008.

still support their state and federal governments through federal payroll taxes, sales taxes, property taxes and gas taxes."[11] Many voters seemed to agree: Obama went on to win the election with 53 percent of the vote, opening a new chapter in the history of efforts to boost the paychecks of America's low-income working families.

The American Recovery and Reinvestment Act of 2009

In addition to regaining the White House, the Democrats solidified their control of the House and Senate in 2008. In the House, they picked up nineteen seats, building on their thirty-one-seat gain in the 2006 midterm elections, which ended twelve years of Republican control. The conservative Blue Dog Coalition also added members, bringing their total from forty-three to fifty-one.[12] In the Senate, the Democrats gained eight seats, giving them a majority of fifty-nine, including two independents, although Democrat Al Franken's victory in Minnesota remained contested until mid-2009. In April 2009, Senator Arlen Specter (R-Pa.) switched parties, and in June the Minnesota Supreme Court ruled that Franken had indeed won his race, confirming a sixty-vote filibuster-proof majority for the Democrats.

Even before taking office, President-elect Obama was forced to confront the deepening economic crisis. He and his advisers worked quickly with Democratic leaders in Congress to draft an economic stimulus plan that would encourage spending by putting money back into the pockets of American workers. House Democrats broadly supported tax relief for working Americans as one major component of an economic stimulus package.[13] However, they were divided over how much tax relief the country could afford.[14] The Blue Dog Coalition warned that some of its members would not support a tax reduction package that added to the projected deficit of $1.2 trillion for fiscal year 2009 unless the Obama administration took steps to address the federal government's rising debt and other long-term fiscal challenges. House Republicans also supported tax relief in principle but did

---

11. Tami Luhby, "Are Tax Credits Welfare?" November 3, 2008 (http://money.cnn.com/2008/10/31/news/economy/taxes_welfare/index.htm).

12. "Blue Dog Coalition Heydays," *CQ Weekly*, January 19, 2009, p. 112).

13. David Clarke, "Democrats Roll Out Stimulus Plan," *CQ Weekly*, January 19, 2009, pp. 126–28.

14. Clea Benson, "Long-Term Options in a Quick Stimulus," *CQ Weekly*, November 24, 2008, pp. 3128–30.

not want to see a boost in the paychecks of the middle class financed through a heavier tax burden on high-income earners.

The stimulus plan introduced in the House in mid-January 2009 combined $275 billion in tax relief with $550 billion in new spending.[15] Within a week, the Ways and Means Committee had approved the tax portion of the package. The bill included the MWP credit, which allowed taxpayers to take 6.2 percent of their earned income, up to $500 for individuals and $1,000 for married couples, as a refundable credit in 2009 and 2010. (In other words, the credit would expire with most of the Bush-era tax reforms.) The credit, which phased out for individuals earning more than $75,000 and couples earning more than $150,000, was expected to cost $145 billion.[16] In addition, Ways and Means agreed to a temporary increase in the EITC for working families with three or more children and expanded eligibility for the refundable portion of the CTC by temporarily reducing the income eligibility threshold from $8,500 to zero for 2009 and 2010.[17] House Republicans found no traction for their proposal for a much smaller plan that would instead cut rates in the two bottom brackets (then 15 percent and 10 percent) by 5 percentage points each, and the stimulus package passed the House without a single Republican vote by the end of January.

In the Senate, modifications to the package were negotiated by a group of moderates from both parties, led by Susan Collins (R-Maine) and Ben Nelson (D-Nebr.), who supported Obama's call to pull the economy out of recession but feared the overall cost of the stimulus package was too large to win a bipartisan Senate majority. The Senate reduced the MWP tax credit from $500 per individual and $1,000 per married couple to $400 and $800, respectively, and slightly lowered the income levels at which the credit would phase out. In addition, rather than eliminate the income eligibility threshold for the refundable CTC, the Senate temporarily reduced it by only $400, from $8,500 to $8,100.[18]

---

15. Lee Hudson Teslik, "Backgrounder: The U.S. Economic Stimulus Plan," *New York Times,* January 27, 2009.

16. U.S. House of Representatives, Committee on Ways and Means, "Tax Relief Included in 'The American Recovery and Reinvestment Plan,'" January 22, 2009 (http://waysandmeans.house.gov/media/pdf/110/taxsum.pdf).

17. Ibid.

18. U.S. Senate, Committee on Finance, "Side-By-Side Chart of Notable Differences between the Senate-Passed and the House-Passed American Recovery and Reinvestment Act of 2009," February 10, 2009 (http://finance.senate.gov/sitepages/baucus.htm).

Table 7-1. *2009 American Recovery and Reinvestment Act:*
Distribution of Selected Tax Benefits, by Cash Income Level
Share of total tax change

Cash income in thousands of 2008 dollars	MWP tax credit	Reduction of the CTC refundability threshold to $3,000	Expansion of the EITC
Less than 10	5.6	12.0	1.6
10–20	11.7	53.6	10.6
20–30	12.4	26.4	29.1
30–40	10.2	5.1	31.6
40–50	8.9	1.4	21.8
More than 50	51.0	1.0	4.5

Source: Urban-Brookings Tax Policy Center Microsimulation Model (version 0308-7).

The final version of the 2009 American Recovery and Reinvestment Act set the MWP credit at the levels stipulated by the Senate and adopted the slightly higher phase-out levels voted by the House. It also temporarily expanded the EITC for families with three or more children by increasing the credit from 40 percent to 45 percent of their first $12,570 in earned income, and raised the level at which the credit began to phase out by $1,880 for married couples. More important, it significantly increased eligibility for the refundable CTC by lowering the eligibility threshold to $3,000 in 2009 and 2010.[19] After its passage, most wage earners received an immediate boost in their paychecks because of the changes made to the federal income tax withholding tables to implement the MWP tax credit. The MWP increased most families' take-home pay by over $65 a month. It could help low-income workers both by boosting their after-tax income and by encouraging them to work. However, much of the benefit of the MWP went to families earning more than $50,000. (See table 7-1). In contrast, the expansion of the EITC largely benefited moderate-income families, and the change in the CTC primarily helped low-income families.

According to the Obama administration, 95 percent of all working families would receive tax relief under the American Recovery and Reinvestment Act. The middle class would benefit the most: 70 percent of the tax

19. U.S. House of Representatives, Committee on Ways and Means, "Summary of H.R. 1, The American Recovery and Reinvestment Act of 2009," February 12, 2009 (http://waysandmeans.house.gov/media/pdf/111/arra.pdf).

benefits would go to the middle 60 percent of American workers. However, more than $150 billion in tax reduction would assist low-income and vulnerable families during the economic recovery, and 2 million families would be lifted above the federal poverty threshold.[20] The temporary expansion of the CTC benefited 13 million low-income children and lifted an estimated 1 million children out of poverty.[21] If the changes to the CTC were allowed to expire, the earnings threshold at which families can claim the refundable credit would rise above $12,000. This would have a devastating effect on low-income working families.

Planning for 2010 and Beyond

The president sought to preserve these gains in his budget for fiscal year 2010, which was regarded as one of the most ambitious policy prescriptions in decades. The $3.6 trillion spending plan called for massive investments in health care, education, and energy, and projected a $1.2 trillion federal deficit. However, as the *Washington Post* reported, President Obama planned to reduce the deficit to $533 billion by the end of his first term "in large part by levying nearly $1 trillion in new taxes over the next decade on the nation's highest earners, defined as families with gross income of more than $250,000 a year."[22]

As promised during the campaign, the Obama 2010 budget blueprint preserved the Bush tax reductions for most middle-class families. It also proposed to make permanent the changes in the EITC and CTC that had just been adopted as part of the stimulus package and to extend the MWP credit. If the MWP were extended, roughly three-quarters of taxpayers would see their taxes fall by an average of $385 in 2012, representing an average boost in after-tax income of 0.7 percent.[23] (Federal tax revenues

20. White House, "American Recovery and Reinvestment Act: A Progressive Plan to Create Jobs and Help Families," February 17, 2009 (www.whitehouse.gov/.../Recovery_Act_Working_Families_2-17.pdf).

21. Arloc Sherman, "Recovery Agreement Temporarily Expands Child Tax Credit for Large Numbers of Children in Every State," February 12, 2009 (www.cbpp.org/cms/index.cfm?fa=view&id=2547).

22. Lori Montgomery, "In $3.6 Trillion Budget, Obama Signals Broad Shift in Priorities," *Washington Post,* February 27, 2009.

23. Urban–Brookings Tax Policy Center, "Tax Topics: 2010 Budget Tax Proposals: Make Permanent the 'Making Work Pay' Tax Credit" (www.taxpolicycenter.org/taxtopics/2010_budget_makingworkpay.cfm [June 29, 2009]).

would also fall by an estimated $640 billion between 2011 and 2018.)[24] However, since the White House did not call for the MWP credit to be indexed, its maximum value for a single filer was expected to fall from $400 to $358 in real terms by 2017, a more than 10 percent drop. For very low income families, this loss would be offset by an increase in their eligibility for the refundable CTC. Over the same period, the real value of the income threshold at which families can start to claim this credit was expected to decline from $3,000 to $2,688.[25]

Although federal income taxes would fall or remain constant for most households under the White House plan, they would rise for high-income taxpayers. After 2010 rates in the top two brackets would revert to their pre-2001 levels. In the same spirit, Obama proposed to reinstate the pre-2001 rules that phased out the personal exemption at high-income levels, to limit the value of itemized deductions for high-income earners, and to impose a 20 percent tax rate on long-term capital gains and qualified dividends. Compared to the existing tax code, under which the 2001–03 tax reductions would virtually all expire after 2010, Obama's proposals would increase income taxes for about 5 percent of all earners. About one-sixth of those in the top quintile of the income distribution and one-fourth of those in the top 1 percent would experience a tax increase: all other earners would continue to experience a boost in the paychecks.[26]

Speaking on tax day—April 15, 2009—the president vigorously defended his program, saying, "We need to end the tax breaks for the wealthiest 2 percent of Americans, so that people like me, who are extraordinarily lucky, are paying the same rates that the wealthiest 2 percent of Americans paid when Bill Clinton was President." Addressing his critics, he argued,

> For too long, we've seen taxes used as a wedge to scare people into supporting policies that actually increased the burden on working people instead of helping them live their dreams. That has to change, and that's the work that we've begun. We've passed tax cuts that will help our economy grow. We've made a clear promise that families that

24. Urban–Brookings Tax Policy Center, "Tax Topics: 'Making Work Pay' Tax Credit" (www.tax policycenter.org/taxtopics/conference_makingworkpay.cfm [August 2009]).
25. Ibid.
26. Urban–Brookings Tax Policy Center, "Make Permanent the 'Making Work Pay' Tax Credit."

earn less than $250,000 a year will not see their taxes increase by a single dime. And we have kept to those promises that were made during the campaign. We've given tax relief to the Americans who need it and the workers who have earned it. And we're helping more Americans move towards their American Dream.[27]

At the same time, Obama reached out to fiscal moderates and conservatives who remained concerned about the cost of his proposals: "We know," he said, "that tax relief must be joined with fiscal discipline. Americans are making hard choices in their budgets, and we've got to tighten our belts in Washington, as well. In addition, that's why we've already identified $2 trillion in deficit reductions over the next decade. And that's why we're cutting programs that don't work, contracts that aren't fair, and spending that we don't need."

The president was speaking not only to Republicans but also to the Blue Dogs who made up one-fifth of the House Democratic caucus. Although the Blue Dogs remained concerned about the deficits envisioned in Obama's 2010 budget, they were won over—at least provisionally—by a pledge by House Democratic leaders to support stricter deficit control measures going forward.[28] In addition, in June 2009, Obama proposed to reenact the pay-as-you-go budgeting rules that were in force from 1990 through 2002. Under this legislation, Congress would be required to offset any increases in entitlement spending or tax cuts with other tax increases or spending cuts.[29]

Beyond concerns about cost, controversy over the refundability of tax credits loomed as a likely stumbling block for the White House's plans. In 2009 nearly 71 million tax units—nearly half the total number—had no tax liability according to the Tax Policy Center.[30] This figure included almost all of those with cash incomes under $10,000 (18.7 million tax units), 84 percent of those with cash incomes between $10,000 and $20,000 (20.6 million tax units), and 62 percent of those with cash

27. White House, "Remarks by the President on Taxes," April 15, 2009 (www.whitehouse.gov/the_press_office/Remarks-by-the-President-on-Taxes-4-15-09/).

28. David Clarke, "Budget Moves on Hard Party Lines," *CQ Weekly,* May 4, 2009, pp. 1036–37.

29. Sheryl Gay Stolberg, "Obama Aims to Revive 'Pay as You Go,'" *New York Times,* June 10, 2009, p. A20.

30. Urban–Brookings Tax Policy Center, "The Numbers: Zero or Negative Liability" (www.taxpolicycenter.org/numbers/displayatab.cfm?Simid=310 [June 29, 2009]).

incomes between $20,000 and $30,000 (12.5 million tax units). In order to provide further support to individuals and families in this group through the federal tax code, the government would have to provide rebates in excess of their liability. Given the Republican record of opposition to "tax welfare," a *New York Times* article predicted in early 2009 that refundable credits were likely to be "the hottest tax issue over the next two years."[31]

31. Edmund L. Andrews, "Changes Up and Down the Ladder," *New York Times*, February 27, 2009.

The Past and Future Politics of Boosting Paychecks

The forging of a political bargain to provide economic support to low-income workers and their families was a critical challenge throughout the twentieth century, and it remains so today. This book has analyzed the political development of two key pillars of this "boosting paychecks" regime: the federal tax system and the minimum wage. These policies have followed separate legislative trajectories over the past century. As a result, they do not add up to a coherent policy framework. However, the effectiveness of the minimum wage at alleviating poverty clearly depends on the workings of the tax system and vice versa. Moreover, the two policy instruments share an underlying political logic. Both have been marked by repeated trade-offs between the demands of effectiveness and political support, and southern Democrats and smaller bipartisan groups of centrists have been critical at every stage of their evolution.

In the case of the federal minimum wage, this has meant slow and piecemeal growth. In the first five decades after its passage as part of the later New Deal, liberal Democrats had to accept limitations on coverage to gain support for even modest increases from conservative southern Democrats and Republicans. In the mid-1990s, the price they paid for minimum wage increases changed to become tax relief for small businesses. Such bargains have allowed the minimum wage to endure through both liberal and conservative periods.

On the tax side of the agenda, tax credits have emerged as the center-piece of efforts to help low-income working families. This development has been fostered by growing reliance on the budget reconciliation process. Through reconciliation—a process first used in 1981—Congress decides which changes in mandatory spending and revenue programs are necessary to reach the overall goals set by the budget resolution for that fiscal year.[1] The process is governed by expedited procedures and restrictions, such as a ban on filibustering in the Senate, and produces huge omnibus packages. "Together, all these rules ensure that a reconciliation bill moves quickly through the legislature, beset by few of the procedural vetogates that lie in wait for the typical piece of legislation."[2] In this environment, tax credits have become a useful and popular way for legislators to fine-tune the dis-tributional impact of tax and spending packages and to deliver benefits to favored political constituencies.[3]

Equally important, the period since the early 1980s has seen the con-solidation of a bipartisan consensus around the idea that working families should be the primary beneficiaries of such forms of federal assistance. This consensus rests on a simple idea: in the United States, if able-bodied par-ents participate in the labor market, their take-home pay should be suffi-cient to lift their families out of poverty. It both drove and was strength-ened by the passage of welfare reform in the shape of the Personal Responsibility and Work Opportunity Reconciliation Act of 1996. This landmark legislation—which replaced Aid to Families with Dependent Children, a program with origins in the 1935 Social Security Act, with Temporary Assistance to Needy Families—shifted the focus of federal ef-forts to support poor families from cash assistance programs, such as wel-fare, to strategies to supplement labor market earnings, such as refundable tax credits.[4]

This consensus notably omits low-income workers without children, who have seen their effective tax rates remain at high levels while low-income working families have found themselves with zero or even negative federal tax liability. It also papers over—sometimes just barely—growing

1. For more background on the reconciliation process, see U.S. House of Representatives, Com-mittee on Rules, Majority Office, "The Budget Reconciliation Process" (www.rules.house.gov/archives/bud_rec_proc.htm).
2. Garrett (2000, p. 720).
3. Kettl (1992).
4. Haveman (2003).

anger over the refundability of some of the credits offered to lower-income workers and their families. These issues will continue to shape the Obama administration's efforts to move toward a new politics of boosting paychecks of working families.

The Past and Future of the Minimum Wage

The original 1938 Fair Labor Standards Act agreement on the federal minimum wage established a particular political and institutional logic that helps explain its subsequent development. Instead of delegating legislative authority to a wage-setting board, Congress chose to retain statutory control over the amount and timing of any increase and the industries and occupations covered by the federal minimum wage. Legislators jealously guarded this power over the following decades. For example, in 1977 Congress refused to index the minimum wage to inflation, and in 1990 it declined to establish a minimum wage advisory board even to recommend cost-of-living adjustments.

By retaining control over its parameters, reluctant converts to the minimum wage were able to maximize the electoral benefits of a highly popular policy while minimizing the negative effects by limiting the costs imposed on business and agricultural groups. Until 1994 this meant that conservative southern Democrats and Republicans, both in Congress and in the White House, were largely able to control the pace of increases in both the level and coverage of the federal minimum wage.[5] This pattern held for increases in the minimum wage in 1949, 1955, 1961, 1966, 1974, 1977, and 1990—all years when Democrats controlled the House.

This pattern began to shift in the 1980s. From 1981 to 1990, when Republicans controlled both the Senate and the White House, the minimum wage remained at $3.35 an hour, and the percentage of workers paid hourly rates at or below the prevailing minimum wage dropped significantly.[6] In 1990 Democrats in Congress secured a two-step increase to $4.25, but only by agreeing to the introduction of a new subminimum training wage—a measure sought by the Bush administration—and the expansion of small business exemptions.[7] Since then a new bargain has been struck linking minimum wage increases with tax relief for small (and

5. Sinclair (1982).
6. Even and MacPherson (2007).
7. "Legislative Summary: Labor," *CQ Weekly*, December 2, 1989, p. 3304.

at times large) businesses. In 1996 conservative House Republican leaders were forced to accept a bargain among centrist Republicans, Democrats, and the Clinton White House to adopt a minimum wage increase in return for $16.2 billion in tax relief over ten years—including significant benefits for some of the nation's largest companies.[8] In 2007 congressional Democrats, who were back in the majority, again packaged a minimum wage increase with small business tax relief and secured its passage by attaching the measure to a supplemental defense spending package. Their partners in this effort were centrist Democrats, Senate Republicans, and President Bush.

Since the late 1960s, the principal casualties of these political dynamics have been the real value of the minimum wage and the earnings of minimum wage workers as measured by their real annual earnings. (See figure 8-1.) For example, the inflation-adjusted value of the minimum wage was 17 percent lower in 2009 than it was in 1968.

Over time the combination of inflation and congressional or presidential inaction has also caused the minimum wage to lose ground relative to average hourly earnings. In the 1950s and 1960s, the minimum wage averaged 50 percent of average hourly earnings. That decreased to 44 percent in the 1970s and hovered around 39 percent in the 1980s and 1990s. By 2009 the minimum wage equaled only 39.2 percent of the average wage for private sector, nonsupervisory workers (figure 8-2).[9] As a result, the minimum wage has become less and less effective at raising the floor for hourly earnings.

At the same time, the number of workers who would be directly affected by a minimum wage increase has declined. The percentage of hourly paid workers earning the prevailing minimum wage or less has trended downward since 1979, when data began to be collected on a regular basis, falling from 13.4 percent in 1979 to 2.2 percent in 2006.[10] That year 59.7 percent of all wage and salary workers were paid at hourly rates, while 1.7 million of these workers earned wages at or below the minimum wage. Of the latter group, roughly half were under twenty-five, and about one quarter were between sixteen and nineteen.

---

8. For the final tax provisions of the minimum wage–tax bill, see Alissa J. Rubin and Jonathan Weisman, "Provisions: Tax Cut, Minimum Wage Law," *CQ Weekly*, September 21, 1996, pp. 2705–08.

9. Kai Filion, "EPI's Minimum Wage Issue Guide," updated July 21, 2009 (www.epi.org/publications/entry/issue_guide_on_minimum_wage).

10. U.S. Department of Labor (2007).

Figure 8-1. *Real Value of the Minimum Wage, 1938–2009*

May 2009 dollars

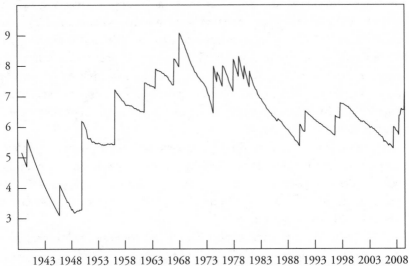

Source: Economic Policy Institute analysis of U.S. Department of Labor data.

Following the passage of the Fair Minimum Wage Act of 2007, the federal minimum wage increased from $5.15 to $5.85 in 2007, from $5.85 to $6.55 in 2008, and again to $7.25 in 2009. Approximately 4.5 million workers experienced an increase in their hourly wage with the last hike.[11]

Since 1980 the minimum wage has been below the federal poverty level for a full-time, full-year worker supporting a family of three (figure 8-3). In 2006 its level relative to the federal poverty threshold was lower than at any time over the prior forty-seven years. For someone working a minimum wage job forty hours a week, the latest three-step increase to $7.25 an hour boosted annual income from roughly $11,000 to $15,000.[12] However, even this latest gain left a family of three about $2,300 below the poverty line unless it also received the Earned Income Tax Credit (EITC), the Child Tax Credit (CTC), and in-kind benefits. During the 2008 campaign, then Senator Obama pledged to increase the minimum wage from $7.25 to $9.50 by 2011 and to index it to inflation. Such an increase would raise

11. Filion, "EPI's Minimum Wage Issue Guide." See also discussion in chapter 6.
12. Xiyun Yang, "Democrats Cheer Wage Hike," *Washington Post*, July 25, 2007, p. D2.

Figure 8-2. *Minimum Wage as a Percent of the Average Wage, 1947–2009*

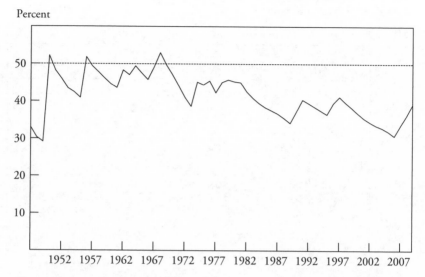

Source: Economic Policy Institute analysis of U.S. Department of Labor and Bureau of Labor Statistics data.

a minimum wage worker's nominal annual earnings from $15,000 to roughly $20,000, and indexing would lock in that gain in future years. But every prior effort to index the minimum wage has been defeated. It remains to be seen whether the new president will be able to make good on his minimum wage commitments.

The Past and Future of Federal Taxes on Individual Income

While the importance of the federal minimum wage as an antipoverty tool has diminished over time, the income tax code has emerged as a central mechanism for boosting the paychecks of low-income working families—and since the mid-1990s, those of moderate- and middle-income families as well.[13] The EITC, in particular, has proven popular with both parties. It has expanded not only as part of omnibus packages that lowered taxes (2001), but also when taxes were increased (1990, 1993), and when other deductions and credits were eliminated (1986). Since 1994 real federal spending on the EITC has outstripped outlays for Aid to Families with Dependent Children

---

13. Gitterman and Howard (2003).

Figure 8-3. *Annual Minimum Wage Earnings and Poverty Level for Family of Three, 1938–2009*[a]

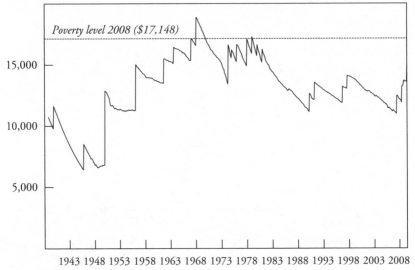

May 2009 dollars

Poverty level 2008 ($17,148)

Source: 2008 poverty thresholds from Census Bureau, in May 2009 dollars.

a. The poverty level is composed of one adult and two children. The poverty level for two adults and one child is roughly the same, $17,132, in May 2009 dollars.

and Temporary Assistance to Needy Families (welfare), and the same has been true of the CTC since 2002 (figure 8-4). Federal spending on the EITC, CTC, and the dependent exemption reached a high of $114.3 billion in 2007. Such numbers have led the Urban Institute to tag "kids, families, and tax policy" as "best friends forever."[14]

These policies had relatively modest roots. Initial attempts to shape the impact of the tax system focused on the personal exemption, the standard deduction, and lower-bracket tax rates. Over time the standard deduction has taken different forms—as a percentage of income, a zero percent tax bracket amount, and a lump-sum amount based on filing status. The personal exemption, in contrast, has been consistently defined as a fixed amount per person that is used to adjust tax liability for family size.

14. Urban Institute, "Kids, Families, and Tax Policy: Best Friends Forever?" Panel discussion, April 16, 2009 (www.urban.org/events/thursdayschild/Kids-Families-and-Tax-Policy.cfm).

Figure 8-4. *Real Federal Spending on the EITC, CTC, and Welfare (AFDC and TANF), Fiscal Years 1976–2010*[a]

Billions of real 2005 dollars

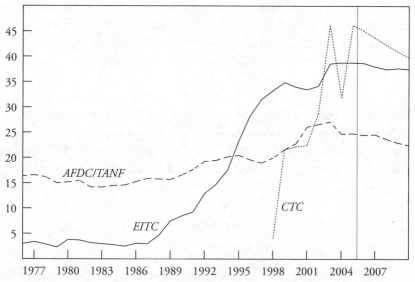

Source: Tax Policy Center, "Spending on the EITC, Child Tax Credit, and AFDC/TANF, 1976–2010" (www.taxpolicycenter.org/taxfacts/displayafact.cfm?Docid=266).

a. AFDC, Aid to Families with Dependent Children; TANF, Temporary Assistance to Needy Families. EITC and CTC aggregate amounts include both outlays and receipts.

Together they exempt from federal tax liability an amount of income that has varied over time.

As a result of these features, the individual income tax code has been broadly progressive throughout its history. Today, on average, households with higher income pay a larger share of their income in taxes.[15] In contrast, the payroll taxes that finance Social Security and Medicare are regressive because they apply from the first dollar of earned income, apply only to labor income, apply at a flat rate, and exempt income above a certain ceiling from Social Security tax. As a result, many low-income families have historically faced high effective tax rates, and many low-income individuals continue to do so today.

15. Jeffrey Rohaly, "The Distribution of Federal Taxes," *Tax Notes*, June 25, 2007 (www.urban.org/UploadedPDF/1001091_distribution_federal_taxes.pdf).

Through the 1960s, the Democratic majority in Congress attempted to lessen the tax burden on low-income working families by increasing the personal exemption and standard deduction and by lowering rates in the bottom brackets. In the 1970s, Congress created a new policy tool in the form of the earned income credit (EIC). The EIC's original mandate, as set forth by an agreement between liberal and conservative Democrats, was to create an added bonus or incentive for low-income people to work and to reduce welfare dependency by inducing individuals receiving federal assistance to support themselves.[16] Specifically, as adopted in 1975, the EIC was intended to offset the Social Security payroll taxes of low-income workers with children. The first EIC was a small credit of up to $400, enacted as part of an economic stimulus package. In 1975, 6.2 million families claimed $1.25 billion in credits.[17] These efforts stimulated internal debate among Democrats over whether the EIC should provide tax relief to all lower-wage earners or target the least skilled workers with children who might otherwise rely on welfare. Ultimately they chose to pursue both goals.

From the Earned Income Credit to Making Work Pay

The original Earned Income Credit, renamed the Earned Income Tax Credit, was made a permanent provision of the federal income tax in 1978, but it was not indexed for inflation. Consequently, the real value of the EITC declined significantly until 1986.[18] That year the Reagan White House reached agreement with Democrats in Congress to eliminate the federal income tax liability of families at or below the federal poverty line. The bipartisan Tax Reform Act of 1986 restored the real value of the EITC to its 1975 level. It also indexed the EITC to inflation, along with income tax brackets, exemptions, and the standard deduction. Consequently, effective tax rates in 1988 (when the Tax Reform Act was fully phased in) moved closer to their level in 1975, although they remained slightly higher because of the increase in payroll taxes over the same period.[19]

Four years later, low-income working families received a further boost when President George H. W. Bush abandoned his "no new taxes" pledge and struck a deal with Democratic leaders in Congress to enact deficit reduction legislation. As part of the 1990 Omnibus Budget Reconciliation

16. U.S. House of Representatives (1975).
17. U.S. House of Representatives (2004).
18. Scholz (2007).
19. Ibid.

Act, Democrats were able to expand the maximum EITC and create a larger credit for families with two or more children. (Before 1990 families with two or more children received the same EITC benefit as families with one child.) In addition, Congress eased some of the rules regarding eligibility for the EITC and directed federal agencies to exclude EITC payments when calculating eligibility for other means-tested benefits.

President Clinton took the antipoverty effects of the EITC yet further by committing his administration to the goal of ensuring that the income of a full-time worker at the federal minimum wage, including the EITC and food stamps, would exceed the federal poverty level.[20] In 1993 he worked with the Democratic majority in Congress to increase the EITC, particularly for families with two or more children. These efforts had considerable impact. In 1986 a single-parent family with two children and income at the federal poverty level owed $2,398 in payroll and income taxes. In 1997 the same family was eligible for a $1,790 refundable income tax credit.[21] In addition, for the first time, the 1993 legislation made low-income childless workers eligible for a small EITC.[22] This childless credit was intended to offset the effect of payroll taxes on low-income workers and to strengthen incentives to work.[23]

Thus, throughout its history, the EITC has helped legislators deliver benefits to low-income families, alter the distributional balance of omnibus tax packages, and thereby secure bipartisan agreement. The 1986 expansion of the EITC resulted from a bipartisan political effort to deal with some of the distributional unfairness of Reagan's across-the-board tax relief in 1981. In 1990 both Republicans and Democrats saw further expansion as a straightforward way to alter the distributional characteristics of the deficit reduction package and head off charges that it essentially benefited high-income earners. The 1993 EITC expansion made it easier for many Democrats to support President Bill Clinton's first budget, which included more spending cuts and deficit reduction than they preferred.

In comparison to the EITC, the CTC has provided little benefit to lower-income working families. Enacted as part of the 1997 Taxpayer Relief Act, the CTC emerged from an agreement between the Clinton

20. Shapiro (1990).
21. Scholz (2007).
22. Greenstein (1990).
23. This effect is offset somewhat by the fact that the EITC imposes high marginal tax rates over its phase-out range.

White House and the Republican Congress to provide income tax relief to more middle- and upper-income earners and out of concern that the income tax code did not make adequate adjustments for family size. Initially, the CTC was only refundable for families with three or more children, and even then a family's refund could be no higher than its payroll tax liability. However, in 2001 President George W. Bush and the Democratic leadership in Congress modified the credit to make it partially refundable for all low-income working families with at least $10,000 in annual earnings.[24] Like many of the 2001 tax changes, this measure was scheduled to sunset in 2010.

No similar modifications were made for the Child and Dependent Care Tax Credit (CDCTC), which was intended to help offset the cost of child care for children under the age of thirteen. Democrats wanted to expand the CDCTC and extend its benefits to low-wage working mothers. Republicans, in contrast, sought to use the legislation to help women stay home with their children. This conflict prevented any significant expansion of the CDCTC. The 2001 Economic Growth and Tax Relief Reconciliation Act increased the ceiling on eligible expenses and raised the rate at which the credit could be claimed (changes that were due to expire at the end of 2010), but it did not make the credit refundable.[25] As a result, the majority of the boost in paychecks from the child and dependent care tax credit continued to flow to middle- and upper-middle-income families.[26] In 2009 the Obama administration proposed to make the CDCTC more progressive by increasing it and making it fully refundable so that families with child care expenses could claim the credit regardless of their tax liability. However, this measure was not included in the 2009 American Recovery and Reinvestment Act (ARRA).

Instead the Obama White House worked with Democratic leaders in Congress to create the temporary Making Work Pay (MWP) tax credit as part of the ARRA. The MWP credit, which the president has proposed to make permanent, is a refundable tax credit of up to $400 for all working individuals and up to $800 for married couples. Its primary purpose is to offset Social Security and Medicare payroll taxes. Unlike the EITC, this refundable credit is offered to moderate- and middle-income workers and families as well as lower-income families. Moreover, unlike the CTC, it

24. Esenwein and Shvedov (2007, pp. 1–6).
25. Rohaly (2007).
26. Ibid.

helps childless workers and married couples, as well as families with children, suggesting a possible turn toward greater universalism in the future politics of boosting paychecks.

Changes in the Tax Burden of Low-Income Families

As a result of provisions such as the EITC and CTC, the tax burden facing low-income families has declined significantly over the past four decades. Between 1960 and 1974, the typical family at the federal poverty threshold owed federal income tax in every year except 1972.[27] The amounts were substantial in some years: in 1963 poor families paid more than 5 percent of their income. However, since the 1990s, the tax entry threshold for a family of four has exceeded the federal poverty threshold (figure 8-5). For families with two children, the tax entry threshold is more than twice the poverty threshold. In contrast, the tax entry threshold is only slightly above the federal poverty threshold for married couples without children and below the poverty threshold for single filers.[28] This is due largely to the differential impact of the EITC and more recently the CTC.

Today many low-income working parents owe no federal income tax. Almost half of all children and 80 percent of children in single-parent households live in tax units with no federal income tax liability.[29] The average effective federal tax rate—tax paid as a percentage of cash income—is negative for the bottom two quintiles of the income distribution. Thus federal income taxes for low-income working families as a percentage of family income are at a twenty-year low.

In contrast, federal payroll taxes remain high. In 2006 federal payroll taxes were higher for families at all income levels than they were twenty years ago. About two-thirds of all earners owed more in payroll taxes (including both the employee and the employer shares) than in federal income tax. Among households with wage income, 86 percent had higher payroll taxes than federal income taxes, including almost all of those with incomes below $40,000 and 94 percent of those with incomes below $100,000. If only the employee portion of payroll taxes is considered, 56 percent of wage earners paid more payroll tax than income tax, including nearly 80 percent of earners with incomes below $50,000.[30]

27. Scholz (2007).
28. Ibid.
29. Bachelder, Goldberg, and Orszag (2006).
30. Burman and Leiserson (2007).

Figure 8-5. *Relationship between Tax Entry Thresholds and Poverty,*
1980–2017

Percent of poverty threshold

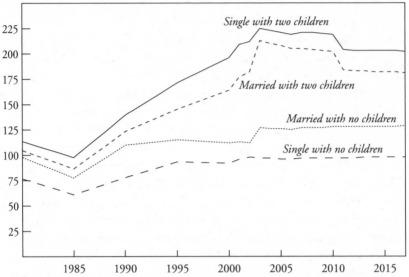

Source: Tax Policy Center, "Relationship between Tax Entry Thresholds and Poverty, Selected Years
1980–2020" (www.taxpolicycenter.org/taxfacts/displayafact.cfm?Docid=471).

Nonetheless, combined income and payroll tax rates for low-income
working families have seen a marked decline. By the mid-1970s, average
effective tax rates on poor families could exceed 13 percent, largely due to
the payroll tax, which nearly doubled from 6 percent to 11.7 percent
between 1960 and 1974. Since then, the total direct taxes paid by low-
income families have fallen significantly, especially since the late 1990s. By
2006 the average combined income and payroll tax rate for married couples with two children and income at the federal poverty threshold had
fallen to negative 17 percent.[31]

The Importance of Having Children

To illustrate both this trend and its limits, Kevin Hassett and Anne
Moore analyzed the total tax liability of three hypothetical low-income
households: a married couple with two children, a single mother with two

31. Hassett and Moore (2005).

children, and an unmarried adult with no children. In the first case, they assumed that the husband worked full time at $8.50 an hour, earning an annual income of $17,000, and that the wife earned $5.15 an hour (the federal minimum wage between 1997 and 2008), earning $10,300 annually. In the second case, the single mother was assumed to earn $7 an hour, or $14,000 a year for full-time work. In the third case, the unmarried adult, like the husband of the married couple, was assumed to earn $8.50 an hour and $17,000 a year.[32]

In 1979 the married couple with two children paid about $5,236 in total income and payroll taxes; by 2004 their liability had fallen to $1,208. Similarly, the single mother saw her after-tax income rise over time as federal tax subsidies for work increased. By 2004 her net subsidy amounted to $2,613, or 19 percent of total income. However, the total tax liability for an unmarried adult with no children declined only slightly and was still positive, at $3,923 in 2004 (figure 8-6).

Married couples with and without children faced similar federal tax rates until the mid-1980s when the expansion of the EITC reduced tax rates for low-income families with two children. Since then the EITC has accomplished one of its original goals: to offset rising payroll taxes for low-income workers with families. However, the tax rate for those without children has remained remarkably steady at about 15 percent, meaning that low-income childless workers bear a disproportionate amount of the tax burden.[33]

The maximum EITC for childless workers, $438 in 2008, was less than one-sixth the size of the maximum EITC for a family with one child, and less than one-tenth the size of the maximum EITC for families with two or more children. In part because the childless single workers' EITC is so limited, the poorest fifth of childless adults pay more than four times as large a share of their income in federal taxes, on average, as do low-income families with children.[34] Thus the EITC's current structure offers minimal support

32. Ibid. The authors constructed measures of taxes paid for these families over time by using two complementary approaches. First, they used the National Bureau of Economic Research Tax Simulation Model to estimate the tax liability for a hypothetical family for each year from 1979 to 2004. Second, they constructed an alternative measure of average tax paid from the Internal Revenue Service's Statistics of Income.

33. Jason Furman, "Tax Reform and Poverty," *Tax Notes*, June 12, 2006 (www.americanprogress.org/kf/furman.pdf).

34. Aviva Aron-Dine and Arloc Sherman, "Ways and Means Committee Chairman Charles Rangel's Proposed Expansion of the EITC for Childless Workers: An Important Step to Make Work Pay," October 25, 2007 (www.cbpp.org/files/10-25-07tax.pdf).

Figure 8-6. *Tax Liability for Three Family Types, 1979–2004*[a]

Constant 2004 dollars

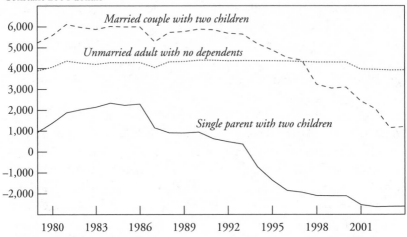

Source: Hassett and Moore (2005).

a. Figure shows total tax liability, including federal income, payroll, and state income taxes. Total income level per family type, in 2004 dollars: married couple with two children, $27,300; unmarried adult with no dependents, $17,000; single parent with two children, $14,000.

for single earners. Moreover, childless workers qualify for few if any other government benefits. They generally are ineligible for means-tested cash and medical assistance funded in whole or in part by the federal government; such assistance is limited to families with children, the elderly, and those with disabilities. Thus tax relief for low-income childless workers is an increasingly important issue of tax fairness.[35]

Continued attention to the impact of federal tax reform on low-income workers and their families is important due to the persistence of poverty and wage stagnation at the bottom of the income distribution. The tax entry threshold is the amount of income a family can earn before owing federal income taxes. The poverty threshold is considered to be the minimum dollar amount needed for individuals, married couples, or families to meet basic needs. The interaction of these two metrics offers a very important way to measure how the tax system has treated low-income families. When the tax entry threshold fell below the poverty threshold, we might be concerned that low-income families were being asked to pay too much in

35. Gitterman, Gorham, and Dorrance (2008).

Figure 8-7. *Income Tax Threshold (with EITC and CTC) as a Percentage of Federal Poverty Threshold, Selected Years, 1980–2015*[a]

Percent of threshold

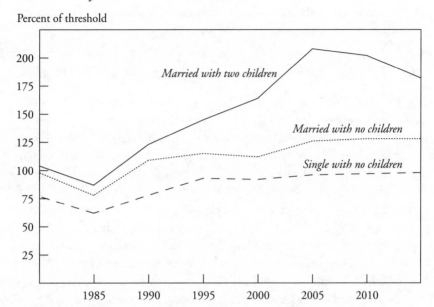

Source: Tax entry thresholds calculated by Urban-Brookings Tax Policy Center, February 9, 2009; poverty thresholds from U.S. Census Bureau, *Current Population Survey*, various years.

a. The income tax entry threshold is the income level at which a household begins to owe income tax. Assumes all income is wages; children qualify for EITC and CTC and no childcare expenses. Calculations only include EITC and CTC in years in which they were effective. The EITC for families with children was first effective in 1975; individuals with no children first claimed the EITC in 1994. The CTC was first effective in 1998.

federal income taxes.[36] As figure 8-7 shows, the tax entry threshold for a family of four has exceeded the poverty threshold since 1990. A married couple with no children begins paying taxes after their income reaches the poverty threshold; but a single person with no children begins paying taxes before his or her income reaches the federal poverty threshold.

Regular increases in the minimum wage are particularly important to the economic welfare of this group of single workers, given the current limitations of the childless EITC. As Richard Freeman argues, an appropriately set minimum wage can be a modestly effective redistributive

36. Elaine Maag, "Relationship between Tax Entry Thresholds and Poverty," *Tax Notes*, March 15, 2004 (www.taxpolicycenter.org/.../1000625_TaxFacts_031504.pdf).

tool—a risky but potentially profitable investment—particularly if it is linked with other social policies that support low-income earners.[37] In sum, the income tax code and minimum wage can coexist and reinforce one another "when work alone is not enough."[38]

Crafting a New Bargain to Support Low-Income Workers and Families

What shape might a new policy bargain to support low-income workers and their families take? One alternative is a uniform family-oriented income tax credit that would replace the current panoply of credits. For example, Adam Carasso, Jeff Rohaly, and Eugene Steuerle of the Tax Policy Center have proposed merging the EITC and the CTC in an "Earned Income Child Credit" that would be available to working families with children age eighteen and under.[39] The new credit would offer benefits similar to the current EITC and CTC, but it would provide more relief at the bottom of the income distribution and phase out at somewhat lower income levels than under current law. Similarly, David Ellwood and Jeffrey Liebman of Harvard's Kennedy School of Government favor the creation of a new "Working Family Tax Credit" that would combine a more generous EITC at the bottom end of the income scale with a more generous child credit ($1,500) in the middle of the distribution ($20,000 to $110,000 for married couples) and phase down to a credit of $1,000 per child for high-income earners.[40]

A single credit amalgamating the EITC, CTC, and even the Child and Dependent Care Tax Credit would simplify the tax system and make it easier for families to claim the benefits for which they qualify. Currently the interaction of the EITC, CTC, and CDCTC makes it difficult for most low- and moderate-income working families to understand their child-related tax benefits. Therefore, many variants of a single credit have been proposed, including Katie Campbell and Will Marshall's "Family Tax Credit" and Robert Cherry and Max Sawicky's "Universal Unified Child Credit."[41]

Equally important, most single credit proposals reflect the principle of "targeting within universalism": they provide tax benefits to most families

37. Freeman (1996).
38. Haveman (2003).
39. Carasso, Rohaly, and Steuerle (2003).
40. Ellwood and Liebman (2000).
41. Campbell and Marshall (2007, pp. 1–10); Cherry and Sawicky (2000).

but target more support at the lower end of the income distribution. According to proponents of this approach, it would reinforce political support for assistance to low-income working families by linking it to programs that also benefit middle- and even upper-income households. In this way, strategic policymakers could broaden and strengthen the coalition in favor of federal income support for America's working families. More broadly, Theda Skocpol suggests that by making a range of universal benefits, such as health coverage, paid family leave, and affordable child care, available to low- and middle-income families, policymakers could set in place the cornerstones of a powerful coalition in support of all working families.[42]

Such policies would do little or nothing to help childless workers. However, a different approach advocated by Michael Lind of the New America Foundation would offer tax relief to this group. In a 2007 article titled "Share the Credit," Lind suggested that policymakers should make all Americans who pay federal payroll taxes eligible for every existing income tax credit—"the child tax credit, the home mortgage interest deduction, all of them."[43] His argument was as much about politics as it was about policy: "Democrats should take a leaf from the Republican playbook and position themselves as the party of deep tax cuts for working Americans. What the Reaganites did for affluent income tax payers, Democrats (and like-minded Republicans) can do for America's working-class majority." According to Lind, under the "Total Tax Credit" system,

> The biggest winners would be those who could claim the most TTC deductions: home-owning families with dependent children. But even single, childless renters who don't pay income tax, or pay only a small amount, could benefit as well—for example, from tax credits for savings. In this way, today's tax credit system exclusively for income tax payers would be turned overnight from a professional-class gated community into a mainstream middle-class neighborhood.[44]

The MWP credit takes a step in this direction by offering payroll tax relief to nearly all workers, regardless of family status. Under the ARRA,

---

42. Skocpol (1991). Similarly, William Julius Wilson argues that advocates seeking to alleviate poverty and enhance economic security should support broad social policies that include whites and people of color, and middle-income as well as economically disadvantaged families. See Wilson (1987).

43. Lind (2007).

44. Ibid.

the MWP provides a refundable tax credit equal to 6.2 percent of earnings (the employee share of the Social Security payroll tax), up to a maximum credit of $400 for individuals ($800 for couples). Under Obama's proposed 2010 budget, the MWP would reduce income taxes for three-fourths of all tax units in 2012 by an average of $385, raising average after-tax income by 0.7 percent. The credit is modestly progressive: after-tax income would rise by 2.3 percent for the poorest 20 percent of households, compared with 1 percent for the middle quintile, and 0.2 percent for the top quintile.[45] More dramatically, as the president has repeatedly claimed, 95 percent of all working families will receive a tax cut as a result of the MWP, and 70 percent of the tax benefits will go to the middle 60 percent of American workers.

Looking to the Future

Political scientists are notoriously bad at seeing the future. Nonetheless, I will venture two predictions about the policy and the politics of boosting paychecks. On the policy side, it is safe to conclude that federal income tax credits will remain at the heart of the debate about boosting paychecks for some time to come. This is due in no small measure to the enduring popularity of the EITC and the CTC. The prevailing wisdom among political analysts is that narrowly targeted income transfers and direct spending programs, such as direct cash assistance to poor families, have enjoyed only sporadic political support. They tend to be enacted or expanded in periods of partisan imbalance and to be vulnerable to retrenchment when elections shift the balance of power. However, the refundable EITC is a notable counterexample. It has been expanded under both Democratic and Republican administrations, often with bipartisan support. According to Robert Greenstein, director of the Center for Budget and Policy Priorities, the EITC's design—"a middle ground of maintaining a targeted program structure while incorporating near-poor and moderate-income working families that are struggling themselves"—has helped broaden its political appeal.[46] This design is likely to inspire future policymakers. However, the EITC has not been immune from political opposition, and the

---

45. See Urban–Brookings Tax Policy Center, "Tax Topics: 2010 Budget Tax Proposals: Make Permanent the 'Making Work Pay' Tax Credit" (www.taxpolicycenter.org/taxtopics/2010_budget_making workpay.cfm).

46. Greenstein (1991).

attacks on the program suggest the challenges other tax credits may face. Notably, some Republicans remain steadfastly opposed to the concept of refundable tax credits.

Many critics of refundability would agree with George Yin, former chief of staff of the Joint Committee on Taxation , that "programs should not be hidden in the tax system and therefore be subject to a lower level of scrutiny. If as a transfer program the EITC would not garner a sufficient level of political support to remain viable, there is no reason that it should continue to exist in the tax system and in the process be administered inefficiently."[47] In addition, critics typically advance four arguments. First, some question the extent to which the federal government should engage in redistribution between different income groups. Second, some argue that the tax system should be used only to raise revenue, not to provide subsidies. Third, some argue that refundable credits increase administrative and compliance costs on net and are particularly subject to fraud and abuse.[48] Finally, some believe that all Americans should pay at least some tax, even if just one dollar, as a duty of citizenship and so that they feel some stake in governmental decisions.[49] This last argument, coined the rise of the zero-filers, is perhaps the most daunting for proponents of refundable tax credits. In 2009 nearly half of all tax units will pay no income tax. Almost 90 percent of households with children that earn between $30,000 and $40,000 will pay no tax, reflecting, in part, the value of the refundable earned income and child tax credits.[50]

The challenge of navigating this treacherous ground leads to my second prediction, which is about the politics of supporting low- and moderate-income workers and their families. Since the early 1980s, despite growing polarization, both Republicans and Democrats have found their way around partisan gridlock to reach bipartisan bargains on issues as contentious as tax policy and the minimum wage. In each case, centrists in both parties have played a key role in forcing their more liberal and conservative colleagues to make the concessions such bargains require. This pattern is likely to continue into the future.

---

47. Yin (1996, p. 316).

48. Outrage over high error rates has prompted the Internal Revenue Service to embark on an effort to "precertify" EITC filers. See U.S. Department of the Treasury (2003); Greenstein (2003).

49. Batchelder, Goldberg, and Orszag (2006).

50. Roberton Williams, "Who Pays No Income Tax?" July 2, 2009 (www.taxpolicycenter.org/publications/url.cfm?ID=1001289).

There has been so much uncertainty lately in American politics. Since 1990 we have experienced divided control of government with a Republican president, unified Democratic control of government under President Clinton, divided government with a Democratic president, unified Republican control, divided control of government with a Republican president, and now unified Democratic control of government.

With rare exceptions, neither party had a sufficient majority or sufficient internal unity to legislate on its own in the past three decades. Instead, Republicans and Democrats achieved rough parity in Congress. In the Senate, party control switched several times between 1981 and 2006, and not once did the majority party have the sixty votes necessary to end a filibuster. On the House side, Democrats enjoyed a 50- to 100-seat margin during the 1970s and 1980s, but when the Republicans became the majority party in 1994, their margin of control was considerably slimmer. If they had lost an additional ten races in any election between 1996 and 2004, they would have lost control of the House. The Democrats took back the House in 2006 by gaining thirty-one seats, and two years later they had a seventy-nine-seat margin in the House and held a sixty-vote majority in the Senate, but even then, their filibuster-proof majority depended on the support of two former Republicans.

Throughout this period, the divide between Democratic and Republican members of Congress deepened, reaching levels of partisan conflict not witnessed since the 1920s. Relatively little attention has been paid to the effects of polarization on public policy outcomes. Some political scientists conclude that polarization is not ideologically neutral; it has had a conservative effect on economic and social policy. Others argue that the main effect of polarization has been to produce less public policy. However, most agree that polarization leaves centrists in both parties with the ever more important and demanding role of brokering policy and political bargains. Since 1994 a number of groups have taken on this task. Most recently, the principal players have been the Main Street Partnership and the Blue Dogs. Founded in 1998, the Main Street Partnership comprises centrist Republicans with a fiscally conservative background. The Democratic Blue Dog Coalition, which was formed in 1995, also includes many fiscal conservatives and descends from the Boll Weevils, a group of southern Democrats who played a critical role in the early 1980s by supporting President Ronald Reagan's tax reduction packages. Since 1996, twenty-four Blue Dogs have won their seats by defeating Republican incumbents.

These moderate Democrats, together with a bipartisan group of centrists in the Senate, hold the key to the fate of President Obama's agenda. If history is any guide, they will take the lead in forging a new bargain around efforts to help low-income workers and families that balances partisan distributional and electoral goals. In the process, they will write the next chapter in the story of boosting the paychecks in America. For Republicans and Democrats, those advocating for red states or blue states, what is at stake is making working pay and creating a viable middle class—something that's always been a source of pride for all Americans.

References

Alm, James, and Leslie A. Whittington. 1996. "The Rise and Fall and Rise . . . of the Marriage Tax." *National Tax Journal* 49, no. 4: 571–89.
———. 1999. "For Love or Money? The Impact of Income Taxes on Marriage." *Economica* 66 (August): 297–316.
Anderson, John E. 2007. *U.S. Tax Reforms and Their Effects on Average Tax Rates.* Rochester, N.Y.: Social Science Electronic Publishing.
Arnold, Douglas. 1990. *The Logic of Congressional Action.* Yale University Press.
Atrostic, B. K., and James R. Nunns. 1990. "Measuring Tax Burden: A Historical Perspective." In *Fifty Years of Economic Measurement: The Jubilee of the Conference on Research in Income and Wealth*, edited by Ernst R. Berndt and Jack E. Triplett, pp. 343–420. Cambridge, Mass.: National Bureau of Economic Research.
Baack, Bennett D., and Edward J. Ray. 1985. "Special Interests and the Adoption of the Income Tax in the United States." *Journal of Economic History* 45, no. 3: 607–25.
Bakija, Jon, and C. Eugene Steuerle. 1991. "Individual Income Taxation since 1948." *National Tax Journal* 44, no. 4: 451–75.
Bartels, Larry M. 2004. *Partisan Politics and the U.S. Income Distribution.* Working Paper. New York: Russell Sage Foundation (February).
———. 2005. "Homer Gets a Tax Cut: Inequality and Public Policy in the American Mind." *Perspectives on Politics* 3, no. 1: 15–31.
Batchelder, Lily L. 2003. "Taxing the Poor: Income Averaging Reconsidered." *Harvard Journal on Legislation* 40, no. 2: 395–452.

Batchelder, Lily L., Fred T. Goldberg Jr., and Peter R. Orszag. 2006. "Reforming Tax Incentives into Uniform Tax Refundable Credits." Policy Brief 156. Brookings.

Beach, William W., and others. 2008. "The Obama and McCain Tax Plans: How Do They Compare?" Center for Data Analysis Report 08-09. Washington: Heritage Foundation (October)

Berkowitz, Edward D. 1996. "Social Security and the Financing of the American Welfare State." In *Funding the Modern American State, 1941–1995: The Rise and Fall of the Era of Easy Finance,* edited by W. Elliot Brownlee, pp. 148–93. New York: Woodrow Wilson Center Press and Cambridge University Press.

Bernstein, Jared, and Isaac Shapiro. 2006. "Nine Years of Neglect: Federal Minimum Wage Remains Unchanged for Ninth Straight Year, Lowest Level in More Than Half a Century." Issue Brief 227. Washington: Economic Policy Institute (August 31).

Bernstein, Michael. 1987. *The Great Depression: Delayed Recovery and Economic Change in America, 1929–1939.* Cambridge University Press.

Black, Merle. 2004. "Transformation of the Southern Democratic Party." *Journal of Politics* 66, no. 4: 1001–17.

Blakey, Roy, and Gladys Blakey. 1940. *The Federal Income Tax.* London: Longmans, Green.

Blank, Rebecca M. 2000. "Fighting Poverty: Lessons from Recent U.S. History." *Journal of Economic Perspectives* 14, no. 2: 3–19.

———. 2007. "Employment, Job Opportunities, and Inequality among Workers in the U.S. Economy." Testimony to the House Financial Services Committee. U.S. House of Representatives, Hearings on the State of the Economy, the State of the Labor Market and Monetary Policy (February). Washington: Government Printing Office.

Brady, David W., and Charles Bullock. 1980. "Is There a Conservative Coalition in the House?" In *The Modern American Congress, 1963–1989,* edited by Joel Silbey, pp. 505-15. New York: Carlson.

Brady, David. 1988. *Critical Elections and Congressional Policy Making.* Stanford: Stanford University Press.

Brownlee, W. Elliot. 1996. "Tax Regimes, National Crisis, and State-Building in America." In *Funding the Modern American State, 1941–1955: The Rise and Fall of the Era of Easy Finance,* edited by W. Elliot Brownlee, pp. 37–106. New York: Woodrow Wilson Center and Cambridge University Press.

———. 2004. *Federal Taxation in America: A Short History.* New York: Woodrow Wilson Center and Cambridge University Press.

Buehler, Sara J. 1998. "Child Care Tax Credits, the Child Tax Credit, and the Taxpayer Relief Act of 1997: Congress' Missed Opportunity to Provide Parents Needed Relief from the Astronomical Costs of Child Care." *Hastings Women's Law Journal* 9, no. 2: 189–209.

Burman, Leonard E. 2001. "Treasury's New Distribution Presentation." Washington: Urban Institute (March 23).

Burman, Leonard E., and Greg Leiserson. 2007. "Two-Thirds of Tax Units Pay More Payroll Tax than Income Tax." Urban Institute–Brookings Tax Policy Center (April 9).

Burman, Leonard, Elaine Maag, and Jeff Rohaly. 2002. "The Effect of the 2001 Tax Cut on Low- and Middle-Income Families and Children." Urban Institute–Brookings Tax Policy Center.

Burman, Leonard E., and others. 2002. "The AMT: Out of Control." Urban Institute–Brookings Tax Policy Center (September).

————. 2008. "An Updated Analysis of the 2008 Presidential Candidates' Tax Plans." Urban Institute–Brookings Tax Policy Center (July).

Campbell, Christiana M. 1962. *The Farm Bureau and the New Deal.* Urbana: University of Illinois Press.

Campbell, Colin, and William Peirce. 1980. "The Earned Income Tax Credit." Special Analysis. Washington: American Enterprise Institute.

Campbell, Katie M., and Will Marshall. 2007. "Making Work Pay: For Men, Too." Policy Report. Washington: Progressive Policy Institute (November).

Carasso, Adam, Jeffrey Rohaly, and C. Eugene Steuerle. 2003. "Tax Reform for Families: An Earned Income Child Credit." Welfare Reform and Beyond Policy Brief . Brookings (July).

Card, David, and Alan B. Krueger. 1995. *Myth and Measurement: The New Economics of the Minimum Wage.* Princeton University Press.

Center on Budget and Policy Priorities. 1997. "Behind the Numbers: An Examination of the Tax Foundation's Tax Day Report." Washington: Tax Foundation (April).

Cherry, Robert, and Max B. Sawicky. 2002. "Giving Tax Credit Where Credit Is Due: A 'Universal Unified Child Tax Credit' That Expands the EITC and Cuts Taxes for Working Families." Briefing Paper 91. Washington: Economic Policy Institute (April).

Clinton, William J. 1996. "Statement of the President on Signing the Small Business Job Protection Act." *Weekly Compilation of Presidential Documents* 32, no. 34: 1475.

Congressional Budget Office. 1982. "Effects of Tax and Benefit Reductions Enacted in 1981 for Households in Differed Income Categories" (February).

————. 1994. "An Economic Analysis of the Revenue Provisions of OBRA-93," CBO paper (January).

————. 2004. "Effective Federal Tax Rates: 1979–2001" (April).

————. 2006. "Changes in Low-Wage Labor Markets between 1979 and 2005." Publication 2745 (December).

Congressional Quarterly. 1965. *Congress and the Nation, 1945–1964,* vol. 1. Washington.

Dark, Taylor. 1994. "Organized Labor and the Carter Administration: The Origins of Conflict." In *The Presidency and Domestic Policies of Jimmy Carter,* edited by Herbert Rosenbaum and Alexej Urginsky, pp. 761–82. Westport, Conn.: Greenwood Press.

Daugherty, Carroll R. 1939. "The Economic Coverage of the Fair Labor Standards Act." *Law and Contemporary Problems* 6, no. 3: 407–15.

Davig, Troy A., and C. Alan Garner. 2006. "Middle Income Tax Rates: Trends and Prospects." *Economic Review,* Q4: 5–30.

Derthick, Martha. 1979. *Policymaking for Social Security.* Brookings.

Dodyk, Paul M. 1971. "The Tax Reform Act of 1969 and the Poor." *Columbia Law Review* 71, no. 5: 758–802.

Douglas, Paul, and Joseph Hackman. 1938. "The Fair Labor Standards Act of 1938." *Political Science Quarterly* 53, no. 4: 491–515.

Dunbar, Amy, and Susan Nordhouser. 1991. "Is the Child Care Credit Progressive?" *National Tax Journal* 44, no. 4: 519–28.

Ellwood, David T. 1989. *Poor Support: Poverty in the American Family.* 3rd ed. New York: Basic Books.

Ellwood, David, and Jeffrey Leibman. 2000. "The Middle-Class Parent Penalty: Child Benefits in the U.S. Tax Code." Working Paper 8031. Cambridge, Mass.: National Bureau of Economic Research (December).

Ellwood, David, and Isabel Sawhill. 2000. "Fixing the Marriage Penalty in the EITC." Economic Papers. Brookings (September).

Esenwein, Gregg, and Maxim Shvedov. 2007. "The Child Tax Credit." Report RS21860. Congressional Research Service, Library of Congress.

Even, William E., and David A. MacPherson. 2007. "Consequences of Minimum Wage Indexing." *Contemporary Economic Policy* 14, no. 4: 67–77.

Farhang, Sean, and Ira Katznelson. 2005. "The Southern Imposition: Congress and Labor in the New Deal and Fair Deal." *Studies in American Political Development* 19 (Spring): 1–30.

Finegold, Kenneth, and Theda Skocpol. 1995. *State and Party in America's New Deal.* University of Wisconsin Press.

Fleck, Robert. 2002. "Democratic Opposition to the Fair Labor Standards Act of 1938." *Journal of Economic History* 62 (March): 25–54.

Fox, Liana. 2006. "Minimum Wage Trends: Understanding Past and Contemporary Research." EPI Briefing Paper 178. Washington: Economic Policy Institute (October).

Fraser, Steve, and Gary Gerstle. 1989. "Introduction." In *The Rise and Fall of the New Deal Order, 1930–1980,* edited by Steve Fraser and Gary Gerstle, pp. ix–xxv. Princeton University Press.

Freeman, Richard. 1994. "Minimum Wages—Again!" *International Journal of Manpower* 15, nos. 2–3 (February–March): 8–25.

———. 1996. "The Minimum Wage as a Redistributive Tool." *Economic Journal* 106, no. 436: 639–49.

Gallup, George H., ed. 1996. *The Gallup Poll: Public Opinion 1996.* Wilmington, Del.: Scholarly Resources.

Garrett, Elizabeth. 2000. "The Congressional Budget Process: Strengthening the Party-in-Government." *Columbia Law Review* 100, no. 3: 702–30.

Gitterman, Daniel P., Lucy S. Gorham, and Jessica L. Dorrance. 2008. "*Georgetown Journal* on Expanding the EITC for Single Workers and Couples without Children: Tax Relief for All Low-Wage Workers." *Poverty Law and Policy* 15, no. 2: 245-284.

Gitterman, Daniel P., and Christopher Howard. 2003. "Tax Credits for Working Families: The New American Social Policy." Discussion Paper. Brookings.

Gottschalk, Marie. 2000. *The Shadow Welfare State: Labor, Business, and the Politics of Health Care in the United States.* Cornell University Press.

Graetz, Michael J., and Jerry L. Mashaw. 1999. *True Security: Rethinking American Social Insurance.* Yale University Press.

Gravelle, Jane G. 1992. "Equity Effects of the Tax Reform Act of 1986." *Journal of Economic Perspectives* 6, no. 1: 27–44.

———. 2001. "Across the Board Tax Cuts: Economic Issues." Report RL30779. Congressional Research Service, Library of Congress (September).

———. 2006. "Tax Reform and Distributional Issues." Report RL33285. Congressional Research Service, Library of Congress (February).

Greenstein, Robert. 1991. "Universal and Targeted Approaches to Relieving Poverty: An Alternative View." In *The Urban Underclass*, edited by Christopher Jencks and Paul E. Peterson, pp. 437–59. Brookings.

———. 2001. "The Changes the New Tax Law Makes in Refundable Tax Credits for Low-Income Working Families." Washington: Center on Budget and Policy Priorities.

Greenstein, Robert. 2003. "The New Procedures for the Earned Income Tax Credit." Center on Budget and Policy Priorities (May 20).

Grossman, Jonathan. 1978. "Fair Labor Standards Act of 1938: Maximum Struggle for a Minimum Wage." *Monthly Labor Review* (June): 22–30.

Hacker, Jacob S. 2002. *The Divided Welfare State: The Battle over Public and Private Social Benefits in the United States.* Cambridge University Press.

Hall, Robert, and others. 2003. "The NBR's Recession Dating Procedure." Cambridge, Mass.: National Bureau of Economic Research (October).

Hamersma, Sarah. 2005. "The Work Opportunity and Welfare-to-Work Tax Credits." Tax Policy Issues and Options 15. Urban Institute–Brookings Tax Policy Center (October).

Hansen, John M. 1991. *Gaining Access: Congress and the Farm Lobby, 1919–1981.* University of Chicago Press.

Hart, Vivian. 1994. *Bound by Our Constitution: Women, Workers, and the Minimum Wage.* Princeton University Press.

Hassett, Kevin A., and Anne Moore. 2005. "How Do Tax Policies Affect Low-Income Workers?" Working Paper 05-16. National Poverty Center, University of Michigan (September 6).

Haveman, Robert. 2003. "When Work Alone Is Not Enough." In *One Percent for the Kids: New Policies, Brighter Futures for America's Children,* edited by Isabel Sawhill, pp. 40–55. Brookings.

Haveman, Robert, and Jonathan Schwabish. 2000. "Has Macroeconomic Performance Regained its Antipoverty Bite?" *Contemporary Economic Policy* 19, no. 4: 415–27.

Herzberg, Roberta. 1986. "Blocking Coalitions and Policy Change." In *Congress and Policy Change,* edited by Gerald Wright, Leroy Rieselbach, and Lawrence Dodd, pp. 201–22. New York: Agathon Press.

Himmelberg, Robert. 1976. *The Origins of the National Recovery Administration, 1921–1933.* Fordham University Press.

Hook, Janet. 1984. "Labor Opposition Remains Strong: White House Resurrects Youth Summer Wage." *CQ Weekly* (May 19): 1177.

Hotz, Joseph V., and John K. Scholz. 2000. "Not Perfect, but Still Pretty Good: The EITC and Other Policies to Support the U.S. Low-Wage Labour Market." *OECD Economic Studies* 31: 25–42.

Howard, Christopher. 1994. "Happy Returns: How the Working Poor Got Tax Relief." *American Prospect* 5, no. 17 (spring): 46–54.

———. 1997. *The Hidden Welfare State: Tax Expenditures and Social Policy in the United States.* Princeton University Press.

———. 2007. *The Welfare State Nobody Knows: Debunking Myths about U.S. Social Policy.* Princeton University Press.

Katznelson, Ira, Kim Geiger, and Daniel Kryder. 1993. "Limiting Liberalism: The Southern Veto in Congress." *Political Science Quarterly* 108, no. 2: 283–306.

Kent, Arthur H. 1940–41. "The Revenue Act of 1940." *California Law Review* 160: 163.

Kettl, Donald. 1992. *Deficit Politics.* New York: Macmillan.

Klein, Jennifer. 2003. *For All These Rights: Business, Labor, and the Shaping of America's Public–Private Welfare State.* Princeton University Press.

Kollmann, Geoffrey. 2000. *Social Security: Summary of Major Changes in the Cash Benefit Program.* Legislative History RL30565. Congressional Research Service, Library of Congress (May).

Leff, Mark H. 1984. *The Limits of Symbolic Reform: The New Deal and Taxation, 1933–1939.* Cambridge University Press.

Light, Paul. 2000. "Government's Greatest Achievements of the Past Half Century." Reform Watch Brief 2. Brookings.

Lind, Michael. 2007. "Share the Credit." *American Prospect* (September 3) (www.prospect.org/cs/articles?article=share_the_credit).

Linder, Marc. 1987. "Farm Workers and the Labor Standards Act: Racial Discrimination in the New Deal." *Texas Law Review* 65: 1335–87.

Maag, Elaine. 2004. "Relationship between Tax Entry Thresholds and Poverty." Urban Institute–Brookings Tax Policy Center (March).

Marmor, Theodore, and others. 1990. *America's Misunderstood Welfare State.* New York: Basic Books.

McCarty, Nolan. 2007. "The Policy Effects of Political Polarization." In *The Transformation of American Politics*, edited by Paul Pierson and Theda Skocpol, pp. 223–255. Princeton University Press.

McCubbins, Matthew D., R. G. Noll, and Barry R. Weingast. 1992. "Positive Canons: The Role of Legislative Bargains in Statutory Interpretation." *Georgetown Law Journal* 80: 705–42.

———. 1994. "Legislative Intent: The Use of Positive Political Theory in Statutory Interpretation." *Law and Contemporary Problems* 57, no. 1: 3–49.

McIntyre, Robert. 2000. "Tax Wars: Winners and Losers from the Bush and Gore Tax Plans." *American Prospect* (October 23).

McIntyre, Robert S., and Michael J. McIntyre. 1999. "Fixing the 'Marriage Penalty' Problem." *Valparaiso University Law Review* 33: 907–46.

McLure, Charles E., and George R. Zodrow. 1987. "Treasury I and the Tax Reform Act of 1986: The Economics and Politics of Tax Reform." *Economic Perspectives* 1, no. 1: 44.

Mettler, Suzanne. 1998. *Dividing Citizens: Gender and Federalism in New Deal Public Policy.* Cornell University Press.

Mitrusi, Andrew, and James Poterba. 2000. "The Distribution of Payroll and Income Tax Burdens, 1979–1999." *National Tax Journal* 53 (September, part 2): 765–94.

Nellen, Annette. 2001. "Simplification of the EITC through Structural Changes." In *Study of the Overall State of the Federal Tax System and Recommendations for Simplification*, vol.1, JCS-3-01. Joint Committee on Taxation (April).

Nordlund, Willis J. 1988. "A Brief History of the Fair Labor Standards Act." *Labor Law Journal* 39, no. 11: 715–38.

O'Brien, Ruth. 1998. *Workers' Paradox: The Republican Origins of New Deal Labor Policy, 1886–1935.* University of North Carolina Press.

O'Connor, Brendon. 2002. "Policies, Principles, and Polls: Bill Clinton's Third Way Welfare Politics 1992–1996." *Australian Journal of Politics and History* 48, no. 3: 396–411.

O'Neill, William L. 1995. "Eisenhower and American Society." In *Eisenhower: A Centenary Assessment*, edited by Gunter Bischof and Stephen E. Ambrose, pp. 101–10. Louisiana State University Press.

Patterson, James T. 1967. *Congressional Conservatism and the New Deal: The Growth of the Conservative in Congress, 1933–1939.* University of Kentucky Press.

Paulsen, George. 1996. *A Living Wage for the Forgotten Man: The Quest for Fair Labor Standards, 1933–1941.* London: Associated University Presses.

Pierson, Paul. 1995. "The Creeping Nationalization of Income Transfers in the United States, 1935–1994." In *European Social Policy*, edited by Stephan Leibfried and Paul Pierson, pp. 301–28. Brookings.

Pollack, Sheldon D. 1996. *The Failure of U.S. Tax Policy: Revenue and Politics.* Penn State University Press.

Poole, Keith, and Howard Rosenthal. 1991. "The Spatial Mapping of Minimum Wage Legislation." In *Politics and Economics in the Eighties,* edited by Alberto Alesina and Geoffrey Carliner, pp. 215–50. University of Chicago Press.

Reese, Thomas J. 1980. *The Politics of Taxation.* Westport, Conn.: Quorum Books.

Reichley, A. James. 1981. *Conservatives in an Age of Change: The Nixon and Ford Administrations.* Brookings.

Robertson, David B. 2000. *Capital, Labor, and State: The Battle for American Labor Markets from the Civil War to the New Deal.* Lanham, Md.: Rowman and Littlefield.

Rohaly, Jeffrey. 2007. "Reforming the Child and Dependent Care Tax Credit." Urban Institute–Brookings Tax Policy Center (June).

Ruggles, Patricia. 1990. *Drawing the Line: Alternative Poverty Measures and Their Implications for Public Policy.* Urban Institute Press.

Sammartino, Frank. 2001. "Designing Tax Cuts to Benefit Low-Income Families." Washington: Urban Institute (July).

Sammartino, Frank, Eric Toder, and Elaine Maag. 2002. "Providing Federal Assistance for Low-Income Families through the Tax System: A Primer." Discussion Paper 4. Urban Institute–Brookings Tax Policy Center (July).

Samuelson, Paul A. 1964. *Final Report to the President of the Task Force on Sustaining Prosperity.* Government Printing Office (November).

Sawhill, Isabel, and Adam Thomas. 2001. "A Tax Proposal for Working Families with Children." Policy Brief. Brookings.

Schieber, Sylvester J., and John B. Shoven. 1999. *The Real Deal: The History and Future of Social Security.* Yale University Press.

Scholz, John K. 2007. "Taxation and Poverty: 1960–2006." *Focus* 25, no. 1: 52–57.

Schulman, Bruce. 1991. *From Cotton Belt to Sun Belt: Federal Policy, Economic Development and the Transformation of the South, 1938–1980.* Oxford University Press.

Seltzer, Lawrence H. 1968. *The Personal Exemptions in the Income Tax.* New York: National Bureau of Economic Research and Columbia University Press.

Seltzer, Lawrence. 1997. "The Effects of the Fair Labor Standards Act of 1938 on the Southern Seamless Hosiery and Lumber Industries." *Journal of Economic History* 57, no. 2 (June): 396–415.

Shapiro, Robert J. 1990. "An American Working Wage: Ending Poverty in Working Families." PPI Policy Report. Washington: Progressive Policy Institute (February).

Shelley, Mack C. 1983. *The Permanent Majority: The Conservative Coalition in the U.S. Congress.* University of Alabama Press.

Shoup, Carl S. 1945. "The Revenue Act of 1945." *Political Science Quarterly* 60, no. 4: 481–91.

Sinclair, Barbara. 1978. "From Party Voting to Regional Fragmentation: The House of Representatives, 1933–1956." *American Politics Research* 6: 125–146.

Sinclair, Barbara. 1982. *Congressional Realignment, 1925–1978.* University of Texas Press.

———. 2000. *Unorthodox Lawmaking: New Legislative Processes in the U.S. Congress.* Washington: CQ Press.

Skocpol, Theda, Kenneth Finegold, and Michael Goldfield. 1990. "Explaining New Deal Labor Policy." *American Political Science Review* 84: 1297–315.

Skocpol, Theda. 1991. "Targeting within Universalism: Politically Viable Policies to Combat Poverty in the United States." In *The Urban Underclass*, edited by Christopher Jencks and Paul E. Peterson, pp. 411–36. Brookings.

———. 1995. *Social Policy in the United States: Future Possibilities in Historical Perspective.* Princeton University Press.

Smiley, Gene, and Richard H. Keehn. 1995. "Federal Personal Income Tax Policy in the 1920s." *Journal of Economic History* 55, no. 2: 285–303.

Smith, Ralph, and Bruce Vavrichek. 1986. "The Minimum Wage: Its Relationship to Incomes and Poverty." Congressional Budget Office, Human Resources and Community Development Division (June).

Sobel, Russell S. 1999. "Theory and Evidence on the Political Economy of the Minimum Wage." *Journal of Political Economy* 107, no. 4 (August): 761–85.

Solomon, Carmen D. 1986. "Major Decisions in the House and Senate Chambers on Social Security: 1935–1985." Report 86-193 EPW. Congressional Research Service, Library of Congress (December).

Steinberg, Ronnie. 1982. *Wages and Hours: Labor and Reform in Twentieth-Century America.* Rutgers University Press.

Steinmo, Sven. 1996. *Taxation and Democracy.* Yale University Press.

Steuerle, C. Eugene. 1995. "Can Flat Taxes Be Progressive?" Washington: Urban Institute.

———. 1996. "Financing the American State at the Turn of the Century." In *Funding the Modern American State, 1941–1955: The Rise and Fall of the Era of Easy Finance,* edited by E. Elliot Brownlee, pp. 409–44. New York: Woodrow Wilson Center and Cambridge University Press.

———. 2008. *Contemporary U.S. Tax Policy,* 2d ed. Washington: Urban Institute Press.

Steuerle, C. Eugene. 1990. "Policy Watch: Tax Credits for Low-Income Workers with Children." *Journal of Economic Perspectives* 4, no. 3: 201–12.

Steuerle, C. Eugene, and Michael Hartzmark. 1981. "Individual Income Taxation 1947–1979." OTA Papers. U.S. Treasury Department, Office of Tax Analysis (April).

Stigler, George J. 1946. "The Economics of Minimum Wage Legislation." *American Economic Review* 36, no. 3 358–65.

Stoker, Robert P., and Laura A. Wilson. 2006. *When Work Is Not Enough: State and Federal Policies to Support Needy Workers.* Brookings.

Storrs, Landon. 2000. *Civilizing Capitalism: The National Consumers' League, Women's Activism, and Labor Standards in the New Deal Era.* University of North Carolina Press.

Strayer, Paul. 1955. "The Significance of Exemption and Deductions for Low-Income Taxpayers." Testimony before the Joint Economic Committee. Hearings on Federal Tax Policy for Economic Growth and Stability. 84 Cong. 1 sess.

Talley, Louis Alan. 2001. "Federal Taxation: An Abbreviated History." Report on History of Federal Taxes. Congressional Research Service, Library of Congress (January).

Tempalski, Jerry. 2006. "Revenue Effects of Major Tax Bills." OTA Working Paper 81. U.S. Department of Treasury, Office of Tax Analysis (September).

Toder, Eric. 1998. "The Changing Role of Tax Expenditures: 1980–99." In *Proceedings of the Ninety-First Annual Conference of the National Tax Association.* Washington.

Tomlins, Christopher. 1985. *The State and the Unions.* Cambridge University Press.

U.S. Congress. 1937. Joint Hearings before the Senate Committee on Education and Labor and House of Representatives Committee on Labor. *Fair Labor Standards Act of 1937* (pt.1-3). Washington: Government Printing Office (GPO).

———. 1974. Subcommittee on Fiscal Policy, Joint Economic Committee, U.S. Congress. *Income Security for Americans: Recommendations of the Public Welfare Study.* Washington: GPO.

———. 1997. Joint Economic Committee. *Payroll Taxes and the Redistribution of Income: A Joint Economic Study.* (July). Washington: GPO.

———. 2003. *A Comparison of Tax Distribution Tables: How Missing or Incomplete Information Distorts Perspectives* (December). Washington: GPO.

———. 2007. Joint Committee on Taxation. "Estimated Revenue Effects." Washington: GPO.

U.S. Department of Commerce. 2007. Census Bureau. "Annual Social and Economic Supplement: Selected Characteristics of Households, by Total Money Income in 2006." *Current Population Survey.*

U.S. Department of Labor. 1996. "Making Work Pay: The Case for Raising the Minimum Wage" (March).

———. 2005. Bureau of Labor Statistics. "Characteristics of Minimum Wage Workers: 2004" (April).

———. 2007. Bureau of Labor Statistics. "Characteristics of Minimum Wage Workers: 2006" (March).

———. 2008. Bureau of Labor Statistics. "Establishment Data: Historical Hours and Earnings" (March).

———. 2009. "History of Changes to the Minimum Wage Law." Adapted from *Minimum Wage and Maximum Hours Standards under the Fair Labor Standards Act*, 1988 Report to the Congress under Section 4(d)(1) of the FLSA.

U.S. Department of the Treasury. 1984. *Tax Reform for Fairness, Simplicity, and Economic Growth: The Treasury Department Report to the President* (November).

———. 2003. Internal Revenue Service, "Earned Income Tax Credit (EITC) Program Effectiveness and Program Management FY 1998–FY 2002," Doc 2002-5236 (25 pp.), 2002 TNT 41-12, at 5 (Feb. 28, 2002).

U.S. House of Representatives. 1937. Committee on Labor. *Fair Labor Standards Act* (H.Rpt.1452). Washington: GPO.

———. 1938. Committee on Labor. *Fair Labor Standards Act of 1938*. Conference Report (H.Rpt.2738). Washington: GPO.

———. 1949. Committee on Education and Labor. *Fair Labor Standards Amendments of 1949* (H.Rpt.267). Washington: GPO.

———. 1961a. Committee on Education and Labor. *Fair Labor Standards Amendments of 1961* (H.Rpt.75). Washington: GPO.

———. 1961b. *Fair Labor Standards Amendments of 1961* Conference Report (H.Rpt.327). Washington: GPO.

———. 1966. *Fair Labor Standards Amendments of 1966* Conference Report (H.Rpt.2004). Washington: GPO.

———. 1971a. General Subcommittee on Labor of the Committee on Education and Labor. *To Amend the Fair Labor Standards Act of 1938* (H.R. 7130). Hearings (April 20–29 and May 4–12). Washington: GPO.

———. 1971b. Committee on Education and Labor. *Fair Labor Standards Amendments of 1971* (H.Rpt.92-672). Washington: GPO.

———. 1972. Committee on Education and Labor. *Fair Labor Standards Amendments of 1973* (H.Rpt.93-232). Washington: GPO.

———. 1975. Committee on Ways and Means. *Report Accompanying HR 2166, the Tax Reduction Act of 1975.* (H.Rpt.94-19), 94 Cong. 1 sess.

———. 1977a. Committee on Education and Labor. *Fair Labor Standards Amendments of 1977* (H.Rpt.95-521). Washington: GPO.

———. 1977b. *Fair Labor Standards Amendments of 1977* Conference Report (H.Rpt.95-711). Washington: GPO.

———. 1997. *Hearing on the Internal Revenue Service's 1995 Earned Income Tax Credit Compliance Study*, 105 Cong. 1 sess.

———. 2000. *Green Book*, 17th ed.

———. 2004. *Green Book: Background Material and Data on the Programs within the Jurisdiction of the Committee on Ways and Means*. Washington: GPO.

U.S. Senate. 1942. Committee on Finance. Hearings on H.R. 7378, vol. 1, 77 Cong. 2 sess.

———. 1949. Committee on Labor and Public Welfare. *Fair Labor Standards Act Amendments of 1949* (S.Rpt.640). Washington: GPO.

———. 1959. Subcommittee on Labor of the Committee on Labor and Public Welfare. *To Amend the Fair Labor Standards Act* Hearings (May 7–26 and June 4). Washington: GPO.

———. 1961b. Committee on Labor and Public Welfare. *Fair Labor Standards Amendments of 1960* (S.Rpt.145). Washington: GPO.

———. 1965. Committee on Finance. *Social Security.* Hearings on House Report 6675 (April–May), 89 Cong. 1 sess.

———. 1975. *Report Accompanying HR 2166, the Tax Reform Reduction Act of 1975.* Senate Report 94-36, 94 Cong. 1 sess.

———. 1984. Committee on Labor and Human Resources. *Youth Opportunity Wage Act of 1984* (S.2687). Hearing (June 18).

———. 1989. Committee on Labor and Human Resources. *Minimum Wage Restoration Act of 1989* (S.4) Hearing (March 3). Washington: GPO.

Van Giezen, Robert, and Albert E. Schwenk. 2001. "Compensation from before World War I through the 'Great Depression.'" *Compensation and Working Conditions* (Fall): 19.

Ventry, Dennis J., Jr. 2000. "The Collision of Tax and Welfare Politics: The Political History of the Earned Income Tax Credit, 1969–99." *National Tax Journal* 53, no. 4 (Part 2): 983–1026.

Webster, George D. 1951. "Taxpayer Relief: The Revenue Act of 1951." *Virginia Law Review* 37, no. 8: 1039–81.

Weinstein, Michael. 1980. *Recovery and Redistribution under the NIRA.* New York: Elsevier North-Holland.

Weir, Margaret, Ann S. Orloff, and Theda Skocpol. 1988. *The Politics of Social Policy in the United States.* Princeton University Press.

Wilson, William J. 1987. *The Truly Disadvantaged: The Inner City, the Underclass, and Public Policy.* University of Chicago Press.

Witte, John F. 1985. *The Politics and Development of the Federal Income Tax.* University of Wisconsin Press.

Woodworth, Laurence. 1969. "Tax Simplification and the Tax Reform Act of 1969: Law and Contemporary Problems." *Law and Contemporary Problems* 34, no. 4: 711–25.

Wright, Gavin. 1986. *Old South New South: Revolutions in the Southern Economy since the Civil War.* New York: Basic Books.

Yin, George K. 1996. "The Uncertain Fate of the EITC Program." In *Taxing America*, edited by Karen B. Brown and Mary Louise Fellows, pp. 297–321. New York University Press.

Zeitlin, June H., and Nancy Duff Campbell. 1982. "Strategies to Address the Impact of the Economic Recovery Tax Act of 1981 and the Omnibus Budget Reconciliation Act of 1981 on the Availability of Child Care for Low-Income Families." *Wayne Law Review* 28, no. 4: 1601–67.

Zelizer, Julian E. 1998. *Taxing America: Wilbur D. Mills, Congress, and the State, 1945–1975.* Cambridge University Press.

Index

Page numbers followed by *f* or *t* refer to figure captions or table captions, respectively.

policies, 131, 144–45; projected fiscal plans, 136–39; refundable tax credit plans, 138–39

Omnibus Budget Reconciliation Act (1990), 76–77

Omnibus Budget Reconciliation Act (1993), 89–90

Payroll taxes: historical development, 9, 14–15, 23–25, 31–32, 33–34, 40, 41, 83, 147, 151–52; impact of World War II, 26–27; income taxes relative to, 12, 41, 67–68, 127, 151; outcomes of 1980s reforms, 83, 84; purpose, 9; Reagan administration reforms, 67–69

Personal Responsibility and Work Opportunity Reconciliation Act of 1996, 94, 141

Petri, Thomas E., 79

Policy development: accomplishments of centrist politicians, 18–19; alternative strategies for assisting low-wage workers, 3–4, 156–58; Bush (G. H. W.) administration, 74–77; Carter administration, 38–40, 59–60; conceptualizations of social insurance and assistance instruments, 2–3; Eisenhower administration, 30–31, 51–52; Ford administration, 37–38; future challenges, 19; historical and conceptual development, 3; impact of World War II, 25–27; Johnson administration, 33–34; Kennedy administration, 32–33, 52–54; Nixon administration, 34–37, 56–58; origins of federal income tax, 20–23; outcomes of 1980s reforms, 83–84; payroll tax, 14–15, 23–25, 26–27, 31–32, 33–34, 40, 41; role of moderates and centrists, 159, 160–61; strategies for supporting low-income earners, 1–2; Truman administration, 27–30, 48–50. *See also* Bush (G. W.) administration; Clinton administration; Reagan administration; Tax policy

Political functioning: distributive considerations in tax and wage policies, 2; evolution of U.S. social policy, 3; future strategies for supporting low-income working families, 156–57, 158–61; historical control of Congress, 61*f,* 62*f;* legislative control over minimum wage, 42–43, 47–48; in origins

of minimum wage, 44–48; polarization trends, 18, 160; policy reform efforts of 1990s, 85–86; presidential 2000 campaign pledges, 106–07; Social Security financing, 14–15; in strategies to assist low-income earners, 1–2, 4; tax policy evolution, 17–19, 21–23; timing of minimum wage increases, 48. *See also* Democratic Party; Moderate and centrist politicians; Republican Party

Poole, K., 18

Poverty: definition, 5, 12; federal income tax as antipoverty tool, 33; federal income tax entry threshold, 12, 13, 33, 40–41, 151, 152*f,* 154–55; minimum wage and, 16, 61, 77, 88, 144, 146*f. See also* Low-wage workers and families

Public attitudes and beliefs: obligation to work, 1; support for working families versus workers without children, 2; understanding of tax policies and outcomes, 118–19

Rangel, Charles, 97, 123

Reagan administration: control of Congress, 64–65; distributive outcomes of tax policies, 18, 65, 66, 67, 71, 74, 83; Economic Recovery Tax Act, 65–69; election, 64; minimum wage policies, 62, 77–79; payroll tax reforms, 67–68; philosophy of government, 64; tax policies, 63–74, 148; Tax Reform Act, 70–74; tax relief for low-income working families, 71–72

Refundable tax credits, 7, 158–59

Reid, Harry, 123

Republican Party: Clinton administration policies, 85–86, 89, 90–96, 97, 99–100, 101–04; evolution of federal income tax policies, 21–23, 27–29, 30–31; Ford administration, 37–38; historical control of Congress, 61*f,* 62*f;* household income results of tax policies, 18; minimum wage policies, 18, 43, 45–46, 48–50, 56–57, 60, 62, 78, 79, 101–04; Obama administration and, 133–34; origins of minimum wage, 42–43; payroll tax policies, 27, 31–32. *See also* Bush (G. H. W.) administration; Bush (G. W.) administration;